Learning Redis

Design efficient web and business solutions with Redis

Vinoo Das

BIRMINGHAM - MUMBAI

Learning Redis

First published: June 2015

Production reference: 1230615

Published by Packt Publishing Ltd.
Livery Place
35 Livery Street
Birmingham B3 2PB, UK.

ISBN 978-1-78398-012-3

www.packtpub.com

Credits

Author
Vinoo Das

Reviewers
Dan Cartoon
Munish Kumar Gupta
Paul Irwin
Dae Myung Kang
Jari Timonen

Commissioning Editor
Ashwin Nair

Acquisition Editor
Sonali Vernekar

Content Development Editor
Manasi Pandire

Technical Editor
Mohita Vyas

Copy Editors
Dipti Kapadia
Alpha Singh

Project Coordinator
Nidhi Joshi

Proofreader
Safis Editing

Indexer
Tejal Soni

Graphics
Abhinash Sahu

Production Coordinator
Aparna Bhagat

Cover Work
Aparna Bhagat

About the Author

Vinoo Das has 16 years of experience in the software industry and has worked in various domains, such as telecom, banking, payment gateways, information management, and so on. He is highly motivated and loves to work on new and upcoming technologies. He is currently architecting a platform for an information technology giant, which will enable the company to position the platform at an enterprise level as well as a cloud solution.

I would like to thank my parents and my family for supporting me. I would also like to thank my friends Lokendra and Kartikeya for helping me shape the book. I would also like to thank Packt Publishing and the editors Manasi Pandire and Mohita Vyas for their efforts in shaping up this book.

About the Reviewers

Dan Cartoon grew up in Atlanta, Georgia, but now spends his time in the San Francisco Bay Area as a software engineer. He has worked at social and game-oriented software start-ups as well as at large companies. He enjoys working in the field of machine learning and building large-scale software systems. In his free time, he likes to play various musical instruments and take long walks on Northern California's foggy beaches.

I would like to thank my wife for her patience while I spent even more time in front of the computer reviewing this book. I would also like to thank Salvatore Sanfilippo for creating Redis and releasing it to the world.

Munish Kumar Gupta is a lead architect working for Wipro Technologies. Based in Bangalore, India, his day-to-day work involves solution architecture, application performance engineering, and helping enterprises adopt open source technologies.

He is always looking for patterns while solving problems, writing code, and making optimum use of tools and frameworks. He is the author of *Akka Essentials, Packt Publishing*.

Dae Myung Kang lives in South Korea. He has more than 10 years of experience in the software industry. His interest lies in studying in-memory cache and storage. He currently works as a backend software engineer for Daum Kakao. He is also a keen contributor of Redis/Twemproxy and Apache Tajo.

I would like to thank my wife, Suki, and my son, Hanyul. I will always love you.

Jari Timonen is an experienced software enthusiast with over 10 years of experience in the software industry. His experience includes successful team leadership combined with understanding complex business domains and putting them into practice. He has built enterprise architectures, designed software, and programming. Having started his career in the finance industry, he currently works as a service architect in a telecommunications company. He practices pair programs and is keen on studying new technologies. When he is not building software, he is spending time with his family, fishing, exercising, or flying his radio-controlled model helicopter. He currently holds certifications that include Sun Certified Programmer for the Java 2 Platform, Standard Edition 5, Sun Certified Developer for the Java 2 Platform, Oracle Certified Master, and Java EE 5 Enterprise Architect.

www.PacktPub.com

Support files, eBooks, discount offers, and more

For support files and downloads related to your book, please visit www.PacktPub.com.

Did you know that Packt offers eBook versions of every book published, with PDF and ePub files available? You can upgrade to the eBook version at www.PacktPub.com and as a print book customer, you are entitled to a discount on the eBook copy. Get in touch with us at service@packtpub.com for more details.

At www.PacktPub.com, you can also read a collection of free technical articles, sign up for a range of free newsletters and receive exclusive discounts and offers on Packt books and eBooks.

https://www2.packtpub.com/books/subscription/packtlib

Do you need instant solutions to your IT questions? PacktLib is Packt's online digital book library. Here, you can search, access, and read Packt's entire library of books.

Why subscribe?

- Fully searchable across every book published by Packt
- Copy and paste, print, and bookmark content
- On demand and accessible via a web browser

Free access for Packt account holders

If you have an account with Packt at www.PacktPub.com, you can use this to access PacktLib today and view 9 entirely free books. Simply use your login credentials for immediate access.

Table of Contents

Preface

Learning Redis is meant to be a guide and handbook for developers, architects, solution providers, consultants, engineers, and anyone planning to learn, design, and architect an Enterprise Solution and looking for an in-memory datastore that is agile and fast and extends its capabilities beyond just storing data.

This book starts with an introduction to the evolving landscape of NoSQL, explores commands in easy-to-understand examples, and then uses Redis in a few sample applications, with Redis as the backbone. The later sections of the book focus on the management of Redis for performance and scalability.

This book covers core concepts to design and create fast, agile, and concurrent applications, but it is not meant to be a replacement for the official documentation guide for Redis, published by Redis.io.

What this book covers

Chapter 1, Introduction to NoSQL, covers the ecosystem of NoSQL. It discusses the evolution of the NoSQL landscape and provides an introduction to the various types of NoSQL and their characteristics.

Chapter 2, Getting Started with Redis, taps into the world of Redis. It also covers areas such as the installation of Redis on various platforms and running a sample program in Java to connect to Redis.

Chapter 3, Data Structures and Communicating Protocol in Redis, covers data structures that are available in Redis and the communicating protocol in Redis. It also covers examples that the user can execute and get a feel of using it. By the end of this chapter, you should have a basic feel of the capabilities of Redis.

Chapter 4, Functions in the Redis Server, takes you from learning commands to the various in-built capabilities of Redis. These capabilities include messaging in Redis, transactions, and the pipeline capabilities in Redis, which have differences between them. The chapter also introduces the users to a scripting language called LUA.

Chapter 5, Handling Data in Redis, focuses on the in-depth data handling capability of Redis. This includes the master-slave arrangement, the way data is stored in Redis, and various options it provides to persist data.

Chapter 6, Redis in Web Applications, is all about positioning Redis in web applications. To make it interesting, there are some example applications, which you can take ideas from, about the wide range of use cases where Redis can be used.

Chapter 7, Redis in Business Applications, is all about positioning Redis in business applications. To expand its applicability further in the Enterprise Solution design landscape, some example applications have been explained from which you can see its versatility.

Chapter 8, Clustering, talks about the clustering capability, how the end user can make use of various patterns in clustering for Redis, and use these patterns accordingly in their solutions.

Chapter 9, Maintaining Redis, is all about maintaining Redis in a production environment.

What you need for this book

The following software is required for this book:

- Redis
- JDK 1.7
- Jedis (the Java client for Redis)
- Eclipse, the IDE for development

Who this book is for

This book is meant for developers, architects, solution providers, consultants, and engineers. Primarily the book requires knowledge of Java but it can also be understood by anybody with a bit of programming background.

Apart from this, there is information about how to design solutions and maintain them in production for which coding skills are not required.

Conventions

In this book, you will find a number of text styles that distinguish between different kinds of information. Here are some examples of these styles and an explanation of their meaning.

Code words in text, database table names, folder names, filenames, file extensions, pathnames, dummy URLs, user input, and Twitter handles are shown as follows: "The following code is for the new Hello World program, which is now called `HelloWorld2`:"

A block of code is set as follows:

```
package org.learningredis.chapter.two;

public class Helloworld2  {
  JedisWrapper jedisWrapper = null;
  public Helloworld2() {
    jedisWrapper = new JedisWrapper();
  }

  private void test() {
    jedisWrapper.set("MSG", "Hello world 2 ");

    String result = jedisWrapper.get("MSG");
    System.out.println("MSG : " + result);
  }


  public static void main(String[] args) {
    Helloworld2 helloworld2 = new Helloworld2();
    helloworld2.test();
  }
}
```

New terms and **important words** are shown in bold. Words that you see on the screen, for example, in menus or dialog boxes, appear in the text like this: "Note the last line showing on the Command Prompt: **The servers now ready to accept connections on port 6379**."

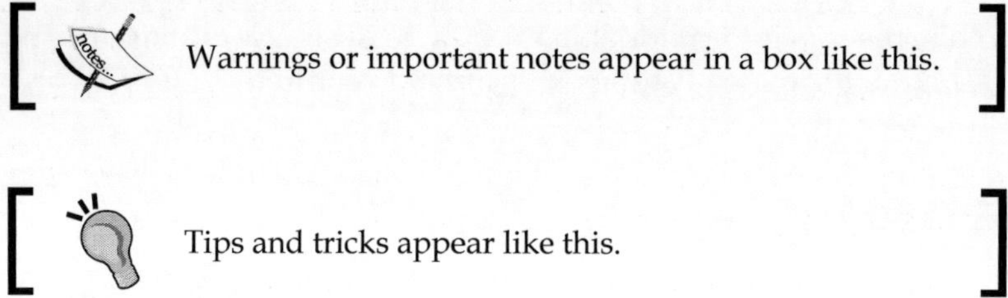

Warnings or important notes appear in a box like this.

Tips and tricks appear like this.

Reader feedback

Feedback from our readers is always welcome. Let us know what you think about this book—what you liked or disliked. Reader feedback is important for us as it helps us develop titles that you will really get the most out of.

To send us general feedback, simply e-mail `feedback@packtpub.com`, and mention the book's title in the subject of your message.

If there is a topic that you have expertise in and you are interested in either writing or contributing to a book, see our author guide at `www.packtpub.com/authors`.

Customer support

Now that you are the proud owner of a Packt book, we have a number of things to help you to get the most from your purchase.

Downloading the example code

You can download the example code files from your account at `http://www.packtpub.com` for all the Packt Publishing books you have purchased. If you purchased this book elsewhere, you can visit `http://www.packtpub.com/support` and register to have the files e-mailed directly to you.

Errata

Although we have taken every care to ensure the accuracy of our content, mistakes do happen. If you find a mistake in one of our books—maybe a mistake in the text or the code—we would be grateful if you could report this to us. By doing so, you can save other readers from frustration and help us improve subsequent versions of this book. If you find any errata, please report them by visiting `http://www.packtpub.com/submit-errata`, selecting your book, clicking on the **Errata Submission Form** link, and entering the details of your errata. Once your errata are verified, your submission will be accepted and the errata will be uploaded to our website or added to any list of existing errata under the Errata section of that title.

To view the previously submitted errata, go to `https://www.packtpub.com/books/content/support` and enter the name of the book in the search field. The required information will appear under the **Errata** section.

Piracy

Piracy of copyrighted material on the Internet is an ongoing problem across all media. At Packt, we take the protection of our copyright and licenses very seriously. If you come across any illegal copies of our works in any form on the Internet, please provide us with the location address or website name immediately so that we can pursue a remedy.

Please contact us at `copyright@packtpub.com` with a link to the suspected pirated material.

We appreciate your help in protecting our authors and our ability to bring you valuable content.

Questions

If you have a problem with any aspect of this book, you can contact us at `questions@packtpub.com`, and we will do our best to address the problem.

1
Introduction to NoSQL

In this chapter, you will learn about the emerging realm of NoSQL and get introduced to various classifications in the NoSQL domain. We will also understand the position of **Redis** in the NoSQL domain. We'll cover the following topics:

- Data in Enterprise
- NoSQL
- Use cases for NoSQL

An Internet-enabled world

We live in interesting times; in the last decade, a lot of changes have happened that have changed the way we experience the world of the Internet and the ecosystem around it. In this chapter, we will focus on some of the reasons that led to progress and discuss the developments happening in the world of data storage.

The following figure is a rough sketch of the evolution process that happened in cyberspace, the data for which is collected from the Internet, and gives a rough idea of the growth experienced in Internet-based services:

	2000 - 2005	2006 - 2009	2010 – present day
Hardware	Pentium series	Dual Core makes an entry , after that cores have been adding up (computer , tablets , smartphones)	
Social Media, Online gaming, Computing, Collaboration.	LinkenIn(2003), Facebook (2004), Youtube (2005), Reddit(2005)	Twitter(2006), Amazon WS(2006), Heroku (2007), Reddit (2005), Google App engine(2008) Wooga (2009)	Twitter:554 million registered users Netflix: 40 million registered users Google search:120 billion monthly Github: 3 million registered users Facebook:1.2 billion monthly users Flipboard: 90 million users LinkedIn: 260 million users
Database	CouchDB(2005) HADOOP(2005)	Cassandra(2008) MongoDB(2009) Riak(2009) Redis(2009)	100+ NoSQL databases.
Internet users	360,985,492 (2000) to 2,405,518,376 (present day and increasing)		

Evolution: Social media, processors and cores, databases (NoSQL)

The preceding chart indicates that the hardware industry saw a paradigm shift during the middle half of the first decade. Instead of new processors coming out with increased clock speeds, the newer generation of processors came with multiple cores and their numbers increased in processors with a subsequent release. Gone were the days when a big machine with lots of memory and a powerful processor could solve any problem or, in other words, when an Enterprise depended on vertical scaling to solve their performance issues. What it signaled, in a way, was that parallel computing was the future and it will be deployed on commodity-based machines.

With the hardware industry signaling the arrival of parallel computing, the newer generation of solutions had to be distributed and parallel in nature. This means that they needed to have logic executed in parallel and data stored in distributed datastores; in other words, horizontal scaling was the way to go. Moreover, with Web 2.0, there was an emergence of social media, online gaming, online shopping, collaborative computing, cloud computing, and so on. The Internet was becoming a ubiquitous platform.

The popularity of the Internet and the number of people using the Internet was increasing by the day, and the amount of time spent on the Internet was also increasing. Another important aspect to be looked at was that users across geographies were coming together in this Internet-enabled world. There are many reasons for this; for one, websites were becoming intelligent and in a way, were engaging end users far effectively than their predecessors. Another factor that was making Internet adoption faster and easier were innovative handheld devices, such as smartphones, tablets, and so on. Nowadays, the kind of compute power these handheld devices have can be compared to that of computers. In this dynamically changing world, Internet-based software solutions and services are expanding the horizon of social media, which brings people together on a common platform. This created a new business domain like social-Enterprise media, where social media bridges with Enterprise. This was definitely going to have an impact on traditional Enterprise solutions.

The Internet effect made Enterprise solutions undergo a metamorphic shift. The shift in Enterprise architecture went from a nuanced set of requirements, typically expected from Enterprise solutions, to adopting newer requirements, which were the bastion of social media solutions. Nowadays, Enterprise solutions are integrating with social media sites to know what their customers are talking about; they themselves have started creating platforms and forums where the customer can come and contribute their impressions about products and services. All this data exchange happens in real time and needs a highly concurrent and scalable ecosystem. To sum it up, Enterprise solutions want to adopt the features of social media solutions, and this has a direct and proportional bearing on the nonfunctional requirements of their architectures. Features such as fault management, real-time big data crunching, eventual consistency, high numbers of reads and writes, responsiveness, horizontal scalability, manageability, maintainability, agility, and so on, and their impact on Enterprise architecture, are being looked at with renewed interest. Techniques, paradigms, frameworks, and patterns that were used in social media architecture are being studied and reapplied in Enterprise architecture.

One of the key layers in any solution (social media or Enterprise) is the data layer. Data, the way it is arranged and managed, and the choice of datastore forms the data layer. From a designer's perspective, data handling in any datastore is governed by perspectives such as consistency, availability, and partition tolerance, or better known as Eric Brewer's **CAP** theorem. While it is desirable to have all the three, in reality, any data layer can have a combination of two of the mentioned perspectives. What this means is that the data in a solution can have many combinations of perspectives, such as availability-partition tolerance (this combination has to forego consistency in data handling), availability-consistency (this combination has to forego partition tolerance which will impact the amount of data that the data layer can handle), and consistency-partition tolerance (this combination has to forego availability).

The CAP theorem has a direct bearing on the behavior of the system, read/write speeds, concurrency, maintainability, clustering patterns, fault tolerance, data loads, and so on.

The most common approach when designing the data model is to arrange it in a relational and normalized way. This works well when the data is in transactional mode, needs consistency, and is structured, that is, it has a fixed schema. This approach of normalizing data appears over-engineered when the data is semistructured, has a tree-like structure, or is schema-less, where consistency can be relaxed. The end result of making semistructured data fit into a structured data model is the explosion of tables and a complicated data model to store simple data.

Due to the lack of alternatives, the solutions have been overtly relying on **RDBMS** to address concerns regarding data handling. The problem with this approach is RDBMS, which was primarily designed to address consistency and the availability perspective of data handling, also started to store data, which had concerns of partition tolerance. The end result was a bloated RDBMS with a very complex data model. This started impacting the nonfunctional requirements of a solution negatively, in the areas of fault management, performance, scalability, manageability, maintainability, and agility.

Another area of concern was **Data Interpretation**, which is very important while designing the data layer. In a solution, the same data is viewed and interpreted differently by a different concerned group. To give a better idea, let's say that we have an e-commerce website that sells products. Three basic functional domains come into play in the design of this data layer; they are inventory management, account management, and customer management. From a core business standpoint, all the domains need **atomicity, consistency, isolation, durability** (**ACID**) properties in their data management, and from the CAP theorem point of view, they need consistency and availability. However, if the website needs to understand its customer in real time, an analytics team needs to analyze data from the inventory management, account management, and customer management domains. Apart from other data, it might collect separately at real time. The way the analytics team views the same data is totally different from the way other teams view it; for them, consistency is less of a concern, as they are more interested in the overall statistics, and a little inconsistent data will have no impact on the overall report. If all the data required for analytics from these domains is kept in the same data model as that for core business, the analytics will run into difficulty because it has to now work with this highly normalized and optimized structured data for business operations. The analytics team will also like to have their data denormalized for faster analysis.

Now, running real-time analytics on this normalized data on a RDBMS system will require heavy compute resources, which will impact the performance of core business during business hours. So, it is better for overall business if separate data models are created for these domains, one for business and one for analytics, where each is maintained separately as they have separate concerns. We will see in subsequent topics why RDBMS is not the right fit for analytics and some other use cases and how NoSQL solves the problem of explosion of data.

The NoSQL primer

Not only SQL or **NoSQL**, as it is popularly called, was coined by Carlo Strozzi in 1998 and was reintroduced by Eric Evans in 2009. This is an exciting area in data handling which, in a way, has filled up the many gaps existing in the data handling layer. Before the emergence of NoSQL as an alternate choice to store data, SQL-oriented databases (RDBMS) were the only choice available for the developers to position or retrofit their data. In other words, RDBMS was one hammer to nail all data problems. When NoSQL and its different categories started emerging, data models and data sizes that were not meant for RDBMS started finding NoSQL as a perfect datastore. There was also a shift in attention from a consistency standpoint; there was a shift was from ACID to BASE properties.

ACID properties represent the consistency and availability of the CAP theorem. These properties are exhibited by RDBMS and stand for the following:

- **Atomicity**: In a transaction, all operations will complete or none will be completed (rollback)
- **Consistency**: The database will be in a consistent state during the start and end of a transaction and cannot leave the state in between
- **Isolation**: There will be no interference among the concurrent transactions
- **Durability**: Once a transaction commits, it will remain so even after the server restarts or fails

BASE properties are exhibited by NoSQL; they represent the availability and partition tolerance of the CAP theorem. They basically give up on the strong consistency shown by RDBMS. BASE stands for following features:

- **Basically available**: This guarantees a response to a request even if the data is in the stale state.

- **Soft state**: The state of the data is always in a position to accept change even when there is no request to change its state. What this means is that suppose there are two nodes holding the same state of a data (the replication of data), if there is a request to change the state in one of the nodes, the state in the other node will not change during the lifespan of the request. The data in the other node will change its state due to an asynchronous process triggered by the datastore, thus making the state soft.
- **Eventually consistent**: Due to the distributed nature of the nodes, the system will eventually become consistent.

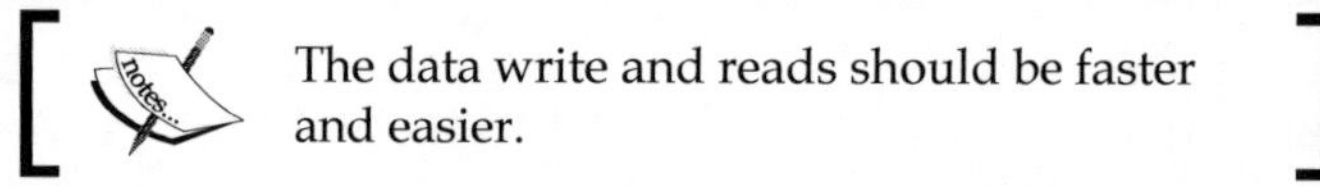

Another interesting development took place in the field of software development. Vertical scalability had reached its limit and solutions had to be designed that were horizontally scalable in nature, so the data layer also had to be distributed and partition tolerant. Apart from that social media solution, online gaming and game theory-based websites (where target marketing was done, that is, users are rewarded based on their purchase history with the site. These kind of sites need real-time analytics) started gaining prominence. Social media wanted the synching of huge amount of data from across geographies in the shortest possible time, and the gaming world was interested in high performance. E-commerce sites were interested in knowing about their customers and products in real time, as well as profiling their customers to know their needs before they could realize the need for it. The categories in NoSQL that emerged based on different data models are as follows:

- Graph-oriented NoSQL
- Document-oriented NoSQL
- Key-value oriented NoSQL
- Column-oriented NoSQL

Graph-oriented NoSQL

Graph databases are a special kind of NoSQL databases. The data models stored by graph databases are graph structures, which are a bit different from other datastores. A graph structure consists of a node, edges, and properties. The way to understand graph databases is to think of them as mindmaps with bidirectional relationships. What this means is that if A is related to B and B is related to C, then C is related to A. Graph databases tend to solve the problems that arise out of relationships formed among unstructured entities at runtime, which can be bidirectional. As compared to this, RDBMS also has a concept of relationships called **table joins**, but these relationships are on structured data and cannot be bidirectional.

Moreover, these table joins add complexity to the data model with foreign keys and have performance penalties on table join-based queries when the dataset grows over a period time. A few of the most promising graph datastores are Neo4i, FlockDB, OrientDB, and so on.

To understand this better, let's take a sample use case and see how easy it becomes to solve complex graph-based business use cases with graph-oriented NoSQL. The following figure is a sample use case, which an e-commerce website might be interested in solving. The use case is to capture visitors' purchase history and people's relationships in the microblogging component of the website.

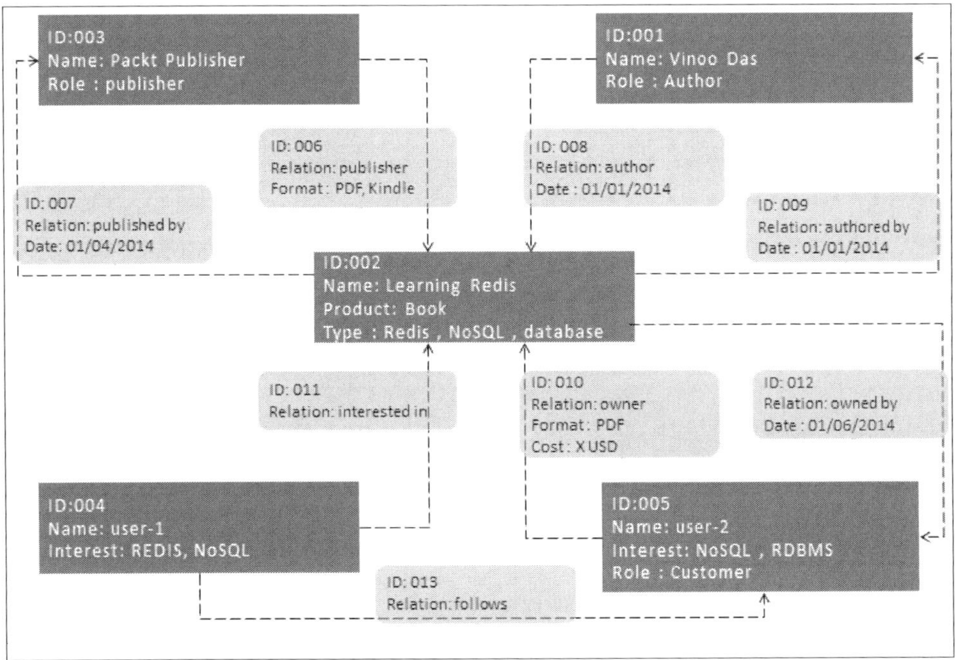

Sample module for graph DB

Business entities such as the publisher, author, customer, product, and so on are represented as nodes in the graph. Relationships such as authored by, author, publisher, published by, and so on are represented by edges in the graph. Interestingly, a nonbusiness node, such as *user-1*, which is from the blogging site, can be represented in the graph along with its relationship, *follows*, with the other node, *user-2*. By combining the business and nonbusiness entities, the website can find target customers for the products. In the graph, both nodes and edges have properties that are used while running analytics.

The following set of questions can be easily answered by a graph database based on the relationships stored in the systems:

- Who authored *Learning Redis*?

  Answer: Vinoo Das

- How are Packt Publishing and *Learning Redis* related?

  Answer: Publisher

- Who has their own NoSQL book published by Packt Publishing?

  Answer: user-2

- Who is following the customer who has purchased *Learning Redis* and is interested in NoSQL?

  Answer: user-1

- List all the NoSQL books that cost less than X USD and that can be bought by the followers of user-2.

  Answer: *Learning Redis*

Document-oriented NoSQL

Document-oriented datastores are designed to store data with the philosophy of storing a document. To understand this simplistically, the data here is arranged in the form of a book. A book can be divided into any number of chapters, where each chapter can be divided into any number of topics, and each topic is further divided into subtopics and so on and so forth.

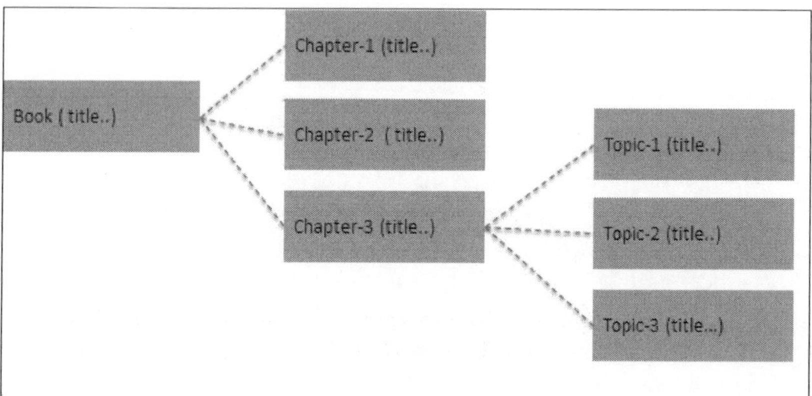

Composition of a book

If the data has a similar structure, that is, it is hierarchical and does not have a fixed depth or schema, then document-oriented datastores are the perfect option to store such data. **MongoDB** and **CouchDB (Couchbase)** are two well-known document-oriented datastores that are getting a lot of attention these days. Like a book, which has indexes for faster searches, these datastores also have the indexes of keys stored in memory for faster searches.

Document-oriented datastores have data stored in the XML, JSON, and other formats. They can hold scalar values, maps, lists, and tuples as values. Unlike RDBMS, where the data is viewed as rows of data stored in a tabular form, the data stored here is in a hierarchical tree-like structure where every value stored in these datastores is always associated with a key. Another unique feature is that document-oriented datastores are schema-less. The following screenshot shows an example which shows how the data is stored in document-oriented datastores. The format in which the data is stored is JSON. One of the beauties of document-oriented datastores is that the information can be stored in the way you think of the data. This, in a way, is a paradigm shift from RDBMS, where the data is broken into various smaller parts and then stored in rows and columns in a normalized way.

```
{
  "learning redis": {
    "publisher": "Packt Publisher",
    "author":"Vinoo Das",
    "page":250,
    "tags":["NoSQL","Redis","Packt Publisher","database"],
    "chapter info":[
        {
                "title":"Introduction to NoSQL",
                "number of pages":20
        },{
                "title":"Installing Redis",
                "number of pages":20
        }
    ]
  }
}
```

Composition of sample data in JASON format

The two most famous document-oriented stores in use are MongoDB and CouchDB, and it will be interesting to pit them against each other in order to have a better overview.

Salient features of MongoDB and CouchDB

Well, the fact that both MongoDB and CouchDB are document-oriented is established, but both differ in various aspects, which will be of interest to people who want to learn about document-oriented datastores and adopt them in their projects. Following are some features of MongoDB and CouchDB:

- **Insertion of small and large data sets**: Both MongoDB and CouchDB are very good for the insertion of small data sets. MongoDB is a tad better than CouchDB when it comes to the insertion of large data sets. Overall, speed consistencies are very good in both of these document datastores.
- **Random reads**: Both MongoDB and CouchDB are fast when it comes to read speeds. MongoDB is a tad better when it comes to reading large data sets.
- **Fault tolerance**: Both MongoDB and CouchDB have comparable and good fault tolerance capability. CouchDB uses **Erlang/OTP** as the underlying technology platform for its implementation. Erlang is a language and a platform that was developed to make fault-tolerant, scalable, and highly concurrent systems. The fact that Erlang act as a backbone for CouchDB gives it a very good fault-tolerant capability. MongoDB uses C++ as the primary language for its underlying implementation. Industry adoption and its proven track record in the area of fault tolerance give MongoDB a good heads-up in this area.
- **Sharding**: MongoDB has an in-built sharding capability, whereas CouchDB does not. Nevertheless, Couchbase, which is another document datastore built on top of CouchDB, has an automatic sharding capability.
- **Load balancing**: MongoDB and CouchDB have a good load balancing capability. However, since the underlying technology, that is the actor paradigm, in CouchDB has a good provision for load balancing, it can be said that the capability in CouchDB scores over the capability in MongoDB.
- **Multi-data center support**: CouchDB has multi-data center support, whereas MongoDB at the time of researching for this book, didn't have this support. However, I guess that in the future, with the popularity of MongoDB, we can expect it.
- **Scalability**: Both CouchDB and MongoDB are highly scalable.
- **Manageability**: Both CouchDB and MongoDB have good manageability.
- **Client**: CouchDB has JSON for data exchange, whereas MongoDB has BSON, which is proprietary to MongoDB.

Column-oriented NoSQL

Column-oriented NoSQL is designed with the philosophy to store data in columns rather than rows. This way to store data is diametrically opposite to the way data is stored in RDBMS, such as in rows. Column-oriented databases are designed from the ground up to be highly scalable and hence, are distributed in nature. They give up on consistency to have this massive scalability.

The following screenshot is a depiction of a small inventory for smart tablets based on our perception; here, the idea is to show how the data is stored in RDBMS as compared to the data stored in a columnar database:

Product ID	Product Name	Unit Price (INR)	Stock
123	IPAD AIR	37000	100
234	SAMSUNG TAB 3	17000	100
345	KINDLE FIRE	18000	100
456	NEXUS 7	21000	100
567	MS SURFACE	25000	100

Presentation of data in columns and rows

The preceding tabular data is stored in RDBMS in the hard disk, in the format shown here:

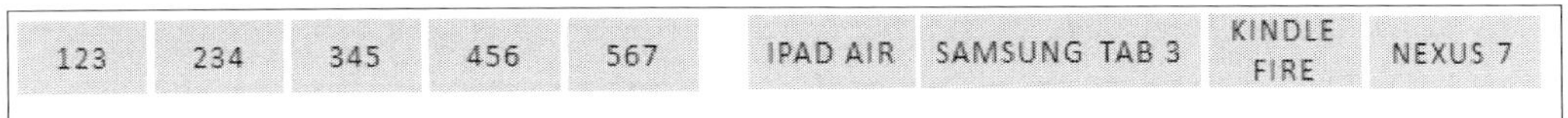

Data serialized as columns

The source of the information in the preceding screenshot is `http://en.wikipedia.org/wiki/Column-oriented_DBMS`.

The same data in a columnar datastore will be stored as shown in the following figure; here, the data is serialized in columns:

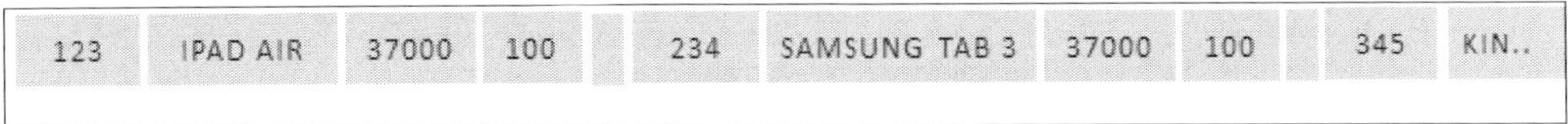

Data serialized as rows

A world where vertical scalability is reaching its limit and horizontal scalability is the way organizations want to adopt to store data, columnar datastores are offering solutions that can store petabytes of data in a very cost-effective way. Google, Yahoo!, Facebook, and so on have pioneered the storage of data in a columnar way, and the proof is in the pudding, that is, the amount of data that these companies store is a well-known fact. HBase and Cassandra are a few of the well-known products that are columnar in nature and can store a huge amount of data. Both the datastores are built with eventual consistency in mind. The underlying language in the case of HBase and Cassandra is Java; it will be interesting to put them against each other in order to have a better overview.

Salient features of HBase and Cassandra

HBase is a datastore that belongs to the category of columnar-oriented datastores. This datastore came into existence after Hadoop became popular with its HDFS file storage system, inspired from the *Google File System* paper published in 2003. The fact that HBase is based on Hadoop makes it an excellent choice for data warehousing and large-scale data processing and analysis. HBase provides a SQL-type interface over the existing Hadoop ecosystem, which is similar to the way we have been viewing data in a RDBMS, that is row-oriented, but the data is stored in a column-oriented way internally. HBase stores row data against a row key, and it is in a sorted order as per the row key. It has components such as the Region Server, which can be plugged to the DataNode provided with Hadoop. This means that the Region Server is collocated with the DataNode and acts as a gateway for interacting with HBase clients. Behind the scenes, the HBase master handles the DDL operations. Apart from this, it also manages the Region assignments and other book keeping activities associated with that. Cluster information and management, which includes state management, is taken care of by Zookeeper nodes. HBase clients interact directly with Region Servers to put and get data. Components such as Zookeeper (used to coordinate between the master and slave nodes), Name Node, and HBase master node do not participate directly in the exchange of data between the HBase client and Region Server nodes.

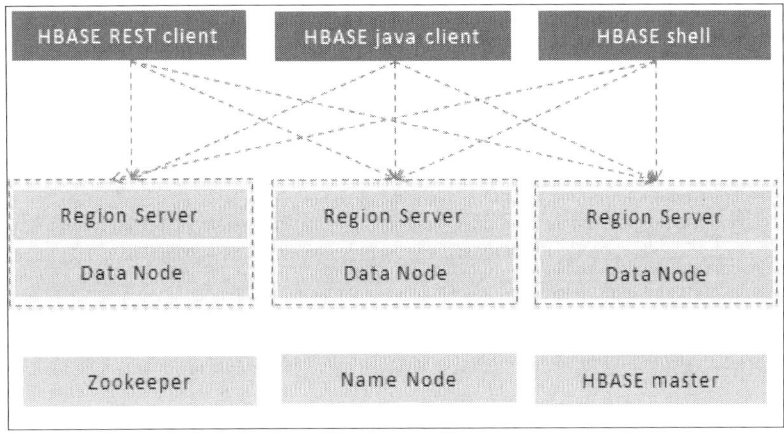

HBASE node set up

Cassandra is a datastore which belongs to the category of columnar-oriented datastores and also shows some features of the key-value datastore. Cassandra, which was initially started by Facebook but later forked to the Apache open source community, is best suited for real-time transaction processing and real-time analytics.

One of the key differentiators between Cassandra and HBase is that unlike HBase, which depends on the existing architecture of Hadoop, Cassandra is standalone in nature. Cassandra takes its inspiration from Amazon's Dynamo to store data. In short, the architectural approach of HBase makes the Region Server and DataNodes dependent on other components such as HBase master, Name Node, Zookeeper, whereas the nodes in Cassandra manage these responsibilities within and thus are not dependent on external components.

A Cassandra cluster can be viewed as a ring of nodes, of which there are a few seeds. These seeds are like any node but are responsible for up-to-date cluster state data. In the event of a seed node going down, a new seed can be elected among the available nodes. The data is distributed evenly across the ring, depending on the hash value of the row key. In Cassandra, data can be queried according to its row-key. Clients for Cassandra come in many flavors; that is, Thrift is one of the most native clients that can be used to interact with the Cassandra ring. Apart from this, there are clients that expose the **Cassandra Query Language** (**CQL**) interface, which has quite a resemblance to SQL.

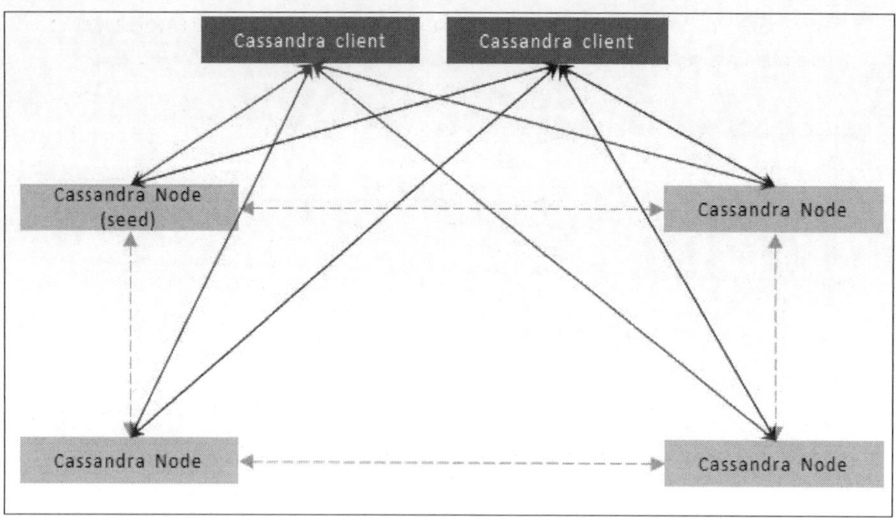

Cassandra nodes set up

- **Insertion of small and large data sets**: Both HBase and Cassandra are very good at the insertion of small data sets. The fact that both these datastores use multiple nodes to distribute writes on top of it. Both of them write the data first to memory-based storage such as RAM, which makes its insertion performance good.
- **Random reads**: Both HBase and Cassandra are fast when it comes to read speeds. In HBase, consistency was one of the key features that was kept in mind when designing the architecture. In Cassandra, data consistency was kept tunable, but one has to sacrifice speed in order to have higher consistency.
- **Eventual consistency**: HBase has strong consistency and Cassandra has eventual consistency, but interestingly, the consistency model in Cassandra is tunable. It can be tuned to have better consistency, but one has to give up performance in the read and write speeds.
- **Load balancing**: HBase and Cassandra have load balancing built into them. The idea is to have many nodes serving read and writes on a commodity grade node. Consistent hashing is used to distribute the load between the nodes.
- **Sharding**: HBase and Cassandra both have sharding capability. This is essential since both claim to give good performance from a commodity grade node, which has limited disk and memory space.
- **Multi-data center support**: Of the two, Cassandra has multi-data center support.

- **Scalability**: HBase and Cassandra have very good scalability, which was one of the design requirements.
- **Manageability**: Of the two, Cassandra has better manageability. This is because in Cassandra, there are nodes to manage but in HBase, there are many components that need to work in tandem, such as Zookeeper, DataNode, Name Node, Region Server, and so on.
- **Client**: Both HBase and Cassandra have clients in Java, Python, Ruby, Node.js, and many more, making it easy to work with heterogeneous environments.

Key value-oriented NoSQL

Key-value datastores are probably one of the fastest and simplest NoSQL databases. In their most simplistic form, they can be understood as a big hash table. From a usage perspective, every value stored in the database has a key. The key can be used to search for values and the values can be deleted by deleting the key. Some popular choices in key-value databases are Redis, Riak, Amazon's DynamoDB, project voldermort, and more.

How does Redis fare in some of the nonfunctional requirements as a key-value datastore?

Redis is one of the fastest key-value stores, which is seeing a very fast adoption throughout the industry, cutting across many domains. Since this book focuses on Redis, let's find out a bit more about how Redis fares in some of the nonfunctional requirements in brief. We will be talking about them in length as the book progresses:

- **Insertion of data sets**: The insertions of data sets is very fast in key-value datastores and Redis is no exception.
- **Random reads**: Random reads are very fast in key-value datastores. In Redis, all the keys are stored in memory. This ensures faster lookups, so the read speeds are higher. While it will be great if all the keys and values are kept in memory, this has a drawback. The problem with this approach is that memory requirements will be very high. Redis takes care of this by introducing something called *virtual memory*. Virtual memory will keep all the keys in the memory but will write the least recently-used values to disk.
- **Fault tolerance**: Fault handling in Redis depends on the cluster's topology. Redis uses the master-slave topology for its cluster deployment. All the data in the master is asynchronously copied to the slave; so, in case the master node goes to the failure state, one of the slave nodes can be promoted to master using the Redis sentinel.

- **Eventual consistency**: Key-value datastores have master-slave topology, which means that once the master is updated, all the slave nodes are updated asynchronously. This can be envisaged in Redis since slaves are used by clients for a read-only mode; it is possible that the master might have the latest value written but while reading from the slave, the client might get the stale value because the master has not updated the slaves. Thus, this lag can cause inconsistency for a brief moment.
- **Load balancing**: Redis has a simple way of achieving load balancing. As previously discussed, the master is used to write data, and slaves are used to read the data. So, the clients should have the logic built into them, have the read request evenly spread across the slave nodes, or use third-party proxies, such as Twemproxy to do so.
- **Sharding**: It is possible to have datasets that are bigger than the available memory, which makes presharding the data across various peer nodes a horizontal scalable option.
- **Multi-data center support**: Redis and key-value NoSQL do not provide inherent multi-data center support where the replications are consistent. However, we can have the master node in one data center and slaves in the other data center, but we will have to live with eventual consistency.
- **Scalability**: When it comes to scaling and data partitioning, the Redis server lacks the logic to do so. Primarily, the logic to partition the data across many nodes should reside with the client or should use third-party proxies such as Twemproxy.
- **Manageability**: Redis as a key value NoSQL is simple to manage.
- **Client**: There are clients for Redis in Java, Python, and Node.js that implement the **REdis Serialization Protocol** (**RESP**).

Use cases of NoSQL

Understand your business first; this will help you to understand your data. This will also give you deep insights on the kind of data layer that you need to have. The idea is to have a top-to-bottom design methodology. Deciding on the persistence mechanism first and then fitting the data for the business use case in that persistence mechanism is a bad idea (bottom-to-top design methodology). So, define your business requirements first, decide on the roadmap for the future, and then decide on the data layer. Another important factor to take into consideration when understanding the business requirements specification is to factor the nonfunctional requirements for every business use case, which I believe is paramount.

Failing to add a nonfunctional requirement in the business or, functional requirement causes problems when the system goes to performance test or worse, when it goes live. If you feel that the data model requires NoSQL from a functional requirement standpoint, then ask a few questions as follows:

- What type of NoSQL do you need for the data model?
- How big can the data grow, and how much scalability is required?
- How will you handle node failure? What is its impact on your business use case?
- Which is better data replication or infrastructure investment when data is growing?
- What are the strategies for handling read/write loads and how much concurrency is planned?
- What is the level of data consistency required for the business use case?
- How will the data reside (on a single data center or multiple data centers across geographies)?
- What are the clustering strategies and data synch strategies?
- What are the data backup strategies?
- What kind of network topology do you plan to use? What is the impact of network latency on performance?
- How comfortable is the team in handling, monitoring, administrating, and developing in the polyglot persistence environment?

Here's the summary of some of the NoSQL databases and how they are placed as per the CAP theorem. The following chart does not claim to be exhaustive, but is a snapshot of the most popular ones:

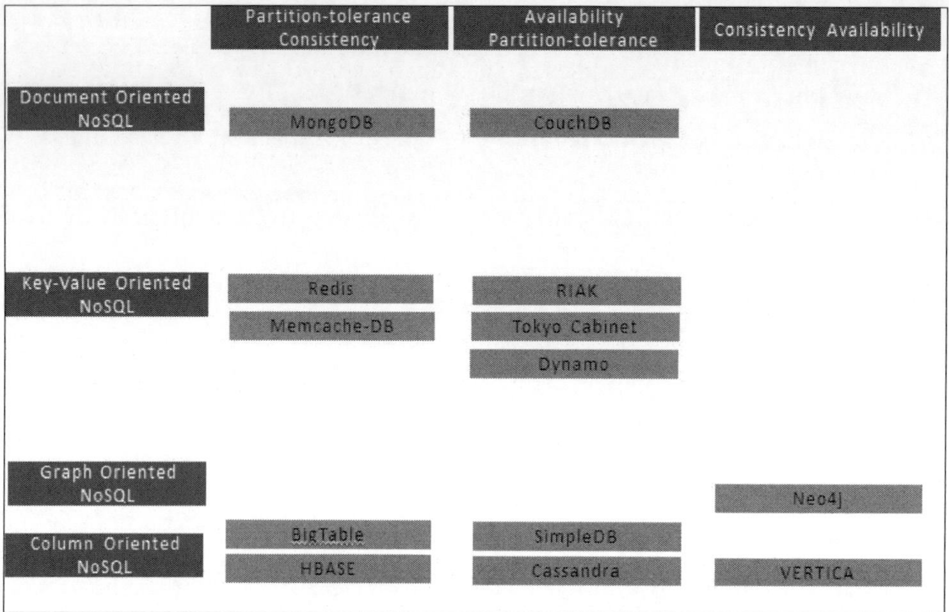

Partition-tolerance Consistency
Availability Partition-tolerance
Consistency Availability
Document Oriented NoSQL
MongoDB
CouchDB
Key-Value Oriented NoSQL
Redis
Memcache-DB
RIAK
Tokyo Cabinet
Dynamo
Graph Oriented NoSQL
Neo4J
Column Oriented NoSQL
BigTable
HBASE
SimpleDB
Cassandra
VERTICA

NoSQL databases placed as per CAP theorem

Let's analyze how companies are using NoSQL, which will give us ideas on how we can use NoSQL in our solutions effectively:

- **Big data**: This very term evokes a picture of hundreds and thousands of servers crunching petabytes of data for analysis. The use case for big data is self-evident and simple to argue for using NoSQL datastores. Columnar databases, one of the patterns of NoSQL, are the obvious choice for this kind of activity. Being distributed in nature, these solutions also have no single point of failure, parallel computing, write availability, and scalability. The following is a sample list of the different types of use cases where companies have successfully used columnar datastores in their business:
    - Spotify uses Hadoop for data aggregation, reporting, and analysis
    - Twitter uses Hadoop to process tweets and log files
    - Netflix uses Cassandra for their backend datastore in order to stream services

  - Zoho uses Cassandra to generate inbox previews for mail services
  - Facebook uses Cassandra for its Instagram operations
  - Facebook uses HBase in its message infrastructure
  - Su.pr uses HBase for real-time data storage and the analytics platform
  - HP IceWall SSO uses HBase to store user data in order to authenticate users for their web-based single sign-on solution

- **Heavy read/write**: This nonfunctional requirement instantly gives us the impression of a social or a gaming website. For Enterprises where this is a requirement, they can take inspiration for the choice of NoSQL.
  - LinkedIn uses Voldermort (the key-value datastore) to cater to millions of read and writes per day under a few milliseconds
  - Wooga (a social network game and mobile developer) uses Redis for its gaming platform; some of the games have a million plus users in a day
  - Twitter caters to 200 million tweets a day and uses NoSQL, such as Cassandra, HBase, Memcached, and FlockDB, and also uses RDBMS, such as MySQL
  - Stack overflow uses Redis to cater to 30 million registered users in a month

- **Document store**: The growth of Web 2.0 adoption and the rise in Internet content is creating data that is schema-less in nature. Having NoSQL (document-oriented) specially designed to store this kind of data makes the job of a developer simpler and the solution more stable in nature. Following are the examples of some companies that use different document stores:
  - SourceForge uses MongoDB to store front pages, project pages, and download pages; Allura on SourceForge is based on MongoDB
  - MetLife uses MongoDB for datastore for *the wall*, a customer service platform
  - Semantic News Portal uses CouchDB to store news data
  - Vermont public radio website's homepage uses CouchDB to stores news headlines, commentaries and more
  - AOL advertising uses Couchbase (a new avatar of CouchDB) to serve billions of impressions a month for 100 million plus users

- **Real-time experience and e-commerce platform**: Shopping carts, user profile management, voting, user session management, real-time page counters, real-time analytics, and more are the services that are being offered by companies to give real-time experience to the end user. Following are the examples of some companies that use real-time experience and e-commerce platform:
    - Flickr push uses Redis to push real-time updates
    - Instagram uses Redis to store hundreds and millions of media content against keys and to serve them in real time
    - Digg uses Redis for its page views and user clicks solution
    - Best Buy uses Riak for its e-commerce platform

Summary

In this chapter, you saw how the Internet world is undergoing a paradigm shift, the evolution of the NoSQL world, and how social media is championing NoSQL adoption. You also saw the various alternatives in the NoSQL world and how they equate. Finally, you saw how Redis maps up in the NoSQL ecosystem.

In the next chapter, we will take a plunge into the world of Redis.

2

Getting Started with Redis

Redis is a key-value-based NoSQL datastore developed by Salvatore Sanfilippo, launched in 2009. The name Redis comes from **REmote DIctionary Server**. Redis is a high-performing single thread server in C.

Redis can be installed on all POSIX-compliant Unix systems. Though there is no production grade release of a Windows system, it can still be installed in a Windows environment for development purposes. In this chapter, we will install Redis in Windows and Mac OS environments, write programs in Java, and play with the in-built client that comes along with the distribution.

Installing Redis on Windows

Microsoft Open Tech group has ported Redis and maintains it for win32/win64 machines. There are two ways in which we can get started with installing Redis on Windows, and these are listed as follows:

- Working with prebuilt binaries
- Getting the code and compiling it in the Microsoft environment

For the impatient, downloading the binaries of Redis 2.8 is an easier option. First things first, we need to do the following in order to get started:

1. Go to `https://github.com/MSOpenTech/redis` and download the ZIP file under the **Clone in Desktop** button. For this book, we are going to download the latest version of Redis, that is, the `redis-2.8.zip` file.
2. Right-click on the link and save it in a suitable location on your Windows machine. I have saved it at `F:\sw2\redis\redis-2.8.zip`.

3. Right-click and unzip the compressed file to a suitable folder. I have named the folder as `redis-2.8`, and the folder structure after unzipping looks similar to what is shown in the following screenshot:

Name	Date modified	Type	Size
bin	9/28/2014 5:27 PM	File folder	
deps	9/28/2014 5:26 PM	File folder	
msvs	9/28/2014 5:26 PM	File folder	
src	9/28/2014 5:26 PM	File folder	
tests	9/28/2014 5:26 PM	File folder	
utils	9/28/2014 5:26 PM	File folder	
.gitignore	9/24/2014 3:58 AM	GITIGNORE File	2 KB
00-RELEASENOTES	9/24/2014 3:58 AM	File	27 KB
appveyor.yml	9/24/2014 3:58 AM	YML File	1 KB
BUGS	9/24/2014 3:58 AM	File	1 KB
CONTRIBUTING	9/24/2014 3:58 AM	File	2 KB
COPYING	9/24/2014 3:58 AM	File	2 KB
INSTALL	9/24/2014 3:58 AM	File	1 KB
license.txt	9/24/2014 3:58 AM	TXT File	2 KB
Makefile	9/24/2014 3:58 AM	File	1 KB
MANIFESTO	9/24/2014 3:58 AM	File	5 KB
README	9/24/2014 3:58 AM	File	5 KB
README.md	9/24/2014 3:58 AM	MD File	5 KB
redis.conf	9/24/2014 3:58 AM	CONF File	34 KB
runtest	9/24/2014 3:58 AM	File	1 KB
runtest-sentinel	9/24/2014 3:58 AM	File	1 KB
sentinel.conf	9/24/2014 3:58 AM	CONF File	7 KB

Folder structure after unzipping the compressed file

4. Get inside the `bin` folder. You will find the `release` folder; when you click on it, you will have a list of the files inside this folder, as shown in the following screenshot:

Name	Date modified	Type	Size
dump.rdb	9/28/2014 7:09 PM	RDB File	1 KB
Redis on Windows.docx	9/19/2014 12:08 PM	Microsoft Word D...	18 KB
Redis Release Notes.docx	9/19/2014 3:30 PM	Microsoft Word D...	14 KB
redis.windows.conf	9/19/2014 12:08 PM	CONF File	29 KB
redis-2.8.17.zip	9/24/2014 3:58 AM	Compressed (zipp...	1,291 KB
redis-benchmark.exe	9/19/2014 3:22 PM	Application	418 KB
redis-check-aof.exe	9/19/2014 3:22 PM	Application	284 KB
redis-check-dump.exe	9/19/2014 3:22 PM	Application	295 KB
redis-cli.exe	9/19/2014 3:22 PM	Application	456 KB
redis-server.exe	9/19/2014 3:21 PM	Application	1,198 KB
RedisService.docx	9/19/2014 12:08 PM	Microsoft Word D...	16 KB
sentinel28.conf	9/28/2014 5:46 PM	CONF File	8 KB
stdout	9/28/2014 5:28 PM	File	0 KB

Folder structure inside the bin/release folder

5. Open Command Prompt and run `redis-server.exe`. Provide the `redis-server.exe --maxheap 1024mb` heap size and you should see a console window popping up, similar to the following screenshot. In the case of Windows 7, the user might be asked to trust the software to proceed further.

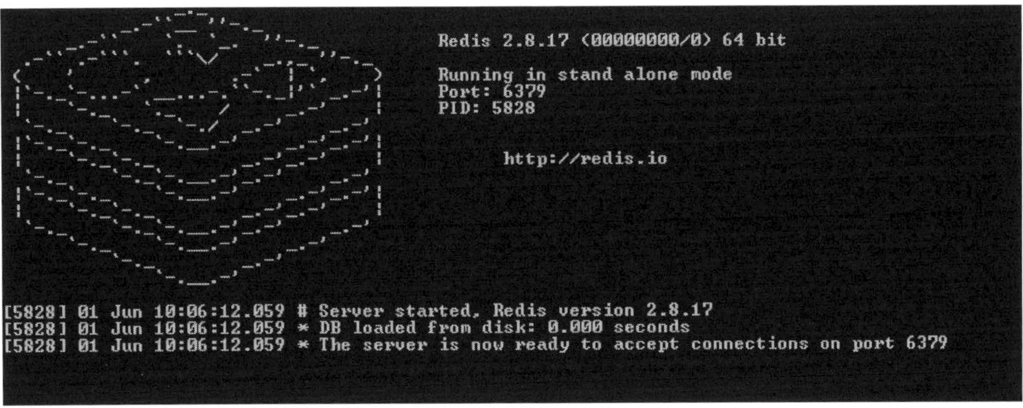
Redis 2.8.17 (00000000/0) 64 bit
Running in stand alone mode
Port: 6379
PID: 5828
http://redis.io
[5828] 01 Jun 10:06:12.059 # Server started, Redis version 2.8.17
[5828] 01 Jun 10:06:12.059 * DB loaded from disk: 0.000 seconds
[5828] 01 Jun 10:06:12.059 * The server is now ready to accept connections on port 6379

Redis server's default startup

6. Note the last line showing on the Command Prompt: **The servers now ready to accept connections on port 6379**.
7. Now, let's start a prebuilt client, which is shipped with the distribution, and connect to the server. The client that we will execute is a command-line interpreter, and when we click on it, the client program will be launched:

```
G:\sw\redis2.8\redis-2.8\bin\release>redis-cli.exe
127.0.0.1:6379> _
```

The Redis client is started with the Redis server running

8. Your simple installation is complete (clustered setup and other management topics will be taken up in later chapters).

Downloading the example code

You can download the example code files from your account at `http://www.packtpub.com` for all the Packt Publishing books you have purchased. If you purchased this book elsewhere, you can visit `http://www.packtpub.com/support` and register to have the files e-mailed directly to you.

Installing Redis on Mac OS

Installing Redis is really simple on a Mac OS. Follow these steps and you are good to go:

1. Download the package from Internet. For this, you can use the following command: `wget http://download.redis.io/releases/redis-2.8.3.tar.gz`
2. Untar the compressed `tar xzf redis-2.8.3.tar.gz` file.
3. This will create a folder; go to the folder by issuing the `cd redis-2.8.3` command.
4. Compile the file by issuing the `make` command. This will compile the binaries and create a folder structure, as shown in the following screenshot:

```
vinoo-dass-MacBook-Pro:redis-2.8.3 vinoodas$ ls
00-RELEASENOTES CONTRIBUTING    INSTALL         Makefile        deps            runtest         src             utils
BUGS            COPYING         MANIFESTO       README          redis.conf      sentinel.conf   tests
vinoo-dass-MacBook-Pro:redis-2.8.3 vinoodas$
```

Folder structure for a Mac distribution

5. Type the `src/redis-server` command; this will start the server, as shown in the following screenshot:

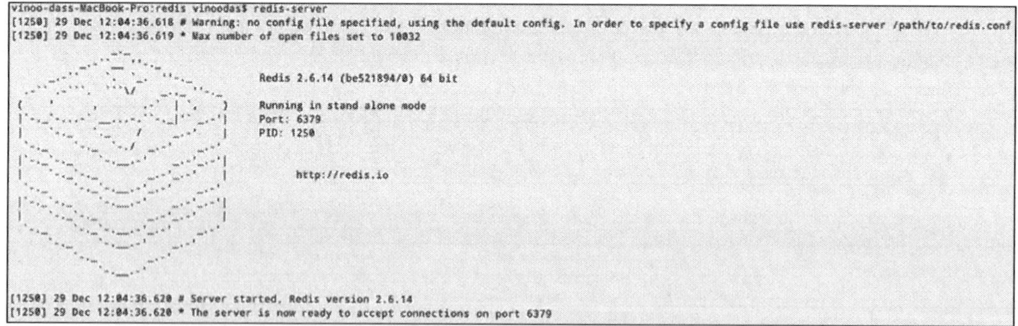

vinoo-dass-MacBook-Pro:redis vinoodas$ redis-server
[1250] 29 Dec 12:04:36.618 # Warning: no config file specified, using the default config. In order to specify a config file use redis-server /path/to/redis.conf
[1250] 29 Dec 12:04:36.619 * Max number of open files set to 10032
Redis 2.6.14 (be521894/0) 64 bit
Running in stand alone mode
Port: 6379
PID: 1250
http://redis.io
[1250] 29 Dec 12:04:36.620 # Server started, Redis version 2.6.14
[1250] 29 Dec 12:04:36.620 * The server is now ready to accept connections on port 6379

Starting the Redis server in the Apple environment

6. Your Redis server is running and it is ready to accept the requests in port 6379. Open another terminal and go the same folder form where you installed Redis. Type the command `src/redis-client`; this will start the client shell, as shown in the following screenshot:

```
vinoo-dass-MacBook-Pro:redis-2.8.3 vinoodas$ src/redis-cli
127.0.0.1:6379>
127.0.0.1:6379>
127.0.0.1:6379>
127.0.0.1:6379>
```

Redis client started in Apple environment

7. Your client is ready and you are ready for the Hello World program, but before you continue, it's better to understand a bit more about the configuration file called `redis.conf`.

Introduction to redis.conf

Redis ships with the `redis.windows.conf` file, which is located in the parent folder that was created when the distribution's ZIP/tarfile was uncompressed. Any customization needed by the server on startup can be done through this configuration file. If you need to include the `redis.conf` file, then provide the path to the file while the server starts up as an argument.

The following message will be displayed on the Command Prompt when you provide the configuration file at startup:

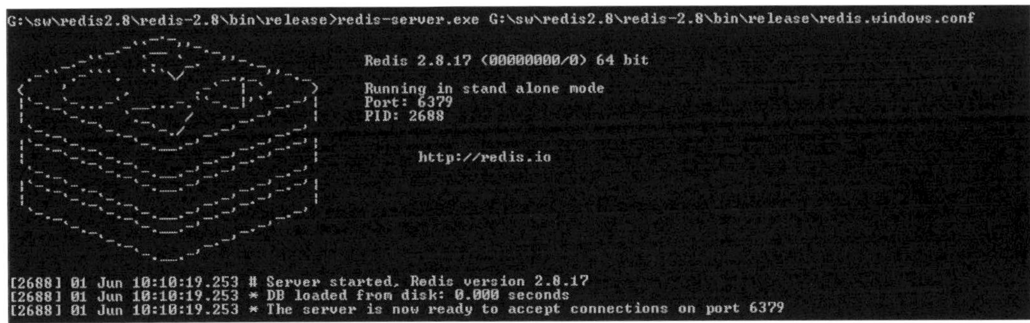
G:\sw\redis2.8\redis-2.8\bin\release>redis-server.exe G:\sw\redis2.8\redis-2.8\bin\release\redis.windows.conf
Redis 2.8.17 (00000000/0) 64 bit
Running in stand alone mode
Port: 6379
PID: 2688
http://redis.io
[2688] 01 Jun 10:10:19.253 # Server started, Redis version 2.8.17
[2688] 01 Jun 10:10:19.253 * DB loaded from disk: 0.000 seconds
[2688] 01 Jun 10:10:19.253 * The server is now ready to accept connections on port 6379

Redis server startup with config path during the startup

Redis, as mentioned, is a Unix-based software, which is ported to the Windows environment. A lot of configuration parameters are meant for the Unix environment; nevertheless, it is always good to know about the parameters that will be beneficial to you when moving to a Unix-based environment. These parameters are explained as follows:

- **Port 6379**: This number indicates that the server will listen to messages coming on port 6379. This port number can be changed to suit your project setup, and the server will listen for messages on that port. This will require a server restart.

- **# bind 127.0.0.1**: This is the IP address that you want your server to bind to. By default, this parameter is commented, which means that the server will listen to all the interfaces for messages.
- **Timeout 0**: This means that the server will not close the connection if the client is in an idle state.
- **tcp-keepalive 0**: This is a command to the server in order to keep the connection with the client open. You can make it `SO_KEEPALIVE`, which will indicate the server to send an `ACK` message to the client.
- **loglevel notice**: This is the log level that you want your server to have. The levels of logs that you can have are debug, verbose, notice, and warning.
- **logfile stdout** : This is the channel to which you want to send your log messages, to the command line in Windows or the terminal in the case of Unix-based systems.
- **syslog-enabled no**: If this is changed to *yes*, this will send the message to the system log.
- **dir**: This should be set to the working directory where the user wants to run the Redis server. This in turn will tell the Redis server to create files, such as server files appropriately.

Rest of the configuration parameters can be treated as advanced parameters, and we shall be using most of them in subsequent chapters when the need arises.

Hello World in Redis

This section will excite programmers the most. Let's get our hands dirty and punch in some code. But, before that, we have to understand that Redis works on a client-server model and uses the Redis protocol to communicate with the server. For the client to connect to the server, the client has to know the location of the server. For this section, I am going to show samples using the redis-cli and Java clients.

Hello World using redis-cli

Start the Redis client Command Prompt (make sure that the server is running). Type in the following commands, as shown in the following screenshot, and see the outcome:

```
G:\sw\redis2.8\redis-2.8\bin\release>redis-cli.exe
127.0.0.1:6379> set MSG "Hello World"
OK
127.0.0.1:6379> get MSG
"Hello World"
127.0.0.1:6379> _
```

Trying simple Set and Get commands using the Redis client

There are three parts to the command we wrote. They are explained as follows:

- Set: This command is used to set a value in the Redis server
- MSG: This is the key for the message to be stored in the Redis server
- Hello World: This is the value stored in the server for the MSG key

So, this clears a pattern that we have to keep in mind when working with Redis. Remember, Redis is a key-value NoSQL datastore. The syntax for this is COMMAND <space> KEY <space> VALUE.

Continuing with the Hello world program, we will do something more. Let's type in set MSG Learning Redis we get an error message, and when we type set MSG "Hello World", the value that the server is going to return is OK:

```
G:\sw\redis2.8\redis-2.8\bin\release>redis-cli.exe
127.0.0.1:6379> set MSG "Hello World"
OK
127.0.0.1:6379> get MSG
"Hello World"
127.0.0.1:6379> set MSG Learning Redis
(error) ERR syntax error
127.0.0.1:6379>
```

Overwriting the key with a new value

The old value is overwritten with the new value for the given key. Let's add another dimension to this sample, that is, open another client to the already existing client Command Prompt we have opened. In the second Command Prompt, let's type the command and key as get MSG. The value it's going to return is again "Hello World". This is shown in the following screenshot:

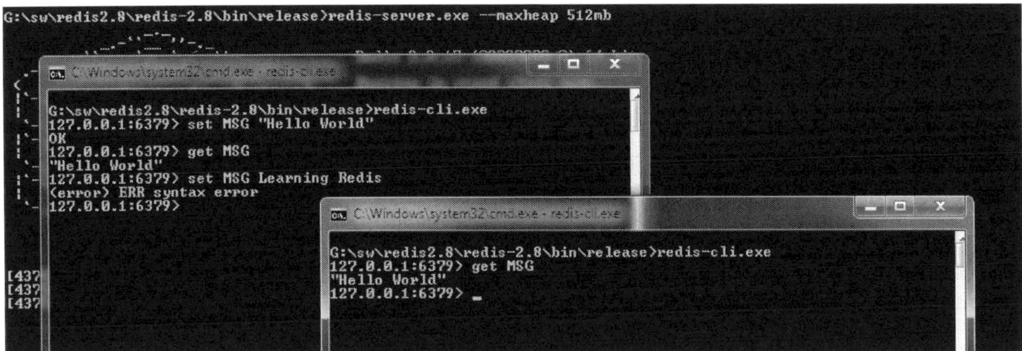

Writing in one client and reading it in another client

At this point, one will wonder what happens if we write a number as a value, maybe to store some timestamp, instead of a string.

Let's have the new command's key value as `set new_msg 1234`, and when we write the command key to retrieve the value as `get new_msg`, we get the result `"1234"`. Notice the double quotes around the value; this tells us something more about Redis and the way it stores the data, that is, every value stored in Redis is of the type string:

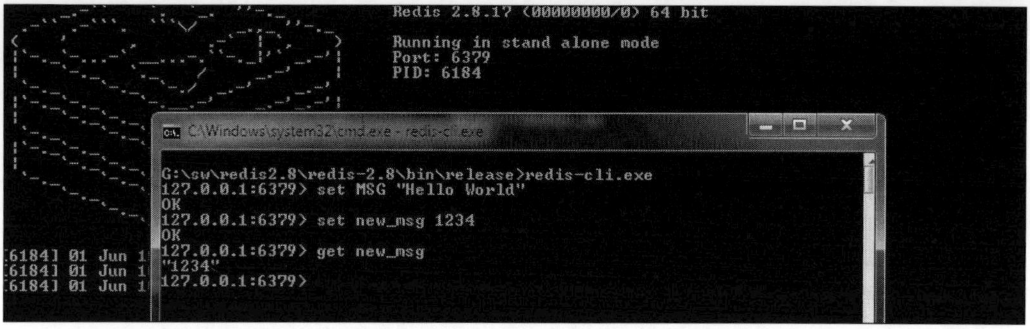

```
G:\sw\redis2.8\redis-2.8\bin\release>redis-cli.exe
127.0.0.1:6379> set MSG "Hello World"
OK
127.0.0.1:6379> set new_msg 1234
OK
127.0.0.1:6379> get new_msg
"1234"
127.0.0.1:6379>
```

Getting an integer value as a string

The redis-cli tool comes in handy for debugging the solution and executing commands to check the system and solution.

The next question that needs to be answered is how to access Redis programmatically.

Hello World using Java

In the previous section, you learned how to work with the `redis-cli.exe` application in order to connect to the Redis server. In this section, we will introduce a Java client API to connect to the Redis server and fire some commands. In all reality, for Redis to be used in a solution, it needs an API to connect to the server. There are some other attributes that an API needs rather than just connecting to the server, passing on commands and command parameters, and returning the result, but we will cover this in later chapters.

The Java client API chosen to demonstrate the examples in this book is Jedis.

There are three steps to run the `"Hello World"` example in Java. They are explained in the sections that follow.

Installing Jedis and creating an environment

Jedis is *Apache License 2.0* Java client for Redis. This client will be used for the samples demonstrated in this book. So, the most important thing to get for this client is that you need to make sure that you have a development environment. For this book, we have chosen Eclipse as the development environment (`http://www.eclipse.org/downloads/`). If you don't have Eclipse, you can grab a copy and install it (it's free and licensed). The examples of this book will work equally well with other integrated development environments. Now, perform the following steps:

1. Open Eclipse and create a project called `learning redis`, as shown in the following screenshot:

Creating a project in Eclipse

2. If you are using Maven, then add the following dependencies for Jedis:

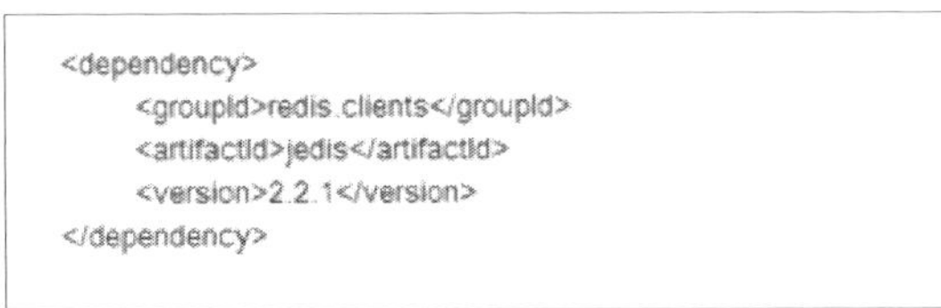

```
<dependency>
    <groupId>redis.clients</groupId>
    <artifactId>jedis</artifactId>
    <version>2.2.1</version>
</dependency>
```

Maven dependencies for Jedis

If you are using any other build tools, follow the instructions to add the dependency for Jedis accordingly.

Writing the program

The following program in Java is written with Redis as a datastore:

```
package org.learningredis.chapter.two;

import redis.clients.jedis.*;

public class HelloWorld {
  private JedisPool pool = new JedisPool(new JedisPoolConfig(),
"localhost");

  private void test() {
    try
        {
            Jedis jedis = pool.getResource();
            jedis.set("MSG", "Hello World");
            String result = jedis.get("MSG");
            System.out.println(" MSG : " + result);
            pool.returnResource(jedis);

        }
        catch (Exception e)
        {
            System.err.println(e.toString());
        }finally{
             pool.destroy();
        }

  }

    public static void main(String args[])
    {
        HelloWorld helloWorld = new HelloWorld();
        helloWorld.test();
    }

}
```

Make sure that your Redis server is up and running. In this sample, the port used here is the default port 6379.

Let's understand, step by step, what we are doing in the program:

1. We are setting up a pool of connections to connect to the Redis server. The pool is configured to the default IP address to which the server will bind.
2. We take a resource from the pool (the client stub that wraps the connection).
3. We set the key-value into it. This will push the value to be inserted into the Redis datastore.
4. We ask/get the value based on the key. In this case, the value inserted against the key in the previous step.
5. We return the resource into the pool for reuse and close the pool.

Shutting down the server

As with any server, shutting down the server gracefully is very important. There are a couple of things that need to be kept in mind before you shut down any Redis server, which are explained here:

1. Close all the client connections. For our Java program, we indicate the client to close all the connections by writing `"pool.destoy();"`.
2. The next thing that we need to do is to go to the client prompt and order a server shutdown.
3. If you intend to use Redis as a cache server, then the data it holds need not be saved. In this case, just type `shutdown nosave`. This will flush out all the data in the memory and free it.
4. If you intend to save the data so that you can use it later, then you have to pass the `shutdown save` command. This will persist the data in the `RDB` file even if no save points are configured, which we will cover in later chapters.

The following figure shows what happens in the example from the resource life cycle perspective:

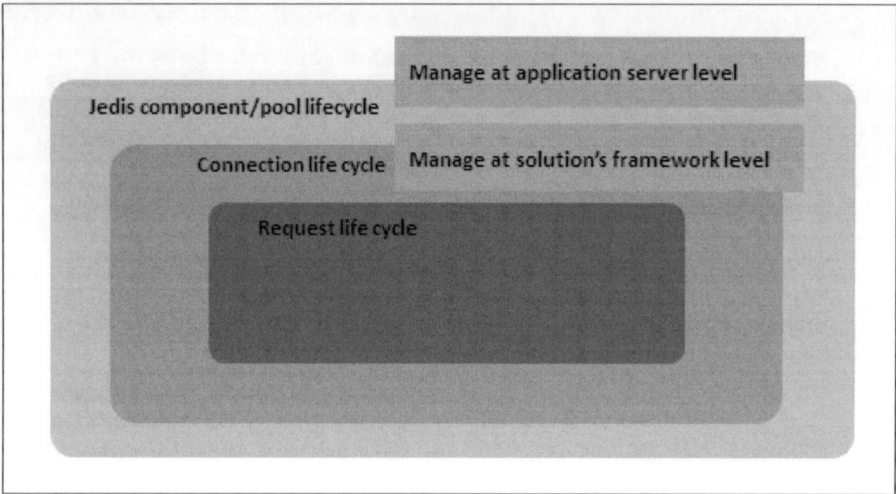

Managing a resource for the Jedis client

We have three resources that we have to consider during the life cycle. They are explained as follows:

- **Jedis connection pool**: This is the pool that should get created when the system/application starts up. This allocates the resources for the pool. The application server life cycle should manage the life cycle of the pool.
- **Connection**: In Jedis, the client stub created wraps the connection and acts as a client for Redis. In the program listed earlier, the client stub is referenced as *Jedis* which is obtained in the `pool.getResource()` statement.
- **Request life cycle**: This is where the command is getting executed. So, what is basically happening here is that using the Redis protocol, the command and the payload is being sent to the server. The payload consists of either the key, if it's a "getter," or the key and the value, if it's a "setter". The life cycle is managed with a positive acknowledgement from the server. It can be a success or an exception if it's a failure. In a way, we don't need explicit life cycle management for this statement.

How do we manage connections in Jedis, and what will happen if we don't manage them?

The answer to the question *what will happen if we don't manage it* is simple. The pool will run out of connections and the client application will suffer. We have seen connection-related problems in areas such as JDBC, where the application suffers when there are no connections for the client to connect to server. It's always the server that reserves the memory for a connection, and closing the connection is an indication for the server to release the memory.

The answer to the question *how do we manage connections in Jedis* is a bit more interesting and requires some code changes. We will take the previous code example and make changes to it, where we will handle connection resource management. For the following example, I am adding a wrapper, but in your applications, you can have more exotic recipes to address the concern mentioned. That is, you can use Spring to inject a connection or use `cglib` to dynamically create a proxy, which will set the connection before the command and return the connection after the command.

The following code is for the new Hello World program, which is now called `HelloWorld2`:

```
package org.learningredis.chapter.two;

public class Helloworld2  {
  JedisWrapper jedisWrapper = null;
  public Helloworld2() {
    jedisWrapper = new JedisWrapper();
  }

  private void test() {
    jedisWrapper.set("MSG", "Hello world 2 ");

    String result = jedisWrapper.get("MSG");
    System.out.println("MSG : " + result);
  }


  public static void main(String[] args) {
    Helloworld2 helloworld2 = new Helloworld2();
    helloworld2.test();
  }
}
```

The following is the wrapper code that handles the connection:

```
package org.learningredis.chapter.two;

import redis.clients.jedis.Jedis;
import redis.clients.jedis.JedisPool;

import redis.clients.jedis.JedisPoolConfig;

public class JedisWrapper {
  static JedisPool pool = new JedisPool(new JedisPoolConfig(),
"localhost");");");");");

  public void set(String key,String value){
    Jedis jedis = pool.getResource();
        jedis.set(key, value);
        pool.returnResource(jedis);
  }

  public String get(String key){
    Jedis jedis = pool.getResource();
        String result = jedis.get("MSG"); ");");");");
        pool.returnResource(jedis);
        return result;
  }
}
```

Two things becomes clear in this case, which are explained here:

- We don't have to manage the connection/resources, since this will be taken care of by the `wrapper` class
- The number of lines of code gets reduced, since we don't have to repeat the code for resource management

Loading a test Hello World program in Redis

Well, you have seen an example of a `Hello world` program in Java and the command line. But it's always good to add a load test dimension to your `Hello World` program. Redis comes with a tool called `redis-benchmark`, which can be found in the release folder.

The following command is going to make 100,000 calls to the Redis server:

```
redis-benchmark -n 100000 -q script load "redis.call('set','MSG' , "load testing hello world")"
```

Load testing of Hello World

The result is the total number of requests handled in a second for your machine. This tool comes in very handy for load testing your target environment. This is the snapshot of the result I got when I executed it in my Windows machine, and this will vary depending on the configuration of your machine and OS:

```
====== PING_INLINE ======
  10000 requests completed in 0.38 seconds
  50 parallel clients
  3 bytes payload
  keep alive: 1

90.60% <= 15 milliseconds
100.00% <= 15 milliseconds
26666.67 requests per second

====== PING_BULK ======
  10000 requests completed in 0.36 seconds
  50 parallel clients
  3 bytes payload
  keep alive: 1

91.13% <= 15 milliseconds
100.00% <= 15 milliseconds
27777.78 requests per second

====== SET ======
  10000 requests completed in 0.30 seconds
  50 parallel clients
  3 bytes payload
  keep alive: 1

92.01% <= 15 milliseconds
100.00% <= 15 milliseconds
33670.04 requests per second
```

Tool performing the load test

What happened over here is that `redis-benchmark` opened up 50 parallel connections to the Redis server and fired 10,000 requests. The requests contain Redis commands and a 3-byte payload. The approximate results get printed for analysis; in my case, the 10,000 `Set` commands took an overall of 0.30 seconds, that is, 33,670 requests were catered to per second.

Summary

Redis is a simple key-value oriented NoSQL, which can be used as a cache server and as a persistence server. This chapter showcased how simple it is to install Redis in multiple environments, including Windows (Redis can also be used in cloud environments, such as Amazon EC2). The installation for Windows should be used for development and sampling purposes only.

Redis has an interesting set of data structures, and it is sometimes called the data structure server. The next chapter will cover data structure in detail.

3
Data Structures and Communicating Protocol in Redis

The previous chapter dealt with installation of Redis and running some simple programs. Since Redis is a datastore, so it's important to understand how Redis treats data by providing data structures to handle and store them. Also important is how Redis deals with data while communicating it to a client such as the communication protocol.

Data structures

Data structure, as the word suggests, means a structure for storing data. In the world of computing, data is always organized in a way that makes sense to the program storing it. Data structure can vary from a simple sequential arrangement of characters to a complex map where keys are not arranged sequentially, but on the basis of an algorithm. Data structures are often composite in nature, which means that one data structure can hold other data structure, which is a map holding another map.

The key influencing factors in designing a data structure are performance and memory management of the data structure. Some of the common examples of data structures are lists, sets, maps, graphs and trees, tuples, and so on. As programmers, we have used data structures in our programs time and again. In an object-oriented world, a simple *object* is also a data structure since it contains data, and logic to access those data. Every data structure is governed by an algorithm which decides the efficiency and functional capability of it. So, if the algorithm can be classified then it would give a clear idea on the performance of data structure; when data is pumped into the data structure or when data is read or when data is deleted from the data structure.

Big O notation is a means to classify the algorithm (data structure) on its performance when the data grows. From Redis perspective, we will be classifying the data structure on the basis of these following notations:

- `O (1)`: Time taken by the command on a data structure is constant irrespective of the amount of data it contains.
- `O (N)`: Time taken by the command on a data structure scales linearly on the amount of data it contains, where `N` is the number of elements.
- `O (log (N))`: Time taken by the command on a data structure is logarithmic in nature, where `N` is the number of elements. Algorithms exhibiting this are highly efficient and used to find elements in sorted arrays. This can be interpreted to be fairly constant with time.
- `O (log (N) + M)`: Time taken by the command is dependent on logarithmic value, where `M` is the total number of elements in the sorted sets and `N` is the range from which the search has to find. This can be interpreted to be fairly dependent on the value of `M`. With increase in the value of `M`, time taken for search would increase.
- `O (M log (M))`: Time taken by the command is log-linear in nature.

Data types in Redis

Redis, a data structure server has many in-built data types, which makes it a bit different from other key-value NoSQL datastores in the ecosystem. Unlike other NoSQL, Redis provides the users with many in-built data types which provide a sematic way of arranging their data. Think of it like this; while designing a solution we need domain objects which in a way shape up our data layer. After deciding on the domain objects, we need to design the structure for our data that will be saved in the data store for which we need some predefined data structures. The advantage of this is that it saves time and efforts of the programmers to externally create and manage this data. For example, suppose in our program there is a requirement for a Set like data structure. Using Java, we can easily use an in-built data structure such as Set. If we were to put this data as a key-value, we will have to put the entire set against a key. Now if we were to sort this Set, the normal way would be to extract the data out and programmatically sort the data, which can be cumbersome. It would be good if the data store itself gives a mechanism to sort the data internally. Redis has the following data types built into it for storing data:

- String
- Hashes
- Lists

- Sets
- Sorted Sets

The following figure represents the data types that can be mapped to a key. The key itself is of type string in Redis and the values it can store can be any one of them as shown:

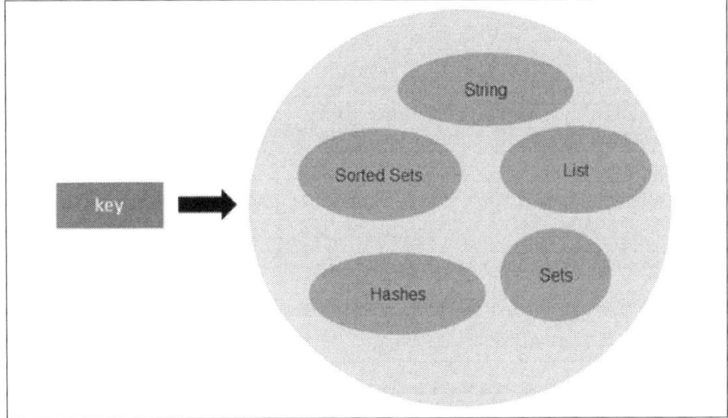

Representation of key and the values it can store

The string data type

String types are the basic data types in Redis. Though misleading in terminology, string in Redis can be considered as a byte array which can hold string, integers, images, files, and serializable objects in them. These byte arrays are binary safe in nature and the maximum size they can hold is 512 MB. In Redis, strings are called **Simple Dynamic String** (**SDS**), which in C language is implemented as `Char` array with some other attributes, such as `len` and `free`. These strings are binary safe too. The SDS header file is defined in `sds.h` file as following:

```
struct sdshdr {
            long len;
           long free;
              char buf[];
          };
```

So any string, integer, bitmap, image files, and so on, in Redis are stored in `buf[]` (`Char` array), the `len` stores the length of the buffer array, and `free` stores additional bytes for storage. Redis has an in-built mechanism to detect the type of data stored in the array. More information on this can be found at `http://redis.io/topics/internals-sds`.

The commands in Redis for the string can be categorized in the following parts:

- **Setters and getters commands**: These are the commands that can be used to set or get values in Redis. There are commands for single key-value as well as multiple key-values. For single get and set, following commands can be used:
    - `Get` key: This key gets the value for a key. Time-based performance for this command is `O (1)`.
    - `Set` key: This key sets a value against a key. Time-based performance for this command is `O (1)`.
    - `SETNX` key: This key sets a value against a key if key doesn't exist - no overwrite is done. Time-based performance for this command is `O (1)`.
    - `GETSET` key: This key gets the old value and sets a new value. Time-based performance for this command is `O (1)`.
    - `MGET key1` key: This key gets all the corresponding values of keys. Time-based performance for this command is `O (N)`.
    - `MSET` key: This key sets all the corresponding values of keys. Time-based performance for this command is `O (N)`, where `N` is the number of keys to be set.
    - `MSETNX` key: This sets all the corresponding values of keys if all the don't keys exist, that is if one key exists then no values are set. Time-based performance for this command is `O (N)`, where `N` is the number of keys to be set.
- **Data clean commands**: These are the commands that can be used for managing the lifecycle of a value. By default, the values for the key do not have an expiry time. However, if you have a use case where values need to have life duration, then use the following keys:
    - `SET PX/ EX`: Removes the values and the key gets expired after expiry time in milliseconds. Time based performance for this command is `O (1)`.
    - `SETEX`: Removes the values and the key gets expired after the expiry time in seconds. Time-based performance for this command is `O (1)`.
- **Utility commands**: Following are some of these commands:
    - `APPEND`: This command appends to the existing value or sets if it does not exist. Time-based performance for this command is `O (1)`.
    - `STRLEN`: This command returns the length of the value stored as string. Time-based performance for this command is `O (1)`.

- SETRANGE: This command overwrites the string at the given offset. Time-based performance for this command is O (1), provided the length of the new string does not take long time to copy.
- GETRANGE: This command gets the substring value from the given offsets. Time-based performance for this command is O (1), provided the length of the new substring is not too big.

A sample program to demonstrate the simple usage of commands for a string is given as follows. Execute the program and analyze the result yourself.

```
package org.learningredis.chapter.three.datastruct;
import redis.clients.jedis.Jedis;
import redis.clients.jedis.JedisPool;
import redis.clients.jedis.JedisPoolConfig;
public class MyStringTest {
  private JedisPool pool = new JedisPool(new JedisPoolConfig(),
"localhost");
  Jedis jedis = null;

  public Jedis getResource() {
    jedis = pool.getResource();
    return jedis;
  }
  public void setResource(Jedis jedis){
    pool.returnResource(jedis);
  }
  public static void main(String[] args) throws InterruptedException {
    MyStringTest myStringTest  = new MyStringTest();
    myStringTest.test();

  }
  private void test() throws InterruptedException {
    Jedis jedis = this.getResource();
    String commonkey = "mykey";
    jedis.set(commonkey, "Hello World");
    System.out.println("1) "+jedis.get("mykey"));
    jedis.append(commonkey, " and this is a bright sunny day ");
    System.out.println("2) "+jedis.get("mykey"));
    String substring=jedis.getrange(commonkey, 0 , 5);
    System.out.println("3) "+"substring value = "+substring);
    String commonkey1 = "mykey1";
    jedis.set(commonkey1, "Let's learn redis");
    for(String value : jedis.mget(commonkey,commonkey1)){
      System.out.println("4) "+" - "+ value);
```

```
    }
    jedis.mset("mykey2","let's start with string","mykey3","then we
will learn other data types");
    for(String value : jedis.mget(commonkey,commonkey1,"mykey2","myk
ey3")){
       System.out.println("5) "+"   -- "+ value);
    }
    jedis.msetnx("mykey4","next in line is hashmaps");
    System.out.println("6) "+jedis.get("mykey4"));
    jedis.msetnx("mykey4","next in line is sorted sets");
    System.out.println("7) "+jedis.get("mykey4"));
    jedis.psetex("mykey5", 1000, "this message will self destruct in
1000 milliseconds");
    System.out.println("8) "+jedis.get("mykey5"));
    Thread.currentThread().sleep(1200);
    System.out.println("8) "+jedis.get("mykey5"));
    Long length=jedis.strlen(commonkey);
    System.out.println("9) "+" the length of the string 'mykey' is " +
length);
    this.setResource(jedis);
  }
}
```

The commands in Redis for the integer and float can be categorized in the following parts:

- **Setters and getters commands**: The set of commands is same as what is mentioned for string.
- **Data clean commands**: The set of commands is same as what is mentioned for string.
- **Utility commands**: The commands here will help to manipulate the integer and float values. For integers, this operation is limited to 64 bit signed integers:
    - **APPEND**: This will concatenate the existing integer with the new integer. Time-based performance for this command is `O (1)`.
    - **DECR**: This will decrement the value by one. Time-based performance for this command is `O (1)`.
    - **DECRBY**: This will decrement the value by the given value. Time-based performance for this command is `O (1)`.
    - **INCR**: This will increment the value by one. Time-based performance for this command is `O (1)`.

- ◦ **INCRBY**: This will increment the value by the given value. Time-based performance for this command is `O (1)`.
- ◦ **INCRBYFLOAT**: This will increment the value by the given floating value. Time-based performance for this command is `O (1)`.

Apart from regular number, string, and so on, string data type can store a special type of data structure called **BitSet** or **bitmap.** Let's learn a bit more about them and see their usage.

The BitSet or bitmap data type

These are special space-efficient types of data structure used to store special kind of information. Bitmaps are specially used for real-time analytics work. Though bitmap can only store values in binary (1 or 0) but the fact that they consume less space and the performance for getting value is `O (1)`, makes them very attractive for real-time analytics:

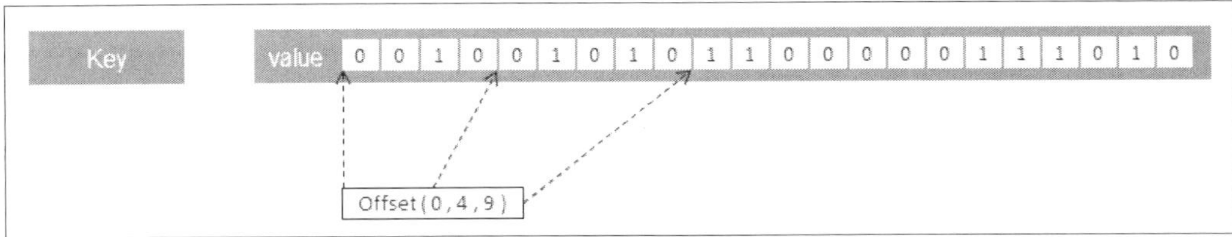

Representation of Bitmap

The key can be any date-based key. Let's say that the key here represents the bitmap about the users who purchased a book on December 12, 2014.

For example, `12/12/2014-user_purchased_book_learning_redis`. Offset here represents a unique integer ID associated with a user. Here we have users associated with number 0, 1, 2...n and so on. Whenever a user makes a purchase, we find the corresponding unique ID of the user, and at that offset position, change the value to `1`.

The following questions can be answered with the help of this space optimizing, high performance bitmap:

- How many purchases were made on December 12, 2014?

  Answer: Count the number of 1 in the bitmap, which is the number of users who made the purchase, say 9.

- Did user associated with ID (offset number) 15 make a purchase?

  Answer: The value at offset 15 is 0, so the user did not make a purchase.

Collection of these bitmaps can be used in union to find answers to more complicated analytics. Let's add another bitmap to an existing sample and let's call it `12/12/2014-user_browsed_book_learning_redis`, for example. Using these two bitmaps, we can find answers to the following questions:

- How many users browsed the product (*Learning Redis*) page?
- How many users purchased the product (*Learning Redis*) page?
- How many users who browsed the product page purchased the book?
- How many users who did not browse the product page purchased the book?

Use case scenario

Redis string can be used to store object IDs. For example, session ID, configuration values as XML, JSON, and so on. Redis string (storing integer) can be used as atomic counters. Redis string (storing bitmaps) can be used as real-time analytics engine.

The Hashes data type

Hashes are Redis version of what a map would do in Java. Hashes in Redis are used to store map of attributes and their values against a key. To understand it better, let's say we have an object called *Learning Redis*; this object will have many properties, such as author, publisher, ISBN number, and so on. To represent this in a storage system, we can store the information as XML, JSON against our key *Learning Redis*. If we require some particular value, for example, author stored against *Learning Redis*, then the entire dataset has to be retrieved and required value has to be filtered out. Doing work this way will not be efficient because lot of data needs to travel via network, and the processing at the client side would increase. Redis provides hashes data structures which can be used for storing such kinds of data. The following figure give a diagrammatic representation of the preceding example:

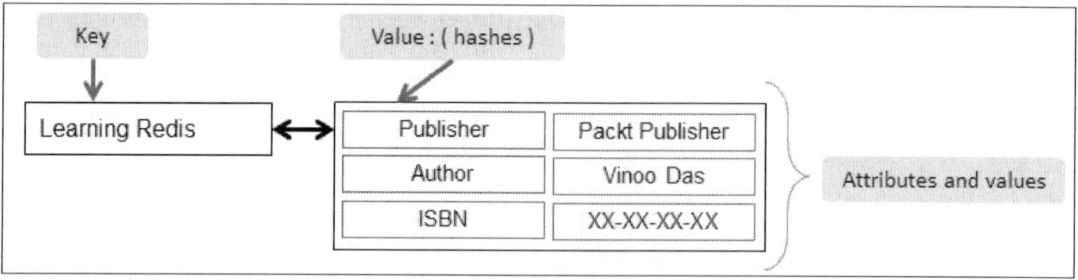

The HAshes data types

Hashes are stored in such a way that they take up less space and each Hash in Redis can store up to 2^{32}–one field-value pairs, that is more than 4 billion.

The commands in Hashes start with `H` and the commands in Redis for the Hashes can be categorized in the following parts:

- **Setters and getters commands**: Following are the commands for this:
    - `HGET`: This command gets the value of a field for a key. Time-based performance for this command is `O (1)`.
    - `HGETALL`: This command gets all the values and fields for a key. Time-based performance for this command is `O (1)`.
    - `HSET`: This command sets the value of a field for a key. Time-based performance for this command is `O (1)`.
    - `HMGET`: This command gets the values for the fields for a key. Time-based performance for this command is `O (N)`, where `N` is the number of fields. However, it's `O (1)` if `N` is small.
    - `HMSET`: This command sets multiple values for respective fields for a key. Time-based performance for this command is `O (N)`, where `N` is the number of fields. However, it's `O (1)` if `N` is small.
    - `HVALS`: This command gets all the values in the Hash for the key. Time-based performance for this command is `O (N)`, where `N` is the number of fields. However, it's `O (1)` if N is small.
    - `HSETNX`: This command sets the value against the field for the key provided the field does not exist. Time-based performance for this command is `O (1)`.
    - `HKEYS`: This command gets all the fields in the Hash for the key. Time-based performance for this command is `O (1)`.
- **Data clean commands**: Following is the command for this:
    - `HDEL`: This command deletes the fields for a key. Time-based performance for this command is `O (N)`, where `N` is the number of fields. However, it's `O (1)` if `N` is small.
- **Utility commands**: Following are the commands for this:
    - `HEXISTS`: This command checks for the existence of a field for a key. Time-based performance for this command is `O (1)`.
    - `HINCRBY`: This command increments the value (provided the value is an integer) of a field for a key. Time-based performance for this command is `O (1)`.
    - `HINCRBYFLOAT`: This command increments the value (provided the value is a float) of a field for a key. Time-based performance for this command is `O (1)`.

- `HLEN`: This command gets the number of fields for the key. Time-based performance for this command is `O (1)`.

A sample program to demonstrate the simple usage of commands for Hashes is given as follows. Execute the program and analyze the result yourself.

```
  package org.learningredis.chapter.three.datastruct;
import java.util.HashMap;
import java.util.Map;
import redis.clients.jedis.Jedis;
import redis.clients.jedis.JedisPool;
import redis.clients.jedis.JedisPoolConfig;
public class MyHashesTest {
  private JedisPool pool = new JedisPool(new JedisPoolConfig(),
"localhost");
  Jedis jedis = null;

  public Jedis getResource() {
    jedis = pool.getResource();
    return jedis;
  }
  public void setResource(Jedis jedis){
    pool.returnResource(jedis);
  }
  public static void main(String[] args)
throws InterruptedException  {
    MyHashesTest myHashesTest  = new MyHashesTest();
    myHashesTest.test();
  }
  private void test() {
    Jedis jedis = this.getResource();
    String commonkey = "learning redis";
    jedis.hset(commonkey, "publisher", "Packt Publisher");
    jedis.hset(commonkey, "author", "Vinoo Das");
    System.out.println(jedis.hgetAll(commonkey));
Map<String,String> attributes = new HashMap<String,String>();
    attributes.put("ISBN", "XX-XX-XX-XX");
    attributes.put("tags", "Redis,NoSQL");
    attributes.put("pages", "250");
    attributes.put("weight", "200.56");
    jedis.hmset(commonkey, attributes);
    System.out.println(jedis.hgetAll(commonkey));
    System.out.println(jedis.hget(commonkey,"publisher"));
    System.out.println(jedis.hmget(commonkey,"publisher","author"));
    System.out.println(jedis.hvals(commonkey));
    System.out.println(jedis.hget(commonkey,"publisher"));
    System.out.println(jedis.hkeys(commonkey));
```

```
        System.out.println(jedis.hexists(commonkey, "cost"));
        System.out.println(jedis.hlen(commonkey));
        System.out.println(jedis.hincrBy(commonkey,"pages",10));
        System.out.println(jedis.hincrByFloat(commonkey,"weight",1.1) + "
    gms");
        System.out.println(jedis.hdel(commonkey,"weight-in-gms"));
        System.out.println(jedis.hgetAll(commonkey));
        this.setResource(jedis);
      }
    }
```

Use case scenario

Hashes provide a sematic interface to store simple and complex data objects in the Redis server. For example, user profile, product catalogue, and so on.

The Lists data type

Redis lists are similar to what linked lists are in Java. This Redis list can have elements added to the head or tail. The performance of doing that is constant or can be expressed as `O (1)`. What it means is that suppose you have a list with 100 elements, the time taken to add elements to the list is equal to the time taken to add elements to a list of 10,000 elements. But on the flip side, accessing elements in the Redis list would result in the scanning of the entire list which means that the performance degrades if the number of items in the list is high.

The advantage of the Redis list getting implemented as a linked list rather than an array list is because Redis list as a data type was designed to have faster writes than reads (a trait shown by all data stores).

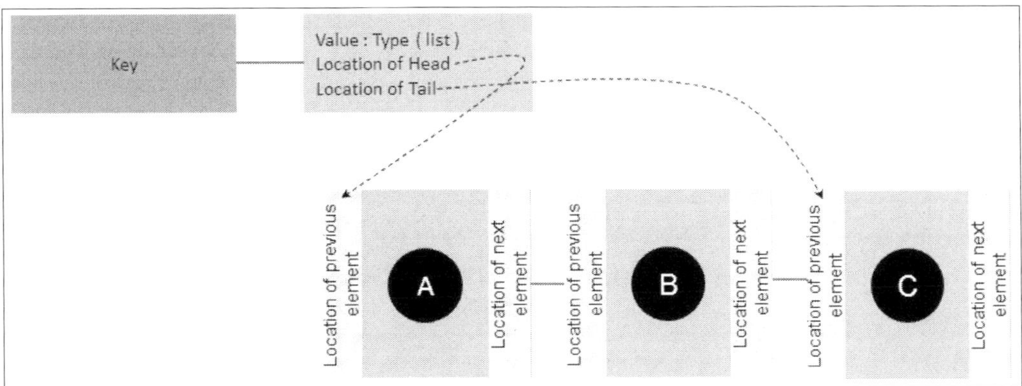

The Lists Data types

The commands in Redis for the lists normally start with `L`. This can also be interpreted that all the commands will execute from *Left or head of the list*, and where the commands are executed from *Right or tail of the list*, they start with R. The commands can be categorized in the following parts:

- **Setters and getters commands**: Following are the examples for this type of commands:
    - `LPUSH`: This command prepends the values to the list from the left of the list. Time-based performance for this command is `O (1)`.
    - `RPUSH`: This command prepends the values to the list from the right of the list. Time-based performance for this command is `O (1)`.
    - `LPUSHX`: This command prepends the values to the list from the left of the list if the key exists. Time-based performance for this command is `O (1)`.
    - `RPUSHX`: This command prepends the values to the list from the right of the list if the key exists. Time-based performance for this command is `O (1)`.
    - `LINSERT`: This command inserts a value in the list after the *pivot* position. This pivot position is calculated from the left. Time-based performance for this command is `O (N)`.
    - `LSET`: This command sets the value of an element in a list based on the index mentioned. Time-based performance for this command is `O (N)`.
    - `LRANGE`: This command gets the sub list of elements based on the start index and the end index. Time-based performance for this command is *O (S+N)*. Here *S* is the start of the offset and *N* is the number of elements we are asking for in the list. What this means is that the time taken to find the element will increase if the offset is farther away from the head and the length of the range is higher.
- **Data clean commands**: Following are the example of this type of commands:
    - `LTRIM`: This command deletes the elements outside the range specified. Time-based performance for this command is `O (N)`. Here `N` is the length of the list.
    - `RPOP`: This command removes the last element. Time-based performance for this command is `O (1)`.
    - `LREM`: This command removes the element at the index point specified. Time-based performance for this command is `O (N)`. Here `N` is the length of the list.

- `LPOP`: This command removes the first element of the list. Time-based performance for this command is `O (1)`.

- **Utility commands**: Following are the commands that come under this type:
  - `LINDEX`: This command gets the element from the list based on the index mentioned. Time-based performance for this command is `O (N)`. Here `N` is the number of elements it has to traverse to reach the element at the desired index.
  - `LLEN`: This command gets the length of the list. Time-based performance for this command is `O (1)`.
- **Advanced command**: Following commands come under this type:
  - `BLPOP`: This command gives the element from the index, which is nonempty, in the sequence of lists mentioned or blocks the call if there is no value in the head till the time at least a value is set or timeout occurs. The alphabet `B` in `BLPOP` hints this call to be blocking. Time-based performance for this command is `O (1)`.
  - `BRPOP`: This command gives the element from the trail which is nonempty in the sequence of lists mentioned or blocks the call if there is no value in the head till the time at least a value is set or timeout occurs. Time-based performance for this command is `O (1)`.
  - `RPOPLPUSH`: This command operates on two lists. Let's say source list and destination list, where it will take the last element on the source list and push it to the first element of the destination list. Time-based performance for this command is `O (1)`.
  - `BRPOPLPUSH`: This command is the *blocking* variety of the `RPOPLPUSH` command. In this, if the source list is empty then Redis will block the operation until a value is pushed into the list or a timeout is reached. These commands can be used to create queues. Time-based performance for this command is `O (1)`.

A sample program to demonstrate the simple usage of commands for lists is given as follows. Execute the program and analyze the result yourself:

```
package org.learningredis.chapter.three.datastruct;
import redis.clients.jedis.Jedis;
import redis.clients.jedis.JedisPool;
import redis.clients.jedis.JedisPoolConfig;
import redis.clients.jedis.BinaryClient.LIST_POSITION;
public class MyListTest {
```

```
  private JedisPool pool = new JedisPool(new JedisPoolConfig(),
"localhost");
  Jedis jedis = null;
  public Jedis getResource() {
    jedis = pool.getResource();
    return jedis;
  }
  public void setResource(Jedis jedis){
    pool.returnResource(jedis);
  }
  public static void main(String[] args) throws InterruptedException {
    MyListTest myListTest  = new MyListTest();
    myListTest.test();
  }
  private void test() {
    Jedis jedis = this.getResource();
    System.out.println(jedis.del("mykey4list"));
    String commonkey="mykey4list";
    String commonkey1="mykey4list1";
    for(int index=0;index<3;index++){
      jedis.lpush(commonkey, "Message - " + index);
    }
    System.out.println(jedis.lrange(commonkey, 0, -1));
    for(int index=3;index<6;index++){
      jedis.rpush(commonkey, "Message - " + index);
    }
    System.out.println(jedis.lrange(commonkey, 0, -1));
    System.out.println(jedis.lindex(commonkey, 0));
    System.out.println(jedis.linsert(commonkey,LIST_POSITION.
AFTER,"Message - 5", "Message - 7"));
    System.out.println(jedis.lrange(commonkey, 0, -1));
    System.out.println(jedis.linsert(commonkey,LIST_POSITION.
BEFORE,"Message - 7", "Message - 6"));
    System.out.println(jedis.lrange(commonkey, 0, -1));
    System.out.println(jedis.llen(commonkey));
    System.out.println(jedis.lpop(commonkey));
    System.out.println(jedis.lrange(commonkey, 0, -1));
    System.out.println(jedis.lpush(commonkey,"Message - 2","Message
-1.9"));
    System.out.println(jedis.lrange(commonkey, 0, -1));
    System.out.println(jedis.lpushx(commonkey,"Message - 1.8"));
    System.out.println(jedis.lrange(commonkey, 0, -1));
    System.out.println(jedis.lrem(commonkey,0,"Message - 1.8"));
    System.out.println(jedis.lrange(commonkey, 0, -1));
```

```
        System.out.println(jedis.lrem(commonkey,-1,"Message - 7"));
        System.out.println(jedis.lrange(commonkey, 0, -1));
        System.out.println(jedis.lset(commonkey,7,"Message - 7"));
        System.out.println(jedis.lrange(commonkey, 0, -1));
        System.out.println(jedis.ltrim(commonkey,2,-4));
        System.out.println(jedis.lrange(commonkey, 0, -1));
        jedis.rpoplpush(commonkey, commonkey1);
        System.out.println(jedis.lrange(commonkey, 0, -1));
        System.out.println(jedis.lrange(commonkey1, 0, -1));
    }
}
```

Use case scenario

List provides with a sematic interface to store data sequentially in a Redis server where the *write* speeds are more desirable than *read* performance. For example, log messages.

The Sets data type

Redis Sets are data structures that are an unordered collection of SDS. The values in Sets are unique and cannot have duplicate value. One of the interesting aspects in terms of performance of Redis Sets is that they show constant timing for adding, removing, and checking for existence of an element. The maximum number of entries that can be in a Set is 2^32,-that is 4 billion per Set. These Set values are unordered in nature. From the look of it, Sets might look like lists, but then they have a different implementation, which makes them perfect candidates for solving problems around Set theory.

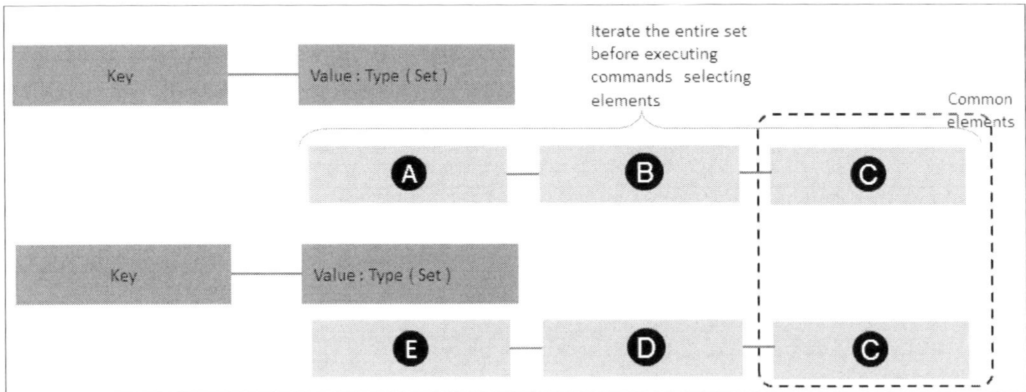

The Sets data types

The commands in Redis for the Sets can be categorized in the following parts:

- **Setters and getters commands**: This type includes the following command:
    - `SADD`: This command adds one or more elements to the Set. Time-based performance for this command is `O (N)`. Here `N` is the number of elements that needs to be added.
- **Data clean commands**: Following are some commands that come under this category:
    - `SPOP`: This command removes and returns a random element from the set. Time-based performance for this command is `O (1)`.
    - `SREM`: This command removes and returns the specified elements from the set. Time-based performance for this command is `O (N)`. Here `N` is the number of elements to be removed.
- **Utility Commands**: Following are the commands that come under this type:
    - `SCARD`: This command gets the number of elements in a Set. Time-based performance for this command is `O (1)`.
    - `SDIFF`: This command gets the list of elements from the first set after subtracting its elements from the other mentioned sets. Time-based performance for this command is `O (N)`. Here `N` is the number of elements in all the sets.
    - `SDIFFSTORE`: This command gets the list of elements from the first set after subtracting its elements from the other mentioned sets. This set is pushed into another Set. Time-based performance for this command is `O (N)`. Here `N` is the number of elements in all the sets.
    - `SINTER`: This command gets the common elements in all the sets mentioned. Time-based performance for this command is `O (N * M)`. Here `N` is the cardinality of the smallest set and `M` is the number of sets. What basically is happening here is that Redis will take the smallest set and look for common elements between this set and other sets. The resultant sets are again compared for common elements, such as the preceding process, until only one set remains with the desired result.
    - `SINTERSTORE`: This command works in the same way as command `SINTER` but here the result is stored in a mentioned set. Time-based performance for this command is `O (N * M)`. Here `N` is the cardinality of the smallest set and `M` is the number of sets.
    - `SISMEMBER`: This command finds if the value is a member of set. Time-based performance for this command is `O (1)`.

- `SMOVE`: This command moves members from one set to another set. Time-based performance for this command is `O (1)`.
- `SRANDMEMBER`: This command gets one or multiple random members from the set. Time-based performance for this command is `O (N)`. Here `N` is the number of members passed.
- `SUNION`: This command adds multiple sets. Time-based performance for this command is `O (N)`. Here `N` is the number of elements in all the sets.
- `SUNIONSTORE`: This command adds multiple sets and stores the result in a set. Time-based performance for this command is `O (N)`. Here `N` is the number of elements in all the sets.

A sample program to demonstrate the simple usage of commands for sets is given as follows. Execute the program and analyze the result yourself:

```
package org.learningredis.chapter.three.datastruct;
import redis.clients.jedis.Jedis;
import redis.clients.jedis.JedisPool;
import redis.clients.jedis.JedisPoolConfig;
public class MySetTest {
  private JedisPool pool = new JedisPool(new JedisPoolConfig(),
"localhost");
  Jedis jedis = null;
  public Jedis getResource() {
    jedis = pool.getResource();
    return jedis;
  }
  public void setResource(Jedis jedis){
    pool.returnResource(jedis);
  }
  public static void main(String[] args) {
    MySetTest mySetTest = new MySetTest();
    mySetTest.test();
  }
  private void test() {
    Jedis jedis = this.getResource();
    jedis.sadd("follow:cricket", "vinoo.das@junk-mail.com","vinoo.
das1@junk-mail.com","vinoo.das3@junk-mail.com");
    System.out.println(jedis.smembers("follow:cricket"));
    System.out.println(jedis.scard("follow:cricket"));
    jedis.sadd("follow:redis", "vinoo.das1@junk-mail.com","vinoo.das2@
junk-mail.com");
    System.out.println(jedis.smembers("follow:redis"));
```

```
        System.out.println(jedis.scard("follow:redis"));
        // intersect the above sets to give name who is interested in
cricket and redis
        System.out.println(jedis.sinter("Cricket:followers","follow:red
is"));
        jedis.
sinterstore("follow:redis+cricket","follow:cricket","follow:redis");
        System.out.println(jedis.smembers("follow:redis+cricket"));
        System.out.println(jedis.sismember("follow:redis+cricket", "vinoo.
das@junk-mail.com"));
        System.out.println(jedis.sismember("follow:redis+cricket", "vinoo.
das1@junk-mail.com"));
        jedis.smove("follow:cricket", "follow:redis", "vinoo.das3@junk-
mail.com");
        System.out.println(jedis.smembers("follow:redis"));
        System.out.println(jedis.srandmember("follow:cricket"));
        System.out.println(jedis.spop("follow:cricket"));
        System.out.println(jedis.smembers("follow:cricket"));
        jedis.sadd("follow:cricket","wrong-data@junk-mail.com");
        System.out.println(jedis.smembers("follow:cricket"));
        jedis.srem("follow:cricket","wrong-data@junk-mail.com");
        System.out.println(jedis.smembers("follow:cricket"));
        System.out.println(jedis.sunion("follow:cricket","follow:redis"));
        jedis.sunionstore("follow:cricket-or-redis","follow:cricket","fol
low:redis");
        System.out.println(jedis.smembers("follow:cricket-or-redis"));
        System.out.println(jedis.sdiff("follow:cricket", "follow:redis"));
    }
}
```

Use case scenario

Sets provides with a sematic interface to store data as a set in Redis server. The use cases for this kind of data would be more for an analytics purpose, for example how many people browse the product page and how many end up purchasing the product.

The Sorted Sets data type

Redis Sorted Sets are very much like Redis Sets in the way that they don't store duplicate values, but the area where they differ from Redis Sets is that the values are sorted on the basis of a score, or integer, float values. These values are provided while setting a value in the Set. The performance of these Sorted Sets is proportional to the logarithm of the number of elements. The data is always kept in a sorted way. This concept is diagrammatically explained in the following figure:

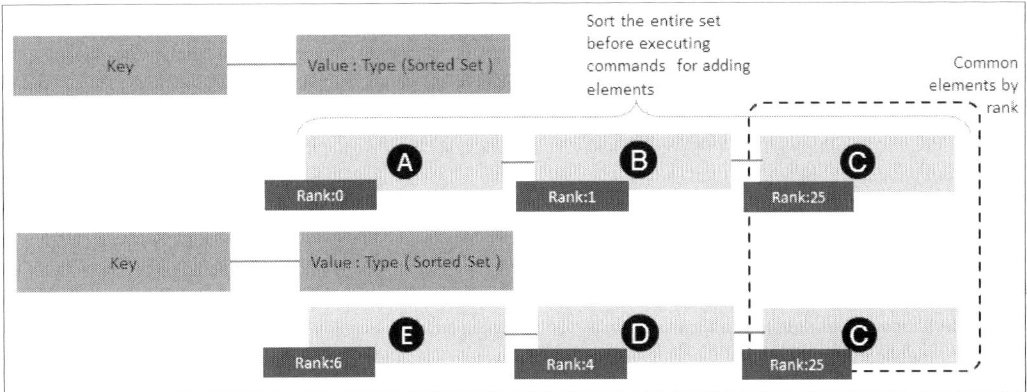

The concept of Sorted Sets

The commands in Redis for the Sorted Sets can be categorized in the following parts:

- **Setters and getters commands**: Following are the commands that come under this category:
    - `ZADD`: This command adds or updates one or more members to a Sorted Set. Time-based performance for this command is `O (log (N))`. Here `N` is the number of elements in the Sorted Sets.
    - `ZRANGE`: This command gets the specified range by rank of elements in the Sorted Set. Time-based performance for this command is *O (log (N) +M)*. Here `N` is the number of elements and `M` is the number of elements returned.
    - `ZRANGEBYSCORE`: This command gets elements from the Sorted Sets within the range by score given. The values in the default Set are ascending by nature. Time-based performance for this command is `O (log (N) +M)`. Here `N` is the number of elements and `M` is the number of elements returned.
    - `ZREVRANGEBYSCORE`: This command gets elements from the Sorted Sets within the score given. Time-based performance for this command is `O (log (N) +M)`. Here `N` is the number of elements and `M` is the number of elements removed.

  - `ZREVRANK`: This command returns the rank of the member in the Sorted Set. Time-based performance for this command is `O (log (N))`.
  - `ZREVRANGE`: This command returns the specified range of elements in the Sorted Set. Time-based performance for this command is `O (log (N) + M)`.
- **Data clean commands**: Following are the commands that come under this category:
  - `ZREM`: This command removes the specified members in the Sorted Set. Time-based performance for this command is `O (M*log (N))`. Here `M` is number of elements removed and `N` is the number of elements in the Sorted Set.
  - `ZREMRANGEBYRANK`: This command removes the members in a Sorted Set within the given indexes. Time-based performance for this command is `O (log (N) * M)`. Here `N` is the number of elements and `M` is the number of elements removed.
  - `ZREMRANGEBYSCORE`: This command removes the members in a Sorted Set within the given scores. Time-based performance for this command is `O (log (N) * M)`. Here `N` is the number of elements and `M` is the number of elements removed.
- **Utility commands**: Following are the commands that come under this category:
  - `ZCARD`: This command gets the number of members in a Sorted Set. Time-based performance for this command is `O (1))`.
  - `ZCOUNT`: This command gets the number of members in a Sorted Set within the score boundaries. Time-based performance for this command is `O (log (N) * M)`. Here `N` is the number of elements and `M` is the result.
  - `ZINCRBY`: This command increases the score of an element in the Sorted Set. Time-based performance for this command is `O (log (N))`. Here `N` is the number of elements in the Sorted Set.
  - `ZINTERSTORE`: This command calculates the common elements in the Sorted Sets given by the specified keys, and stores the result in destination Sorted Set. Time based performance for this command is `O (N*K) + O (M*log (M))`. Here `N` is the smallest Sorted Set, `K` is the number of input Set, and `M` is the number of elements in the result Sorted Set.

- `ZRANK`: This command gets the index of the element in the Sorted Set. Time-based performance for this command is `O (log (N))`.
- `ZSCORE`: This command returns the score of the member. Time-based performance for this command is `O (1)`.
- `ZUNIONSTORE`: This command computes the union of keys in the given Sorted Set and stores the result in the resultant Sorted Set. Time-based performance for this command is `O (N) +O (M log (M))`. Here `N` is the sum of sizes of input Sorted Set and `M` is the number of elements in the Sorted Set.

A sample program to demonstrate the simple usage of commands for Sorted Sets is given as follows. Execute the program and analyze the result yourself:

```
package org.learningredis.chapter.three.datastruct;
import redis.clients.jedis.Jedis;
import redis.clients.jedis.JedisPool;
import redis.clients.jedis.JedisPoolConfig;
public class MySortedSetTest {
  private JedisPool pool = new JedisPool(new JedisPoolConfig(),
"localhost");
  Jedis jedis = null;
  public Jedis getResource() {
    jedis = pool.getResource();
    return jedis;
  }
  public void setResource(Jedis jedis){
    pool.returnResource(jedis);
  }
  public static void main(String[] args) {
    MySortedSetTest mySortedSetTest = new MySortedSetTest();
    mySortedSetTest.test();
  }
  private void test() {
    Jedis jedis = this.getResource();
    jedis.zadd("purchase", 0, "learning-redis");
    jedis.zadd("purchase", 0, "cassandra");
    jedis.zadd("purchase", 0, "hadoop");
    System.out.println(jedis.zcard("purchase"));
    // purchase a 4 books on redis
    jedis.zincrby("purchase", 1, "learning-redis");
    jedis.zincrby("purchase", 1, "learning-redis");
    jedis.zincrby("purchase", 1, "learning-redis");
    jedis.zincrby("purchase", 1, "learning-redis");
```

```
        // purchase a 2 books on cassandra
        jedis.zincrby("purchase", 1, "cassandra");
        jedis.zincrby("purchase", 1, "cassandra");
        // purchase a 1 book on hadoop
        jedis.zincrby("purchase", 1, "hadoop");
        System.out.println(jedis.zcount("purchase", 3, 4));
        System.out.println(jedis.zrange("purchase", 0, 2));
        System.out.println(jedis.zrangeByScore("purchase", 3, 4));
        System.out.println(jedis.zrank("purchase", "learning-redis"));
        System.out.println(jedis.zrank("purchase", "cassandra"));
        System.out.println(jedis.zrank("purchase", "hadoop"));
        System.out.println(jedis.zrevrank("purchase", "learning-redis"));
        System.out.println(jedis.zrevrank("purchase", "cassandra"));
        System.out.println(jedis.zrevrank("purchase", "hadoop"));
        System.out.println(jedis.zscore("purchase", "learning-redis"));
        System.out.println(jedis.zscore("purchase", "cassandra"));
        System.out.println(jedis.zscore("purchase", "hadoop"));
        jedis.zunionstore("purchase:nosql", "purchase");
        System.out.println("-- " + jedis.zrange("purchase:nosql",0,-1));
        System.out.println("-- " + jedis.zrank("purchase:nosql","learning-
    redis"));
        jedis.zrem("purchase:nosql", "hadoop");
        System.out.println("-- " + jedis.zrange("purchase:nosql",0,-1));
        jedis.zremrangeByRank("purchase:nosql", 0,0);
        System.out.println("-- " + jedis.zrange("purchase:nosql",0,-1));
        jedis.zremrangeByScore("purchase:nosql", 3,4);
        System.out.println("-- " + jedis.zrange("purchase:nosql",0,-1));
        this.setResource(jedis);
      }
    }
```

Use case scenario

Sorted Sets provide with a sematic interface to store data as a Sorted Set in Redis server. The use cases for this kind of data would be more in analytics purpose and in the gaming world. For example, how many people played a particular game and categorizing them on the basis of their score.

Communication protocol – RESP

Redis in principle works on a client-server model. So like in every client-server model, the client and the server need to have a protocol to communicate with. Communication protocol can be understood as a message exchange taking place between client and the server (and vice versa) based on some fixed agreement or rule between them. So every communication protocol has to adhere to some syntax and semantics, which should be followed by both the parties (client and server) for the communication to be successful. There is also another dimension to this communication protocol, which is the network layer interaction, or better known as TCP/IP Model. The TCP/IP Model can be divided into four parts:

- Application layer
- Transport layer
- Internet layer
- Network interface

Since the communication protocol between two applications is at application layer, so we intend to focus only on the application layer. The following diagram is a representation of what happens in the communication protocol level at application layer:

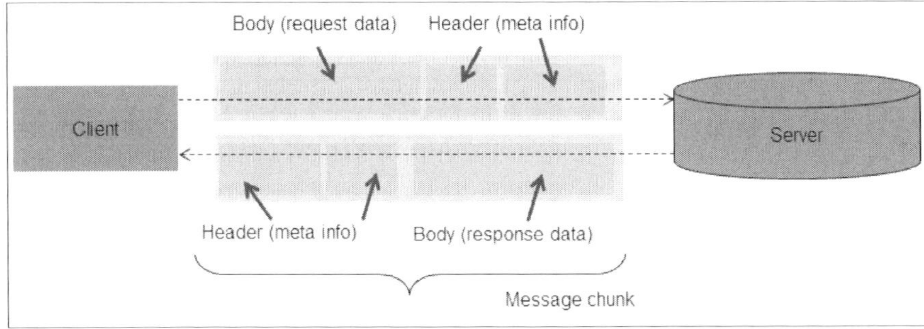

Representation of communication protocol at application layer

In any application protocol, we will have a header and body. The header will contain Meta information about the protocol, that is protocol name, version, security related details, Meta information about the request (number of arguments, type of arguments), and so on, and the body will contain the actual data. The first thing any server will do is to parse the header information. If the header gets successfully parsed, then only rest of the body gets processed. In a way, the server and the client need to have a pipe-like architecture to process header messages.

The protocol used for Redis is fairly simple to understand. This section will focus on the communication protocol used in Redis. By the end of this section, we would have understood the protocol and created a client that connects to Redis server, sends the request, and gets the response from the server. Like in any other protocol, the Redis protocol also has a header (Meta information) and a body part (request data). The request data part consists of information such as command and command data. In response, it will contain parts such as Meta information (if the request was a success or failure) and actual response data payload. The following explains this concept:

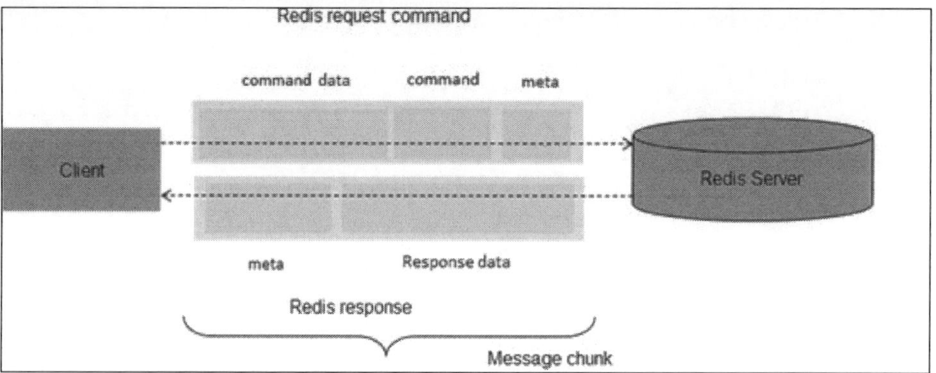

Representation of Meta information and request data

Any request in Redis basically constitutes of two parts, and they are discussed as follows:

- Meta information about the request, say, **Number of arguments**.
- Body part will further have three more pieces of information:
    - Number of bytes for every argument
    - The actual argument
    - **Carriage Return and Line Feeds** (**CRLF**)

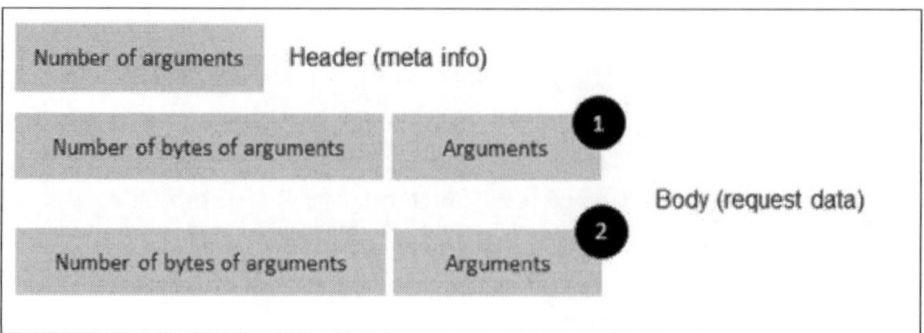

Representation of the body part of a request

So the information that we will hold in the Meta information will be two, since this is the number of the arguments we will be passing as indicative, as shown in the preceding figure. In the body part, we will capture information, such as what is the number of bytes of argument we are sending, that is if the name of the argument is `GET`, then the number of bytes would be `3`.

The response in Redis can be segregated into two types:

- Response for commands which will go and add or manipulate data (no return value is expected):
  - `+` sign suggesting the request was success
  - `-` sign suggesting the request was failure
- Response for commands which will go and fetch data (string type return value is expected):
  - `$-1` will be the response if error is the response
  - `$` and the size of the response if the response is a success followed by the actual string data

As an exercise, let's make a small test client in Java code and record our interactions with the Redis server. The client is just a sample to educate on the Redis protocol and does not intend to replace the client we will use in the book, that is Jedis. Let's get a brief overview of the classes participating in the small test client. For starters, from a design patterns perspective, we will be using command pattern for this sample:

- `Command`: This class is the abstract class and all the command classes will be extended from this class.
- `GetCommand`: This is the class which will fetch the string value for the key given and print the server response and response values.
- `SetCommand`: This is the class which will set the key and the value data for the command and print the server response.
- `ConnectionProperties`: This is the interface which will hold the host and the port address. (This is going to behave more like a properties file.)
- `TestClient`: This is the class that is going to call all the commands.

Following is the domain diagram for the simple test client application. Here the command objects are doing the bulk of the job:

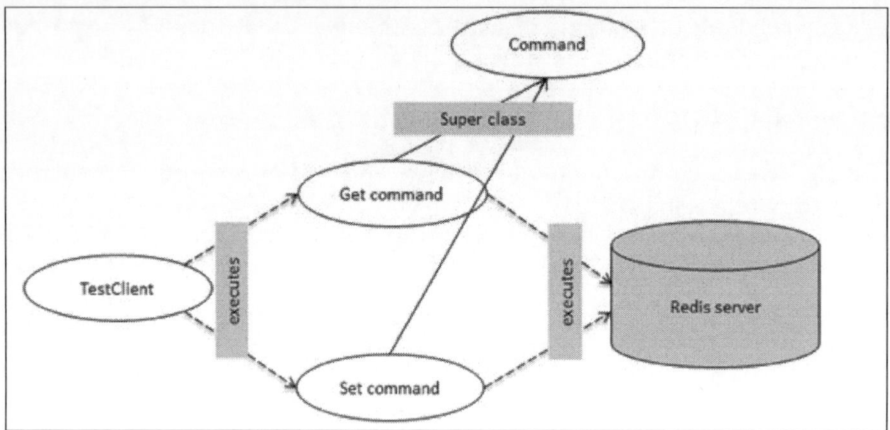

Domain diagram for a simple client application

A look into the code will give more idea and clarity about the simple test client for Redis:

- `ConnectionProperties.java`: This is the class that will hold the configuration value for the host and the port.

```
package org.learningredis.chapter.three;
public interface ConnectionProperties {
  public String host="localhost";
  public int   port =6379;
}
```

- `TestClient.java`: As shown, this is the client which will execute the commands for setting the value and fetching the value.

```
package org.learningredis.chapter.three;
public class TestClient {
  public void execute(Command command){
      try{
        /*Connects to server*/
        command.excute();
      }catch(Exception e){
        e.printStackTrace();
      }
    }
  public static void main(String... args) {
    TestClient testclient = new TestClient();
```

```
        SetCommand set = new  SetCommand("MSG","Hello world : simple
    test client");
        testclient.execute(set);

        GetCommand get = new GetCommand("MSG");
        testclient.execute(get);
        }
    }
```

If everything goes right, following is the message that you should see in your console. Please remember this is a successful operation and your console should look similar to the following screenshot:

```
+ OK
$ 32
Hello world: simple test client
```

Here in this sample, we executed two commands consecutively:

- `SetCommand`
- `GetCommand`

The result of `SetCommand` is `+OK`. The `+` sign indicates that the server has returned a success result followed by the message `OK`.

The result of `GetCommand` is a multi line result. The first line is a string `$32`, which means the size of the result is 32 bytes long, followed by the result `Hello world : simple test client`.

Now, let's attempt to pass a key that does not exist in the `Get` command. The code snippet will look something like shown next (key passed in `wrong-key`, which does not exist):

```
package org.learningredis.chapter.three;
public class TestClient {
  public void execute(Command command){
      try{
        /*Connects to server*/
        command.excute();
      }catch(Exception e){
        e.printStackTrace();
      }
    }
```

```
    public static void main(String... args) {
      TestClient testclient = new TestClient();
      SetCommand set = new  SetCommand("MSG","Hello world : simple test
  client");
      testclient.execute(set);

      GetCommand get = new GetCommand("Wrong-key");
      testclient.execute(get);
      }
  }
```

The result of the preceding code should look something like the `$-1` command. Here the return value is null since the key does not exist. So the length is `-1`. Going forward, we will wrap this message with something more human readable, like `This key does not exist!` Following are some of the classes discussed:

- `Command.java`: This is the abstract class to which all the commands would extend to. This class has the responsibility to instantiate a socket for the implementing commands and create a proper payload to be sent to the Redis server. Understanding this will give us a hint of how actually the Redis server accepts requests.

Representation of Command.java

The first character is the `*` character followed by **number of arguments** that we will pass. This means that if we intend to do a **Set** command, that is **SET MSG Hello**, then the total number of arguments is three here. If we intend to pass a **Get** command such as **GET MSG,** then the number of arguments is two. Followed by the number of arguments, we will use **CRLF** as a separator. The subsequent messages will follow a pattern which will get repeated. The pattern is very simple to understand, that is **$** followed by the length of the argument in bytes followed by **CRLF** followed by argument itself. If we have more arguments, then the same pattern is followed, but then they are separated by CRLF separator. Following is the code for `Command.java`:

```
package org.learningredis.chapter.three;
import java.io.IOException;
import java.net.Socket;
import java.util.ArrayList;
public abstract class Command {
  protected Socket socket;
  public Command() {
    try {
```

```
        socket = new Socket(ConnectionProperties.host,
            ConnectionProperties.port);
      } catch (IOException e) {
        e.printStackTrace();
      }
    }
  public String createPayload(ArrayList<String>
  messageList)
  {
      int argumentSize = messageList.size();
      StringBuffer payload = new StringBuffer();
      payload.append('*');
      payload.append(argumentSize);
      payload.append("\r\n");
      for (int cursor = 0; cursor < messageList.size(); cursor++) {
        payload.append("$");
        payload.append(messageList.get(cursor).length());
        payload.append("\r\n");
        payload.append(messageList.get(cursor));
        payload.append("\r\n");
      }
      return payload.toString().trim();
    }
    public abstract String createPayload();
    public abstract void execute() throws IOException;
  }
```

The code is simple to understand and it does preparation and formatting of the message payload. The `Command` class has two methods that are abstract and need to be implemented by the implementing command. Apart from this, `Command` class creates a new socket based on the properties set in `ConnectionProperties.java`.

- `GetCommand.java`: This is the class that implements the `GET KEY` command. The class extends the `Command.java`. Following is the source code for `GetCommand`:

```
package org.learningredis.chapter.three;
import java.io.BufferedReader;
import java.io.IOException;
import java.io.InputStreamReader;
import java.io.PrintWriter;
import java.util.ArrayList;
public class GetCommand extends Command{
```

```
    private String key;
    public GetCommand(String key) {
      this.key=key;
    }
    @Override
    public String createPayload() {
      ArrayList<String> messageList = new ArrayList<String>();
      messageList.add("GET");
      messageList.add(key);
      return super.createPayload(messageList);
    }
    @Override
    public void excute() throws IOException  {
      PrintWriter out = null;
      BufferedReader in=null;
      try {
      out = new PrintWriter(super.socket.getOutputStream(),true);
      out.println(this.createPayload());
        //Reads from Redis server
  in = new BufferedReader(new
            InputStreamReader(socket.getInputStream()));
            String msg=in.readLine();
            if (! msg.contains("-1")){
              System.out.println(msg);
              System.out.println(in.readLine());
            }else{
            // This will show the error message since the
            // server has returned '-1'
            System.out.println("This Key does not exist !");
        }
      } catch (IOException e) {
        e.printStackTrace();
      }finally{
        out.flush();
        out.close();
        in.close();
        socket.close();
      }
    }
  }
```

The implementing class does two things in principle. First it passes the argument array with a proper value to the super class, which formats it the way Redis will understand, and then, it sends the payload to the Redis server and prints the result.

- `SetCommand`: This is similar to the previous command but in this, we will be setting the value. The class will extend the `Command.java` class. Following is the source code for `SetCommand`:

```
package org.learningredis.chapter.three;
import java.io.BufferedReader;
import java.io.IOException;
import java.io.InputStreamReader;
import java.io.PrintWriter;
import java.util.ArrayList;
public class SetCommand extends Command{
  private String key;
  private String value;
  public SetCommand(String key, String value) {
    this.key=key;
    this.value=value;
  }
  public String createPayload(){
ArrayList<String> messageList = new
                  ArrayList<String>();
    messageList.add("SET");
    messageList.add(key);
    messageList.add(value);
    return super.createPayload(messageList);
  }
  @Override
  public void excute() throws IOException  {
    PrintWriter    out = null;
    BufferedReader in = null;
    try {
      out = new
PrintWriter(super.socket.getOutputStream (), true);
      out.println(this.createPayload());
      //Reads from Redis server
      in = new BufferedReader(new
      InputStreamReader(socket.getInputStream()));
      // This is going to be a single line reply..
      System.out.println(in.readLine());
    } catch (IOException e) {
      e.printStackTrace();
    }finally{
      in.close();
      out.flush();
      out.close();
```

```
            socket.close();
        }
    }
}
```

This command is similar to the previous command in that it does two things in principle. First it passes the argument array in with a proper value to the super class, which formats it the way Redis will understand, and it then, passes the payload to the Redis server and prints the result.

Have fun compiling the program and running it; add more commands and extend it to suit your business requirements. I would strongly recommend using Jedis as it is stable, its community is very active, and it provides implementation for newer commands getting introduced with newer versions of Redis.

Summary

In this chapter, we brushed with various data structures or data types which Redis provides. We also wrote a few programs to see them working and made an attempt to understand how and where these data types can be used. Finally, we understood how Redis communicates with the clients and vice versa.

In the next chapter, we will take our understanding a notch higher and make an attempt to understand Redis Server and the functionality that'll handle it.

4

Functions in the Redis Server

In the previous chapters, we saw some features of Redis Server that make it a key-value NoSQL. We also saw that Redis, apart from storing vanilla key-values, also provides semantics to store data in a structured way. This feature in itself makes Redis stand out in the crowd, since most of the other databases (RDBMS and other NoSQL) don't provide interfaces which programmers can use. Other data stores have a fixed way of storing information, such as documents or maps, and programmers have to convert their data into these semantics to hold information. However, in Redis, programmers can store information in the same sematic that they use in their programs, such as a map, list, and so on. This in way provides a better and an easier way of understanding the program. Apart from that, Redis provides functions which elevate Redis from being just a data store to more like a framework builder, or in other words, more like a Swiss army knife. In this chapter, we will explore these functions and try to understand them.

Following are the functionalities that we would be discussing:

- Real time messaging (Publish/Subscribe)
- Pipeline
- Transaction
- Scripting
- Connection management

Real-time messaging (PUB/SUB)

Enterprises and social media solutions use messaging in a similar way, and in a way, this forms the backbone of any framework or any solution. Messaging also enables us to have architectures which are loosely coupled where components interact via messages and events. Redis provides mechanism to have real time messaging between components. Unlike other messaging systems, the big difference in the messaging model provided in Redis is as follows:

- It does not store the message after delivering it
- It does not store the message if the client (subscriber) was unable to consume it

This can be a disadvantage if compared to a traditional messaging system but is advantageous where data has importance in real time and need not be stored. The message is always sent sequentially. Apart from that, Redis messaging system is simplistic and easy to learn, and does not have the fluff of some of the other messaging systems.

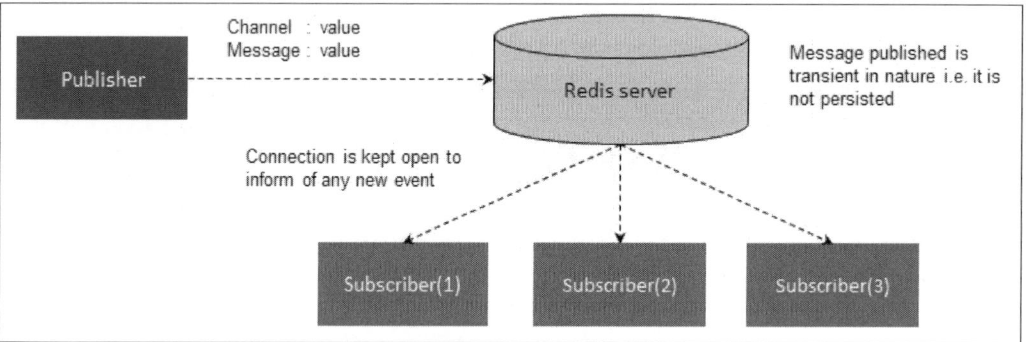

Publish subscribe model of Redis

Following are the commands in Redis that can be used for creating a messaging framework:

- `PUBLISH`: This will post a message to a given channel or pattern.

  The time complexity for this command is given by `O (N+M)`, where `N` is the number of clients who have subscribed to this channel and `M` is the number of patterns the client is subscribed to.

- `SUBSCRIBE`: This subscribes a client to a channel for messages. For example, if a client is subscribed to channel `news.headlines`, then it will get any message published for `news.headlines` channel.

  The time complexity for this command is given by `O (N)`, where `N` is the number of channels the client is subscribed to.

- `PSUBSCRIBE`: This subscribes a client to channels where the pattern name matches the channel name. For example, suppose the channels are registered by the following names:
  - `news.sports.cricket`
  - `news.sports.tennis`

  Then, for a pattern like `news.sports.*`, the subscriber will be getting messages for channels `news.sports.cricket` and `news.sports.tennis`.

  The time complexity for this command is `O (N)`, where `N` is the number of patterns the client is subscribed to.

- `PUBSUB`: This is a command which along with some sub-command helps to take a stock of patterns and channels registered in Redis.

This is only available as of Redis 2.8.0. The Windows version of Redis is based on the 2.6 branch and does not support this command.

  Other `PUBSUB` related commands which help in finding information regarding publishers and subscribers are listed as follows:
  - `PUBSUB CHANNELS [pattern]`: This lists the currently active channels
  - `PUBSUB NUMSUB [channel]`: This lists the number of subscribers to the mentioned channels
  - `PUBSUB NUMPAT`: This lists the number of subscriptions to all the patterns
  - `PUNSUBSCRIBE`: This command unsubscribes the client from a pattern
  - `UNSUBSCRIBE`: This command unsubscribes the client from a channel

Let's have a simple program in Java using Jedis to demonstrate a simple PUB/SUB program. Jedis exposes interface for publishing and has all the functionalities supported by Redis. The interface exposed for subscribing to a message is a bit tricky since the subscriber should be in a ready state before the publisher publishes a message. This is because Redis cannot store message if the subscriber is unavailable. The code for publisher: `SubscriberProcessor.java`:

```
package org.learningRedis.chapter.four.pubsub;
import Redis.clients.jedis.Jedis;
import Redis.clients.jedis.JedisPool;
import Redis.clients.jedis.JedisPoolConfig;
public class SubscriberProcessor implements Runnable{
  private JedisPool pool = new JedisPool(new JedisPoolConfig(),
"localhost");
  private Subscriber subscriber = new Subscriber();
  private Thread simpleThread;
  private Jedis jedis = getResource();
  public Jedis getResource() {
    jedis = pool.getResource();
    return jedis;
  }
  public void setResource(Jedis jedis){
    pool.returnResource(jedis);
  }
  @SuppressWarnings("static-access")
  public static void main(String[] args) {
    SubscriberProcessor test = new SubscriberProcessor();
    test.subscriberProcessor();
    try {
      Thread.currentThread().sleep(10000);
    } catch (InterruptedException e) {
      e.printStackTrace();
    }
    test.unsubscribe();
  }
  private void unsubscribe() {
    simpleThread.interrupt();
    if(subscriber.isSubscribed()){
      subscriber.unsubscribe();
  }
  }
  private void subscriberProcessor() {
    simpleThread = new Thread(this);
    simpleThread.start();
```

```
    }
    @Override
    public void run() {
      while (!Thread.currentThread().isInterrupted()) {
        jedis.subscribe(subscriber, "news");
        //jedis.psubscribe(subscriber, "news.*");
      }
    }
  }
```

The subscriber processor needs to subscribe to a channel. For doing so, it needs to have an instance which is always in a listening mode. In this sample, `Subscriber.java` is the class which does so by extending Jedis PUB/SUB. This abstract class provides methods to manage the life cycle of the subscriber. Next is the code which provides necessary hooks to subscribe to a channel pattern and listen to messages for a channel or a pattern. The code to subscribe to a pattern is commented; to see it in action, we need to uncomment it and comment the code which is subscribing to a channel:

```
package org.learningRedis.chapter.four.pubsub;
import Redis.clients.jedis.JedisPubSub;
public class Subscriber extends  JedisPubSub{
  @Override
  public void onMessage(String arg0, String arg1) {
    System.out.println("on message : " + arg0 + " value = " + arg1);
  }
  @Override
  public void onPMessage(String arg0, String arg1, String arg2) {
    System.out.println("on pattern message : " + arg0 + " channel = "
+ arg1 + " message =" + arg2);
  }
  @Override
  public void onPSubscribe(String arg0, int arg1) {
    System.out.println("on pattern subscribe : " + arg0 + " value = "
+ arg1);
  }
  @Override
  public void onPUnsubscribe(String arg0, int arg1) {
    System.out.println("on pattern unsubscribe : " + arg0 + " value =
" + arg1);
  }
  @Override
  public void onSubscribe(String arg0, int arg1) {
    System.out.println("on subscribe : " + arg0 + " value = " + arg1);
  }
```

```
    @Override
    public void onUnsubscribe(String arg0, int arg1) {
      System.out.println("on un-subscribe : " + arg0 + " value = " +
  arg1);
    }
  }
```

Before you start the publisher to send messages to a channel, it's better to start the subscriber processor, which is going to listen to any message posted to its subscribed channel or pattern. In this case, the subscriber processor will be listening to a news channel or will subscribe to pattern `[news.*]`.

A common class used in these samples is connection manager and the code for the same is listed as follows:

```
package org.learningredis.chapter.four.pipelineandtx;
import redis.clients.jedis.Jedis;
import redis.clients.jedis.JedisPool;
public class ConnectionManager {
  private static JedisPool jedisPool = new JedisPool("localhost");
  public static Jedis get(){
    return jedisPool.getResource();
  }
  public static void set(Jedis jedis){
    jedisPool.returnResource(jedis);
  }
  public static void close(){
    jedisPool.destroy();
  }
}
```

To fire the publishers, use the following code for publisher. The code for publisher, `Publisher.java`, is as follows:

```
package org.learningRedis.chapter.four.pubsub;
import Redis.clients.jedis.Jedis;
import Redis.clients.jedis.JedisPool;
import Redis.clients.jedis.JedisPoolConfig;
public class Publisher {
  private JedisPool pool = new JedisPool(new JedisPoolConfig(),
"localhost");
  Jedis jedis = null;
  public Jedis getResource() {
    jedis = pool.getResource();
    return jedis;
  }
```

```
    public void setResource(Jedis jedis){
      pool.returnResource(jedis);
    }
    private void publisher() {
      Jedis jedis = this.getResource();
      jedis.publish("news", "Houstan calling texas... message published
  !!");
    }
    public static void main(String[] args) {
      Publisher test = new Publisher();
      test.publisher();
    }
  }
```

In this sample, the code will publish a message to a channel called `news`, and to see it working make sure that the subscriber is ready and to publish the message to a pattern, comment the code which publishes to a channel, and uncomment the code which publishes the message to a pattern.

Pipelines in Redis

Redis provides a mechanism for faster execution, called *pipeline*. This groups up all the commands as one command block and sends it to the server for execution. The results of all the commands get queued in a response block and sent back.

Comparing the way pipeline works with multiple individual commands sent across a connection will give us an idea of how pipeline is more efficient and where it needs to be used. Let's assume a scenario where we have to send three commands to Redis. The time taken to send any command to Redis is *X* seconds, so the same amount of time is required to send the response. The total time spent in going and return journey is *2X* seconds. Let's also assume that the time taken for execution is another *X* seconds. Now in the pipeline commands, since we are sending three commands as one block, the time taken for going to Redis is around *X* seconds , the time taken for processing all the three commands is *3X* seconds, and the time taken for the return journey is also *X* seconds. The total time taken in pipeline commands is *5X* seconds. Compare this with a scenario where we have to send individual commands. The time taken for sending a single command and its return journey is equal to *2X* and time taken for including execution is *3X*. Since we are talking of three commands, the total time is equal to *9X*. This *9X* seconds time compared to *5X* seconds proves its efficiency.

One thing we have to keep in mind is that pipeline does guarantee atomicity but only executes multiple commands and returns response in one response block. Following is a simple representation of commands invoked in a pipeline:

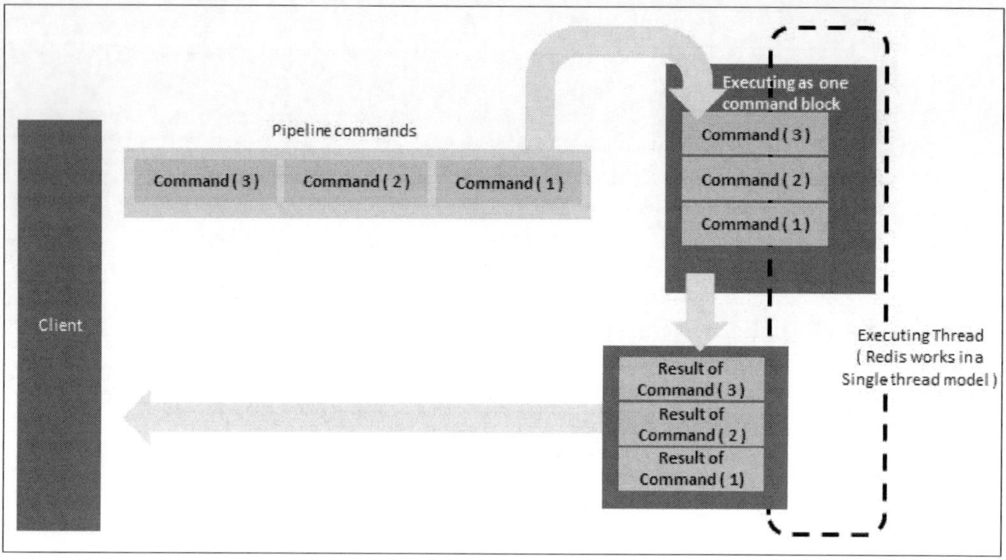

Pipeline in Redis

Next is the representation of multiple commands sent across multiple connections. As we can see, the time taken for sending the response back is saved in case of pipelining the commands:

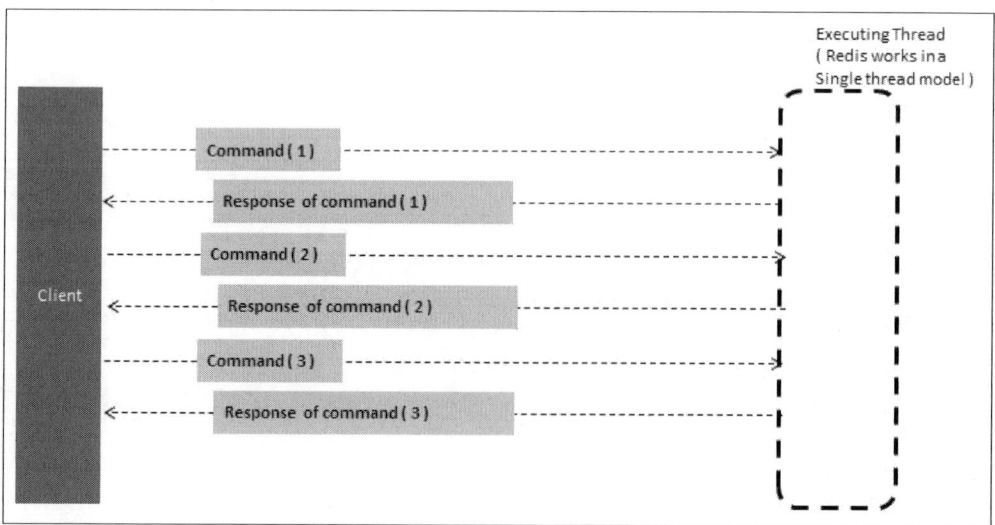

Multiple commands using individual connections in Redis

This way of sending bulk command can be seen in RDBMS also, where we have the provision for sending bulk JDBC as a *batch*. To check this fact, let's write a program and check the time difference between running a program in pipeline and without pipeline:

```
package org.learningRedis.chapter.four.simplepipeline;
import java.util.List;
import Redis.clients.jedis.Jedis;
import Redis.clients.jedis.Pipeline;
public class PipelineCommandTest {
  Jedis jedis = ConnectionManager.get();
  long starttime_withoutpipeline = 0;
  long starttime_withpipeline = 0;
  long endtime_withoutpipeline = 0;
  long endtime_withpipeline = 0;
  public static void main(String[] args) throws InterruptedException {
    PipelineCommandTest test = new PipelineCommandTest();
    test.checkWithoutPipeline();
    Thread.currentThread().sleep(1000);
    test.checkWithPipeline();
    Thread.currentThread().sleep(1000);
    test.getStats();
  }
  private void getStats() {
    System.out.println(" time taken for test without pipeline "+
 (endtime_withoutpipeline - starttime_withoutpipeline ));
    System.out.println(" time taken for test with    pipeline "+
 (endtime_withpipeline - starttime_withpipeline ));
  }
  private void checkWithoutPipeline() {
    starttime_withoutpipeline = System.currentTimeMillis();
    for(int keys=0;keys<10;keys++){
      for(int nv=0;nv<100;nv++){
        jedis.hset("keys-"+keys, "name"+nv, "value"+nv);
      }
      for(int nv=0;nv<100;nv++){
        jedis.hget("keys-"+keys, "name"+nv);
      }
    }
    endtime_withoutpipeline = System.currentTimeMillis();
    // this will delete all the data.
    jedis.flushDB();
  }
  private void checkWithPipeline() {
```

```
        starttime_withpipeline = System.currentTimeMillis();
        for(int keys=0;keys<10;keys++){
          Pipeline commandpipe = jedis.pipelined();
          for(int nv=0;nv<100;nv++){
            commandpipe.hset("keys-"+keys, "name"+nv, "value"+nv);
          }
          List<Object> results = commandpipe.syncAndReturnAll();
          for(int nv=0;nv<results.size();nv++){
            results.get(nv);
          }
        }
        endtime_withpipeline = System.currentTimeMillis();
        jedis.flushDB();
      }
    }
```

The result in my computer is as follows, which of course, may vary depending upon machine configurations used:

```
time taken for test without pipeline 4015
time taken for test with    pipeline 250
```

Pipeline gives the advantage of faster execution but comes with some limitations. This works only when target Redis instance is same, that is, it won't work in a Sharded environment since the connection will be different for every Redis instance. Pipeline also has a lacuna when the commands are not inter-dependent or where custom logic has to be written to form a compound command. In this case also, Redis provides a mechanism of *scripting*, which we will be covering later in the chapter.

Transactions in Redis

Redis as a NOSQL data store provides a loose sense of transaction. As in a traditional RDBMS, the transaction starts with a `BEGIN` and ends with either `COMMIT` or `ROLLBACK`. All these RDBMS servers are multithreaded, so when a thread locks a resource, it cannot be manipulated by another thread unless and until the lock is released. Redis by default has `MULTI` to start and `EXEC` to execute the commands. In case of a transaction, the first command is always `MULTI`, and after that all the commands are stored, and when `EXEC` command is received, all the stored commands are executed in sequence. So inside the hood, once Redis receives the `EXEC` command, all the commands are executed as a single isolated operation. Following are the commands that can be used in Redis for transaction:

- `MULTI`: This marks the start of a transaction block
- `EXEC`: This executes all the commands in the pipeline after `MULTI`

- `WATCH`: This watches the keys for conditional execution of a transaction
- `UNWATCH`: This removes the `WATCH` keys of a transaction
- `DISCARD`: This flushes all the previously queued commands in the pipeline

The following figure represents how transaction in Redis works:

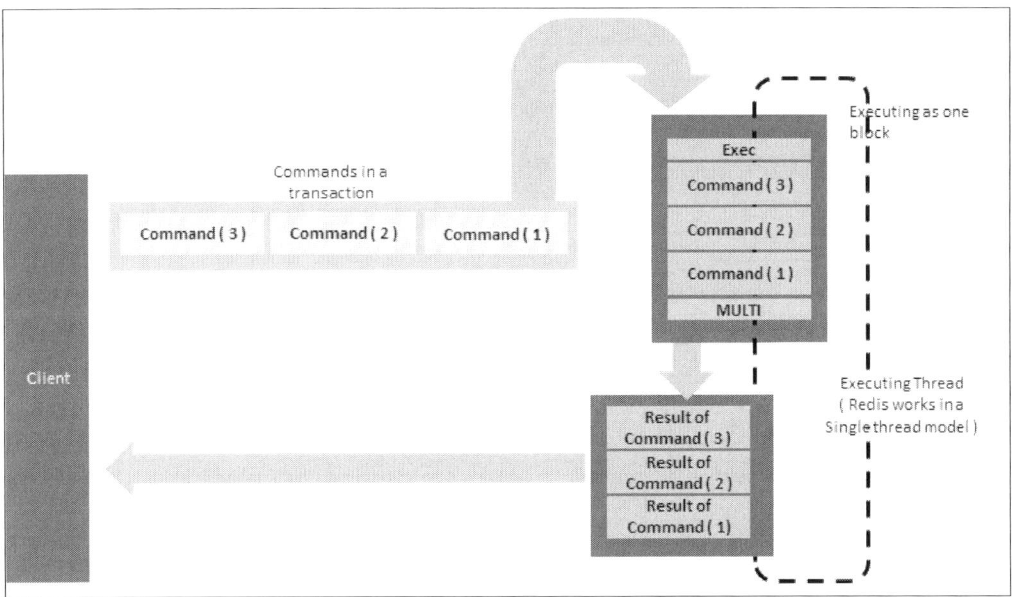

Transaction in Redis

Pipeline versus transaction

As we have seen for many generic terms in pipeline the commands are grouped and executed, and the responses are queued in a block and sent. But in transaction, until the `EXEC` command is received, all the commands received after `MULTI` are queued and then executed. To understand that, it is important to take a case where we have a multithreaded environment and see the outcome.

In the first case, we take two threads firing pipelined commands at Redis. In this sample, the first thread fires a pipelined command, which is going to change the value of a key multiple number of times, and the second thread will try to read the value of that key. Following is the class which is going to fire the two threads at Redis: `MultiThreadedPipelineCommandTest.java`:

```
package org.learningRedis.chapter.four.pipelineandtx;
public class MultiThreadedPipelineCommandTest {
  public static void main(String[] args) throws InterruptedException {
```

```
        Thread pipelineClient = new Thread(new PipelineCommand());
        Thread singleCommandClient = new Thread(new SingleCommand());
        pipelineClient.start();
        Thread.currentThread().sleep(50);
        singleCommandClient.start();
      }
    }
    The code for the client which is going to fire the pipeline commands
    is as follows:
    package org.learningRedis.chapter.four.pipelineandtx;
    import java.util.Set;
    import Redis.clients.jedis.Jedis;
    import Redis.clients.jedis.Pipeline;
    public class PipelineCommand implements Runnable{
      Jedis jedis = ConnectionManager.get();
      @Override
      public void run() {
          long start = System.currentTimeMillis();
          Pipeline commandpipe = jedis.pipelined();
          for(int nv=0;nv<300000;nv++){
            commandpipe.sadd("keys-1", "name"+nv);
          }
          commandpipe.sync();
          Set<String> data= jedis.smembers("keys-1");
          System.out.println("The return value of nv1 after pipeline [ " +
    data.size() + " ]");
        System.out.println("The time taken for executing client(Thread-1)
    "+ (System.currentTimeMillis()-start));
        ConnectionManager.set(jedis);
      }
    }
```

The code for the client which is going to read the value of the key when pipeline is executed is as follows:

```
package org.learningRedis.chapter.four.pipelineandtx;
import java.util.Set;
import Redis.clients.jedis.Jedis;
public class SingleCommand implements Runnable {
  Jedis jedis = ConnectionManager.get();
  @Override
  public void run() {
    Set<String> data= jedis.smembers("keys-1");
    System.out.println("The return value of nv1 is [ " + data.size() +
" ]");
```

```
        ConnectionManager.set(jedis);
      }
    }
```

The result will vary as per machine configuration but by changing the thread sleep time and running the program couple of times, the result will be similar to the one shown as follows:

```
The return value of nv1 is [ 3508 ]
The return value of nv1 after pipeline [ 300000 ]
The time taken for executing client(Thread-1) 3718
```

Please fire FLUSHDB command every time you run the test, otherwise you end up seeing the value of the previous test run, that is 300,000

Now we will run the sample in a transaction mode, where the command pipeline will be preceded by MULTI keyword and succeeded by EXEC command. This client is similar to the previous sample where two clients in separate threads will fire commands to a single key on Redis.

The following program is a test client that gives two threads one with commands in transaction mode and the second thread will try to read and modify the same resource:

```
package org.learningRedis.chapter.four.pipelineandtx;
public class MultiThreadedTransactionCommandTest {
  public static void main(String[] args) throws InterruptedException {
    Thread transactionClient = new Thread(new TransactionCommand());
    Thread singleCommandClient = new Thread(new SingleCommand());
    transactionClient.start();
    Thread.currentThread().sleep(30);
    singleCommandClient.start();
  }
}
```

This program will try to modify the resource and read the resource while the transaction is going on:

```
package org.learningRedis.chapter.four.pipelineandtx;
import java.util.Set;
import Redis.clients.jedis.Jedis;
public class SingleCommand implements Runnable {
  Jedis jedis = ConnectionManager.get();
  @Override
```

```
    public void run() {
      Set<String> data= jedis.smembers("keys-1");
      System.out.println("The return value of nv1 is [ " + data.size() +
" ]");
      ConnectionManager.set(jedis);
    }
  }
```

This program will start with `MULTI` command, try to modify the resource, end it with `EXEC` command, and later read the value of the resource:

```
package org.learningRedis.chapter.four.pipelineandtx;
import java.util.Set;
import Redis.clients.jedis.Jedis;
import Redis.clients.jedis.Transaction;
import chapter.four.pubsub.ConnectionManager;
public class TransactionCommand implements Runnable {
  Jedis jedis = ConnectionManager.get();
  @Override
  public void run() {
      long start = System.currentTimeMillis();
      Transaction transactionableCommands = jedis.multi();
      for(int nv=0;nv<300000;nv++){
        transactionableCommands.sadd("keys-1", "name"+nv);
      }
      transactionableCommands.exec();
      Set<String> data= jedis.smembers("keys-1");
      System.out.println("The return value nv1 after tx [ " + data.
size() + " ]");
    System.out.println("The time taken for executing client(Thread-1)
"+ (System.currentTimeMillis()-start));
    ConnectionManager.set(jedis);
  }
}
```

The result of the preceding program will vary as per machine configuration but by changing the thread sleep time and running the program couple of times, the result will be similar to the one shown as follows:

```
The return code is [ 1 ]
The return value of nv1 is [ null ]
The return value nv1 after tx [ 300000 ]
The time taken for executing client(Thread-1) 7078
```

Fire the `FLUSHDB` command every time you run the test. The idea is that the program should not pick up a value obtained because of a previous run of the program. The proof that the single command program is able to write to the key is if we see the following line: `The return code is [1]`.

Let's analyze the result. In case of pipeline, a single command reads the value and the pipeline command sets a new value to that key as evident in the following result:

```
The return value of nv1 is [ 3508 ]
```

Now compare this with what happened in case of transaction when a single command tried to read the value but it was blocked because of the transaction. Hence the value will be `NULL` or 300,000.

```
The return value of nv1 after tx [0] or
The return value of nv1 after tx [300000]
```

So the difference in output can be attributed to the fact that in a transaction, if we have started a `MULTI` command, and are still in the process of queueing commands (that is, we haven't given the server the `EXEC` request yet), then any other client can still come in and make a request, and the response would be sent to the other client. Once the client gives the `EXEC` command, then all other clients are blocked while all of the queued transaction commands are executed.

Pipeline and transaction

To have a better understanding, let's analyze what happened in case of pipeline. When two different connections made requests to the Redis for the same resource, we saw a result where client-2 picked up the value while client-1 was still executing:

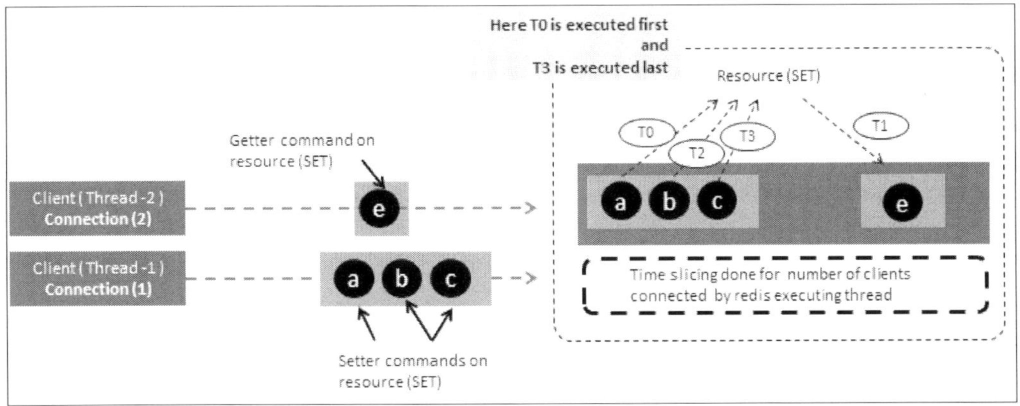

Pipeline in Redis in a multi connection environment

What it tells us is that requests from the first connection which is pipeline command is stacked as one command in its execution stack, and the command from the other connection is kept in its own stack specific to that connection. The Redis execution thread time slices between these two executions stacks, and that is why client-2 was able to print a value when the client-1 was still executing.

Let's analyze what happened in case of transaction here. Again the two commands (transaction commands and `GET` commands) were kept in their own execution stacks, but when the Redis execution thread gave time to the `GET` command, and it went to read the value, seeing the lock it was not allowed to read the value and was blocked. The Redis execution thread again went back to executing the transaction commands, and again it came back to `GET` command where it was again blocked. This process kept happening until the transaction command released the lock on the resource and then the `GET` command was able to get the value. If by any chance, the `GET` command was able to reach the resource before the transaction lock, it got a null value.

Please bear in mind that Redis does not block execution to other clients while queuing transaction commands but blocks only during executing them.

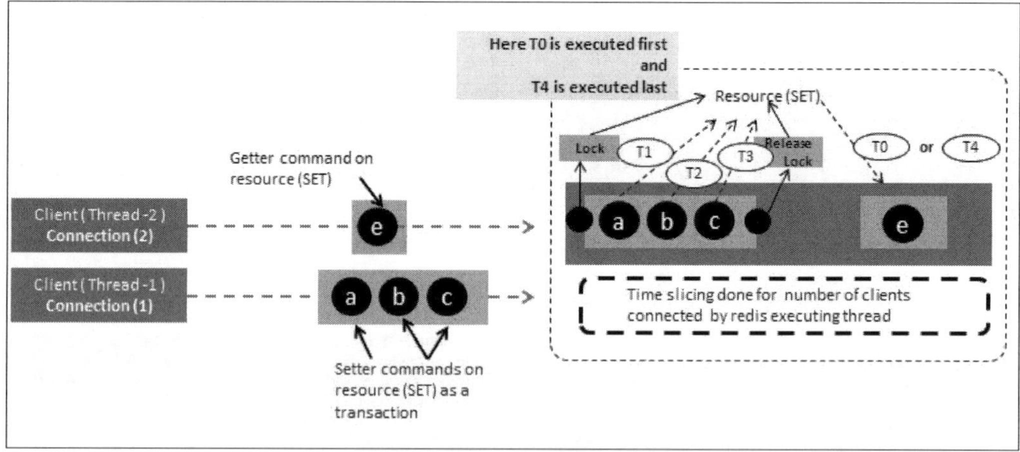

Transaction in Redis multi connection environment

This exercise gave us an insight into what happens in the case of pipeline and transaction.

Scripting in Redis

Lua is a high performing scripting language with interpreter written in C. Redis provides mechanism to extend thc functionality of Redis by providing support for Lua in the server side. Since Redis is implemented in C, it gives a natural synergy for Lua to be offered along with Redis as a server add on. The Lua interpreter shipped along with Redis is with limited capability and following libraries are shipped along with it:

- The `base` library
- The `table` library
- The `string` library
- The `math` library
- The `debug` library
- The `cjson` library
- The `cmsgpack` library

Libraries which can do File I/O and Networking are not included, so you cannot send a message from LUA script in REDIS to another external system.

Before we start with fun stuff, it's always better to have a hang of the language. LUA has its own dedicated site and tons of resources are available to LUA, but the next section concentrates on just enough LUA to get started for Redis.

Brief introduction on Lua

Okay, by now we all know that LUA is an interpreted language and it has support in Redis. To make use of the capability of Redis, let's learn couple of things about LUA. Types and values supported in LUA are as follows:

- **Nil**: Nil is a type with single value *nil*. On comparing it with Java, it can be taken as *null*.
- **Booleans**: These will have either true or false as values.
- **Numbers**: These represent double precession floating point numbers. So we can write our numbers as 1, 1.1, 2e+10, and so on.

- **String**: These represent a sequence of characters as is common in most of the scripting and programming languages. In LUA, strings are immutable in nature; for example, `"Learning Redis"` and `'Learning Redis'`. LUA provides methods in string library to find substring, replace characters, and so on.
- **Tables**: These are like arrays which can be indexed with numbers and strings except *nil*.

Control statements and loops in LUA are as follows:

- The `if then else` statement: As in Java, where we have only `if/else`, LUA supports something similar in the form of `if/then/else`. Following is the code example for it:

```
local  myvariable = 4
local  myothervariable = 5
if myvariable >  myothervariable then
  print("4 is greater than 5".."Please add 2 dots to concatenate
strings")
else
  print("4 is not greater than 5".."Please add 2 dots to
concatenate strings")
end
```

- The `while` loop: This is similar to Java where looping has a similar syntax:

```
local index=1
while index <= 5 do
  print("Looping done interation "..index)
  index=index+1
end
```

- The `repeat` statement: This is similar to `do/while` in Java. This will guarantee at least one time iteration:

```
local index=1
repeat
  print("Looping done interation "..index)
  index=index+1
until index==5
```

- The `for` loop: This is similar to the `for` loop in Java:

```
for i=1,3 do
  print("Looping in for loop ")
end
```

Two keywords in LUA that you will use frequently while executing control statements are `return` and `break`. Following is a simple sample to demonstrate return keyword, getting used in a function:

```
function greaterThanFunction( i , j )
  if i >  j then
    print(i.." is greater than"..j)
    return true
  else
    print(i.." is lesser than"..j)
    return false
  end
end
print(greaterThanFunction(4,5))
```

Next is a simple sample to demonstrate break keyword getting used in a function:

```
local mylist={"start","pause","stop","resume"}
function parseList ( k )
  for i=1,#mylist do
    if mylist[i] == "stop" then break end
    print(mylist[i])
  end
end
print(parseList(mylist))
```

With this minimal understanding of how LUA works, let's run a sample in Redis, and then take the understanding forward. But before that, let's understand how LUA works in Redis.

The following figure describes how LUA works with Redis. To understand how things happen internally, it is important to remember that Redis works in a single thread model and that all the Redis command and LUA logic would execute in a sequence:

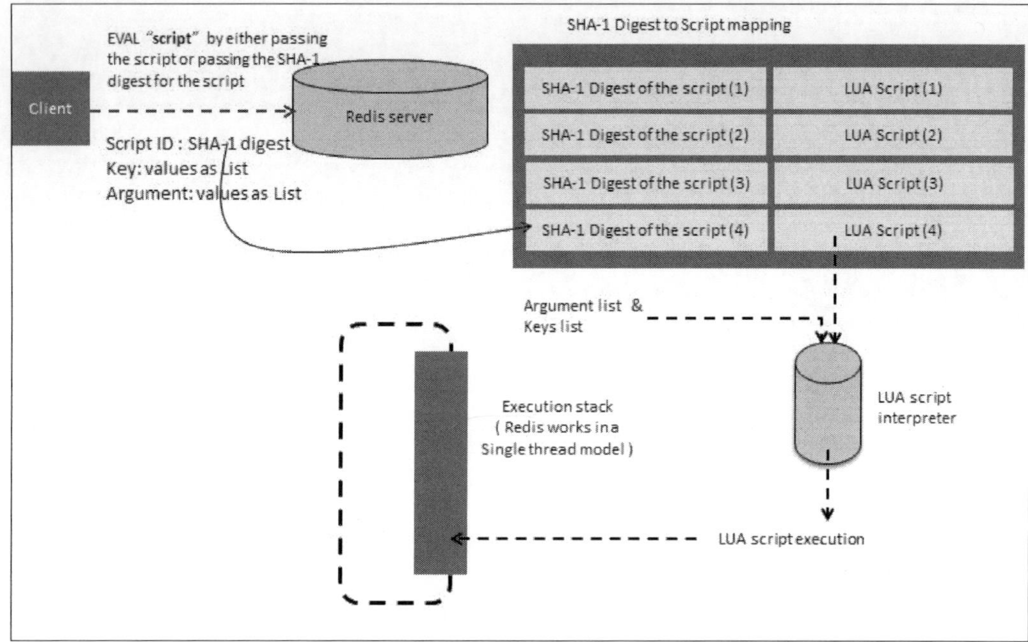

LUA scripting in Redis

When a client sends the script to the Redis server, the script gets validated for its syntax and is stored in an internal map in Redis against a SHA-1 digest. The SHA-1 digest is returned to the client.

Let's try a simple program in LUA which will basically read a value for a key and check if the value is equal to the argument passed. If yes, then it will set it to the second argument passed or else it will set it to the third argument passed to the script. Okay, let's prepare the test environment. Open your Redis command line client and set the value of `msg` key to `"Learning Redis"`:

```
redis 127.0.0.1:6379> set msg "Learning Redis"
OK
```

Preparing for the test executing LUA script

Now with the value of msg set, let's execute the Java program listed as follows:

```
package org.learningRedis.chapter.four.luascripting;
import java.util.Arrays;
import Redis.clients.jedis.Jedis;
import Redis.clients.jedis.JedisPool;
import Redis.clients.jedis.JedisPoolConfig;
public class TestLuaScript {
  public String luaScript = Reader.read("D:\\path\\of\\file\\
location\\LuaScript.txt");
  private JedisPool pool = new JedisPool(new JedisPoolConfig(),
"localhost");
  Jedis jedis = null;
  public Jedis getResource() {
    jedis = pool.getResource();
    return jedis;
  }
  public void setResource(Jedis jedis){
    pool.returnResource(jedis);
  }
  public static void main(String[] args) {
    TestLuaScript test = new TestLuaScript();
    test.luaScript();
  }
  private void luaScript() {
    Jedis jedis = this.getResource();
    String result = (String) jedis.eval(luaScript,Arrays.
asList("msg"),
        Arrays.asList("Learning Redis",
            "Now I am learning Lua for Redis",
            "prepare for the test again"));
    System.out.println(result);
    this.setResource(jedis);
  }
}
```

The code for Reader is a simple Java program which reads program from file location:

```
package org.learningRedis.chapter.four.luascripting;
import java.io.BufferedReader;
import java.io.FileReader;
import java.io.IOException;
public class Reader {
  public static String read(String filepath) {
    StringBuffer string = new StringBuffer();
```

```
        try (BufferedReader br = new BufferedReader(new
    FileReader(filepath)))
        {
          String currentline;
          while ((currentline = br.readLine()) != null) {
            string.append(currentline);
          }
        } catch (IOException e) {
          e.printStackTrace();
        }
        return string.toString();
      }
    }
```

Now let's take a look at the LUA script written in the file `LuaScript.txt` that we would be passing to the Java program:

```
local data= Redis.call('GET',KEYS[1])
if data==ARGV[1] then
  Redis.call('SET',KEYS[1],ARGV[2])
  return "The value that got sent is = "..ARGV[2]
else
  Redis.call('SET',KEYS[1],ARGV[3])
  return "The value that got sent is = "..ARGV[3]
end
```

The first run of the program should give you the following result:

```
The value that got sent is = Now I am learning Lua for Redis
```

The second run of the program should give you the following result:

```
The value that got sent is = prepare for the test again
```

So if you see the messages printed as shown in the preceding code then you actually have successfully executed your first LUA program in Redis. The following are the learnings that we have got with this sample:

- Redis treats LUA script as one function.
- LUA script uses `Redis.call()` method to fire Redis commands.
- Redis commands which return values can be assigned to a local variable. Over here we are assigning the value to a variable called `data`.
- Arrays in LUA start index from `1` not `0`. So you will never have array index such as `ARGV[0]` or `KEYS[0]`.

There are some further restrictions that Redis imposes on the Lua scripting engine which are as follows:

- In Redis, LUA scripts cannot have global variables.
- In Redis, LUA scripts cannot call transaction commands such as `MULTI` or `EXEC`.
- In Redis, LUA scripts cannot access external systems using I/O libraries that come in LUA. The only way it can communicate to external system is via Redis commands such as `PUBLISH`.
- LUA scripts to access system time are not supported via LUA. Instead, use `TIME` command, that is `Redis.call('TIME')`.
- Functions such as `Redis.call('TIME')` are non-deterministic in nature and so are not allowed before a `WRITE` command.
- Nesting of conditions is not allowed since nested condition will end with `END` keyword which impacts the outer conditions which again has to end with `END`.

The following commands are supported for managing the LUA scripts in Redis. Let's have a look at it and understand how they can be used:

- `EVAL`: This command will process the Redis script and the response would be the result of the executed script.
- `EVALSHA`: This command will process the cached script based on SHA-1 digest of the script and the response would be the result of the executed script.
- `SCRIPT EXISTS`: This command will check for the existence of script in the script cache. This check is done by passing SHA-1 digest of the script.
- `SCRIPT FLUSH`: This will flush the LUA script from the script cache.
- `SCRIPT KILL`: This command will kill the script whose execution is taking a lot of time.
- `SCRIPT LOAD`: This command will load the script in the cache and return the SHA-1 digest of the script.

Use case – reliable messaging

By using PUB/SUB capability of Redis, we can create a real time messaging framework but the problem with this is that if the intended subscriber is not available then the message is lost. To overcome this problem, we can take the help of LUA scripting which will store the message if the subscriber is not available.

The implementation of this will vary depending upon the framework design of the solution, but in our case we will take a simplistic approach where every subscriber and publisher will agree upon a channel. When the subscriber goes down, the publisher will store the message in a message box unique to the subscriber. When the subscriber again comes up, it will start consuming the lost messages, as well as the real time messages coming from the publisher. The following figure is representing the steps that we will have to follow to achieve reliable messaging:

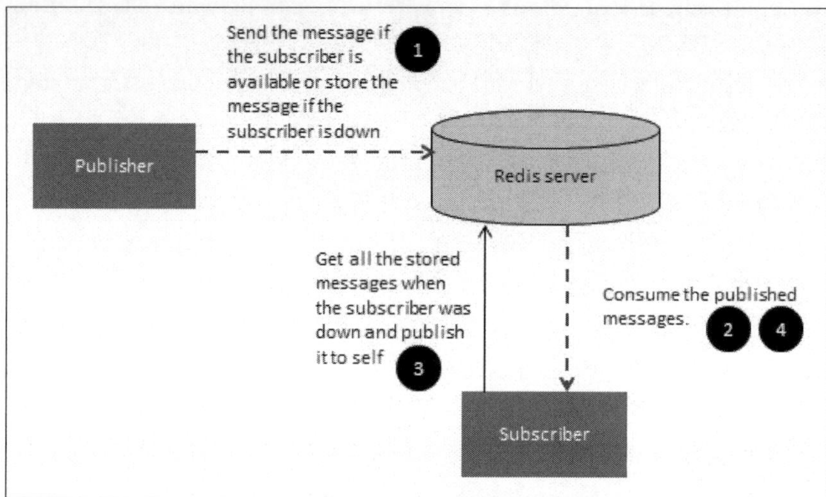

Simple reliable messaging

To begin with, the publisher will send the message to a channel client-1, oblivious to the fact whether the subscriber is in a receiving mode or not. Assuming that the subscriber is running, the messages from the publisher will be consumed in real-time. Then if we bring down the subscriber for a while and publish few more messages, in our case the publisher will be intelligent enough to know if the subscriber is running or not, and sensing that the subscriber is down, it will store the message in a `MSGBOX`.

In the meantime, the moment the subscriber is up and running, the first thing it will do is get the missed messages from the `MSGBOX` and publish it to self. The code for publisher is as follows:

```
package org.learningRedis.chapter.four.pubsub.reliable;
import java.util.Arrays;
import Redis.clients.jedis.Jedis;
import Redis.clients.jedis.JedisPool;
import Redis.clients.jedis.JedisPoolConfig;
import org.learningRedis.chapter.four.luascripting.Reader;
```

```
public class Publisher {
  public String luaScript = Reader.read("D:\\pathtoscript \\RELIABLE-
MSGING.txt");
  private JedisPool pool = new JedisPool(new JedisPoolConfig(),
"localhost");
  Jedis jedis = null;
  public Jedis getResource() {
    jedis = pool.getResource();
    return jedis;
  }
  public void setResource(Jedis jedis){
    pool.returnResource(jedis);
  }
  public static void main(String[] args) {
    Publisher test = new Publisher();
    test.sendingAreliableMessages();
  }
  private void sendingAreliableMessages() {
    Jedis jedis = this.getResource();
    String result = (String) jedis.eval(luaScript,Arrays.asList(""),
        Arrays.asList("{type='channel',publishto='client1',msg='"+Syst
em.currentTimeMillis()+"'}"));
    System.out.println(result);
    this.setResource(jedis);
  }
}
```

The code for the LUA script is as follows:

```
local payload = loadstring("return"..ARGV[1])()
local result = Redis.call("PUBLISH",payload.publishto,payload.msg)
if result==0 then
  Redis.call('SADD','MSGBOX',payload.msg)
  return 'stored messages:  '..ARGV[1]
else
  return 'consumed messages:  '..ARGV[1]
end
```

Following is a brief explanation of the step written in LUA:

1. In the first line we get the message and convert it into a table object. Array index starts with `1` in LUA.
2. We publish the message in the second line and get the result. The result tells us how many subscribers consumed the message.

3. If the result is equal to `0`, then all the listeners were down and we need to persist it. The data type used here is a `Set` and it subsequently returns a message back to the server (this return is optional).
4. If the message was consumed by the subscriber, then the statement in the `Else` is executed.
5. Finally, we `end` the function. (Make sure there is only one `end` in the script. LUA in Redis will not compile if there is more than one `end`.)

Redis will wrap the code in LUA as one function in LUA. The code for `Subscriber` is as follows:

```
package org.learningRedis.chapter.four.pubsub.reliable;
import java.util.Arrays;
import java.util.Set;
import java.util.concurrent.ArrayBlockingQueue;
import java.util.concurrent.BlockingQueue;
import org.learningRedis.chapter.four.luascripting.Reader;
import Redis.clients.jedis.Jedis;
import Redis.clients.jedis.JedisPubSub;
import chapter.four.pubsub.ConnectionManager;
public class SimpleMsgSubscriber {
  static Thread lostMsgWorker;
  static Thread msgWorker;
  public static void main(String[] args) {
    SimpleMsgSubscriber source = new SimpleMsgSubscriber();
  msgWorker = new Thread(source.new MsgProcessor());
lostMsgWorker = new Thread(source.new LostMsgProcessor());
  msgWorker.start();
lostMsgWorker.start();
  }
public class MsgProcessor extends JedisPubSub implements Runnable {
Jedis jedis = ConnectionManager.get();
@Override
public void run() {
  jedis.subscribe(this, "client1");
}
@Override
public void onMessage(String arg0, String arg1) {
  System.out.println("processing the msg = " + arg1);
}
@Override
public void onPMessage(String arg0, String arg1, String arg2) {
    }
```

```
@Override
public void onPSubscribe(String arg0, int arg1) {
    }
@Override
public void onPUnsubscribe(String arg0, int arg1) {
     }
@Override
public void onSubscribe(String arg0, int arg1) {
    }
@Override
public void onUnsubscribe(String arg0, int arg1) {
    }
  }
public class LostMsgProcessor implements Runnable {
    Jedis jedis = ConnectionManager.get();
    @Override
    public void run() {
      String event;
      Jedis jedis = ConnectionManager.get();
      String msg;
      while((msg=jedis.spop("MSGBOX")) != null){
        MessageHandler.push(msg);
      }
    }
  }
  public static class MessageHandler {
    static Jedis jedis = ConnectionManager.get();
        public static void push(String msg)
        {
            String luaScript = "";
            try
            {
                luaScript = read("D:\\path\\to\\file\\RELIABLE-MSGING.
txt");
            }
            catch (IOException e)
            {
                e.printStackTrace();
            }
            String result = (String) jedis.eval(luaScript, Arrays.
asList(""), Arrays.asList("{type='channel',publishto='client1',msg='"
+ msg + "'}"));
        }
```

```
        private static String read(String luaScriptPath) throws
IOException
        {
            Path file = Paths.get(luaScriptPath);
            BufferedReader reader = Files.newBufferedReader(file,
Charset.defaultCharset());
            StringBuilder content = new StringBuilder();
            String line = null;
            while ((line = reader.readLine()) != null)
            {
                content.append(line).append("/n");
            }
            System.out.println("Content: " + content.toString());
            return content.toString();
        }
  }
}
```

The program has following responsibilities and a brief explanation of the program is as follows:

- When it starts it should check if it has any messages in the message box, such as `MSGBOX`, while it was down. If it has messages then its job is to publish it to self.
- The second thing it should do is to listen for messages it has subscribed to.
- For better performance, run the `SCRIPT LOAD` command which will load the script and return a SHA-1 digest, and instead of using `EVAL`, use the `EVALSHA` command, where you pass the same SHA-1 digest. This will prevent the script getting checked for syntax correctness and will be executed directly.

Connection management

In this section we will be focusing on the way we can manage the connection to Redis. The functions provided under connection management in Redis help us to do the following:

- `AUTH`: This command with the password allows the request to be processed if the password matches the configured password. Redis server can be configured with `requirepass` in the `config` file along with the password.
- `ECHO`: This command echoes back the text sent to a Redis instance.
- `PING`: This command replies with `PONG` when sent to a Redis instance.

- `QUIT`: This command kills the connection held by the Redis instance for a client.
- `SELECT`: This command helps in selecting a database in Redis for executing the command. Data in Redis can have separation of concern and this is achieved by creating a silo and storing the data in that. The data in each silo don't interfere and are isolated.

Redis authentication

Adding a simple password to your Redis server via Redis client and testing it via Java client is explained in following steps:

1. Open the Redis client and type `CONFIG SET requirepass "Learning Redis"`. You have set the password for your Redis server as `"Learning Redis"`.
2. Write the following program in Java using Jedis, which will perform some simple getter and setter without authenticating against the Redis server:

```
package org.learningRedis.chapter.four.auth;
import Redis.clients.jedis.Jedis;
public class TestingPassword {
  public static void main(String[] args) {
    TestingPassword test = new TestingPassword();
    test.authentication();
  }
  private void authentication() {
    Jedis jedis = new Jedis("localhost");
    jedis.set("foo", "bar");
    System.out.println(jedis.get("foo"));
  }
}
```

3. The outcome in the console would be `ERR operation not permitted`, or based upon version, you might get `NOAUTH Authentication required`, which is indicative of the fact that since the password was not passed in the request, the operation could not be permitted. To make the program work, the client need, to pass the password for authentication:

```
package org.learningRedis.chapter.four.auth;
import Redis.clients.jedis.Jedis;
public class TestingPassword {
  public static void main(String[] args) {
    TestingPassword test = new TestingPassword();
    test.authentication();
```

```
    }
    private void authentication() {
      Jedis jedis = new Jedis("localhost");
      jedis.auth("Learning Redis");
      jedis.set("foo", "bar");
      System.out.println(jedis.get("foo"));
    }
  }
```

The outcome of the program in the console would be `bar`.

Redis SELECT

Redis provides a mechanism of segregating the Redis server into databases. Instead of an elaborate naming mechanism in some of the databases, Redis has a simple process of dividing the database into separate key spaces, and each key space is represented by an integer.

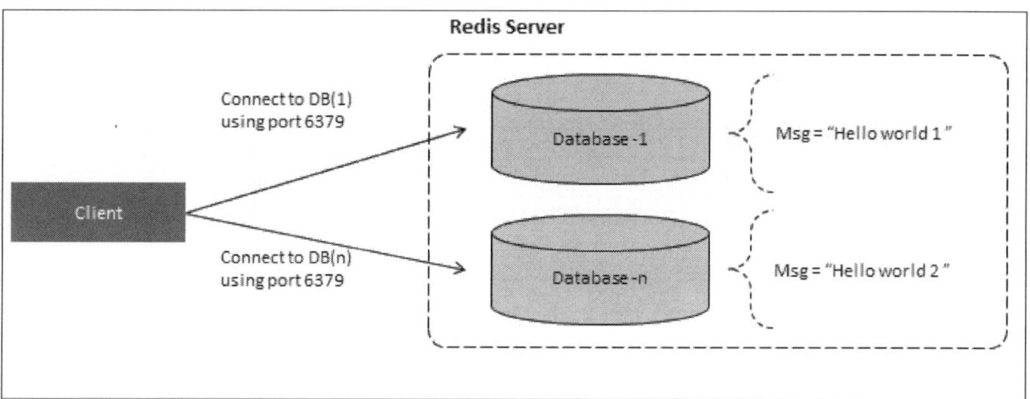

Multiple database in Redis

The program here attempts to store some data in a database and tries to successfully retrieve the data from it. It then changes the database and attempts to retrieve the same data, which of course ends up in failure. Remember to remove any authentication that might be set in the previous program for this code to run or just restart Redis server.

```
package org.learningRedis.chapter.four.selectdb;
import Redis.clients.jedis.Jedis;
public class TestSelectingDB {
  public static void main(String[] args) {
    TestSelectingDB test = new TestSelectingDB();
    test.commandSelect();
  }
```

```
  private void commandSelect() {
    Jedis jedis = new Jedis("localhost");
    jedis.select(1);
    jedis.set("msg", "Hello world");
    System.out.println(jedis.get("msg"));
    jedis.select(2);
    System.out.println(jedis.get("msg"));
  }
}
```

The outcome of this program should be as following:

```
Hello world
null
```

Redis ECHO and PING

Redis provides some utility functions, such as `ECHO` and `PING`, which can be used to check if the server is responding or not, and how much time is it taking in responding to a request. This gives an idea on the latency at network and I/O level.

The following program will demonstrate a sample usage where the `ECHO` and `PING` commands will be fired when no other connections are made to the server, and then again it will fire these commands (`ECHO` and `PING`) when the Redis server is under the load of 100 connections. The outcome when no other connections are made is as follows:

```
PONG in 47 milliseconds
hi Redis  in 0 milliseconds
PONG in 0 milliseconds
hi Redis  in 0 milliseconds
PONG in 0 milliseconds
hi Redis  in 0 milliseconds
PONG in 0 milliseconds
hi Redis  in 0 milliseconds
```

The outcome when 100 other connections are doing activity on the server is as follows:

```
PONG in 16 milliseconds
hi Redis  in 16 milliseconds
PONG in 0 milliseconds
hi Redis  in 15 milliseconds
PONG in 16 milliseconds
hi Redis  in 0 milliseconds
PONG in 15 milliseconds
```

The outcome when 50 other connections are doing activity on the server is as follows:

```
PONG in 15 milliseconds
hi Redis  in 0 milliseconds
PONG in 0 milliseconds
hi Redis  in 16 milliseconds
PONG in 0 milliseconds
hi Redis  in 0 milliseconds
PONG in 16 milliseconds
hi Redis  in 0 milliseconds
PONG in 0 milliseconds
hi Redis  in 15 milliseconds
```

This proves that it is immaterial the amount of activity the Redis server is doing, but depends on the availability of the I/O and network resources. The following program is for reference:

```
package org.learningRedis.chapter.four.echoandping;
import Redis.clients.jedis.Jedis;
public class TestEchoAndPing {
  public static void main(String[] args) throws InterruptedException {
    TestEchoAndPing echoAndPing = new TestEchoAndPing();
    Thread thread = new Thread(new LoadGenerator());
    thread.start();
    while(true){
      Thread.currentThread().sleep(1000);
      echoAndPing.testPing();
      echoAndPing.testEcho();
    }
  }
  private void testPing() {
    long start = System.currentTimeMillis();
    Jedis jedis = new Jedis("localhost");
    System.out.println(jedis.ping() + " in " + (System.
currentTimeMillis()-start) + " milliseconds");
  }
  private void testEcho() {
    long start = System.currentTimeMillis();
    Jedis jedis = new Jedis("localhost");
    System.out.println(jedis.echo("hi Redis ") + " in " + (System.
currentTimeMillis()-start) + " milliseconds");
  }
}
```

The code for `LoadGenerator` is noted as follows for reference:

```
package org.learningRedis.chapter.four.echoandping;
import java.util.ArrayList;
import java.util.List;
import Redis.clients.jedis.Jedis;
public class LoadGenerator implements Runnable{
  List<Thread> clients = new ArrayList<Thread>();
  public LoadGenerator() {
    for(int i=0;i<50;i++){
      clients.add(new Thread(new Sample()));
    }
  }
  @Override
  public void run() {
    for(int i=0;i<50;i++){
      clients.get(i).start();
    }
  }
  public class Sample implements Runnable{
    Jedis jedis = new Jedis("localhost");
    @Override
    public void run() {
      int x=0;
      while(!Thread.currentThread().isInterrupted()){
        jedis.sadd(Thread.currentThread().getName(), "Some text"+new
Integer(x).toString());
        x++;
      }
    }
  }
}
```

We can play around with this program by changing the number of threads and commenting the thread start code in the `TestEchoAndPing`, and seeing the result ourselves. The result is going to show the same consistency as shown in the preceding code.

Summary

In this chapter, we saw how to use Redis, not simply as a datastore, but also as pipeline the commands which is so much more like bulk processing. Apart from that, we covered areas such as transaction, messaging, and scripting. We also saw how to combine messaging and scripting, and create reliable messaging in Redis. This capability of Redis makes it different from some of the other datastore solutions. In the next chapter, we will focus on data handling capabilities of Redis.

5
Handling Data in Redis

Data in business defines the business. What it means is that the way we define, store, interpret, and use data, forms the data platform of our business. It seldom happens that a single piece of data has meaning on its own; it only forms business functionality when combined with other data. So it becomes important that the data is connected, grouped, and filtered in such a way that the same dataset can be used for various aspects of the business.

In order to have a platform which can sustain future requirements, it is pertinent that we define and classify the data in a way which gives us indications on the kind of expectation we have from that data. Data has many facets and it's important to understand those facets to extract full business value from it. For example, stock price of a company is important for the real-time systems to decide whether to buy or sell, and it loses its importance after a few seconds or milliseconds. However, it becomes important for the analytics system to predict its trends. So in a way, the same piece of data at different times has different usage. So it's good practice to take into account the various expectations from the data while strategizing the data architecture.

Classifying data

A general tendency has been to think only in terms of a data model which fits the relational model. This might be a good model for certain classes of data but might prove to be ineffective for another class of data. Since this book is on Redis, we will attempt to classify the data based on certain behaviors and make an attempt to see where Redis fits:

- **Message and event data**: The data classified as message data in business show the following properties:
    - **Data complexity**: Message data has low data complexity as they are usually flat in structure

  - **Data quantity**: Message data usually has high volumes
  - **Persistence**: Message data can be stored in disk and memory
  - **CAP property**: Message data needs to be at least available and partition tolerant
  - **Usability**: Message data can have usability in real-time, soft real-time, and offline and show the property of heavy writes and low reads

  If the requirement for message data is for real-time and soft real-time activity, and the data quantity is not very high then Redis and its messaging capability can be used.

- **Cache data**: The data classified as cache data in business shows the following properties:
  - **Data complexity**: Cache data has low data complexity and is mostly stored as name value pair
  - **Data quantity**: Cache data usually has low to medium volumes
  - **Persistence**: Data can be stored in cache memory
  - **CAP property**: Cache data needs to be at least available and consistent
  - **Usability**: Cache data can have usability in real-time, and show low writes and heavy reads

  Redis is the perfect fit for cache data since it provides data structures which can be used directly by the program for storing the data. Also, the keys in Redis have time to live option which can be used to clean the data in Redis at regular intervals.

- **Meta data**: The data classified as meta data in business shows the following properties:
  - **Data complexity**: Meta data has low data complexity and is mostly stored as name value pair
  - **Data quantity**: Meta data usually has low volumes
  - **Persistence**: Meta data can be stored in memory
  - **CAP property**: Meta data needs to be at least available and consistent
  - **Usability**: Meta data can have usability in real-time and usually show low writes and low to heavy reads

Redis is the perfect fit for meta data since it provides data structures which can be used directly by the program for storing the data. Since Redis is fast and has messaging capability, it can be used for runtime manipulation of the meta data and also act as a central meta data repository. The following figure is a representation of how Redis can be used as meta data store:

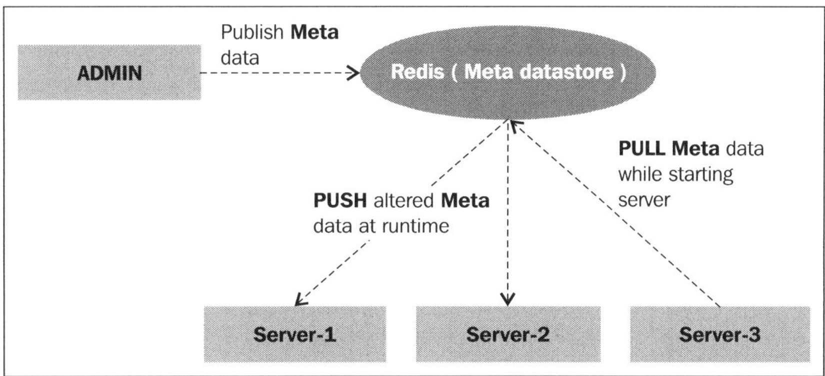

Redis as a meta data store

- **Transactional data**: The data classified as transactional data in business shows the following properties:
    - **Data complexity**: Transactional data has medium to high data complexity and is mostly relational
    - **Data quantity**: Transactional data usually has medium to high volumes
    - **Persistence**: Transactional data can be stored in memory and disk
    - **CAP property**: Transactional data needs to be at least consistent and partition tolerant
    - **Usability**: Transactional data need to show `CRUD` behavior, capabilities that Redis does not have

Redis is not the right datastore for this kind of data. Another point which we can figure out here is that wherever we need partition tolerance as a CAP feature, Redis should not be used.

- **Analytical data**: The data classified as analytical data in business shows the following properties:
    - **Data complexity**: Data complexity can be further segregated on the basis of online analytics and offline analytics. Online analytical data has low to medium data complexity as they can contain graph like relation. Offline analytics have very high data complexity.
    - **Data quantity**: Data here usually has low to high volumes depending upon the kind of analytics we want. Online analytics can have a lower amount of data as compared to offline analytics.
    - **Persistence**: Data can be stored in disk and memory. If online analytics is the requirement, the data is persisted in memory but if the analytics is offline then data needs to persist in the disk.
    - **CAP property**: In case of offline analytics, the data needs to be at least available and partition tolerant, and in case of online analytics, the data needs to be available and consistent.
    - **Usability**: Message data can have usability in real-time, soft real-time, and offline.

  If the requirement is for online analytics, Redis can be used provided the complexity of the data is low.

In the preceding classification of data, we saw some areas where Redis is a good fit and areas where Redis can be avoided. But for Redis to be taken seriously in the business solution environment, it has to show capability for fault tolerance and fault management, replication, and so on. In the next section, we will do in-depth study of how redundancy and fault management can be taken care of.

Master-slave data replication

In any business application, it is paramount that data is kept in a replicated manner since hardware can break at any time without giving any warning. In order to have continuance of the business, it becomes necessary that when the master database goes down, the replicated database can be used instead, which in a way guarantees quality of service. Another advantage of having replicated data is realized when the traffic on one database goes up and it negatively impacts the performance of the solution. In order to provide the performance, it is important to load balance the traffic and reduce the load on each node.

Datastores such as Cassandra provide master-master configuration where all the nodes in the topology are like masters and the replication of data takes place based on token hash generated on the basis of key, and for that to happen nodes in the topology are partitioned based on token ranges.

Redis, unlike master-master breed of datastores, has a simpler master-slave arrangement. What it means is that master is the node which will write all the data and then replicate the data into all the slave nodes. The replication takes place asynchronously which means that the moment a data is written into the master, the slaves are not written synchronously but a separate process writes them asynchronously, so the update is not immediate; in other words **eventual consistency**. But there is advantage in this kind of arrangement in terms of performance. If the replication is synchronous then when an update is made to the master, the master has to update all the slaves and then only the update will be marked as a success. So if there are more slaves then the updates become more time consuming.

The following figure represents the process of master-slave replication in Redis. To have a better understanding of the process, let's say that at time **T0**, the value of a Set represented by **Msg** is **"Hello"** in the master node as well as in all the slave nodes (**S1**, **S2**, **S3**). When an insert command **SADD** is made to insert value (**"Hello again"**) to the Set at time **T1**, the value **Msg** becomes **Hello Hello again** at time **T2** but the value of **Msg** at slave nodes is still **"Hello"**. The new value is successfully inserted into the master node and the reply code for a successful insertion is sent back to the client. Meanwhile, the master will start inserting all the slaves with the new value and this happens in time **T3**. So at time **T3**, all the nodes (master and slaves) are updated with the new value. The time lag between the master getting updated and the slaves getting updated is very small (in milliseconds).

To have a better understanding of how master-slave would work in Redis, let's revisit the previous chapter where we discussed real-time messaging in Redis. To apply the same functionality in this case, we can think that all the slave nodes have been subscribed to the master node and when the master node gets updated, it publishes the new data to all the slave nodes.

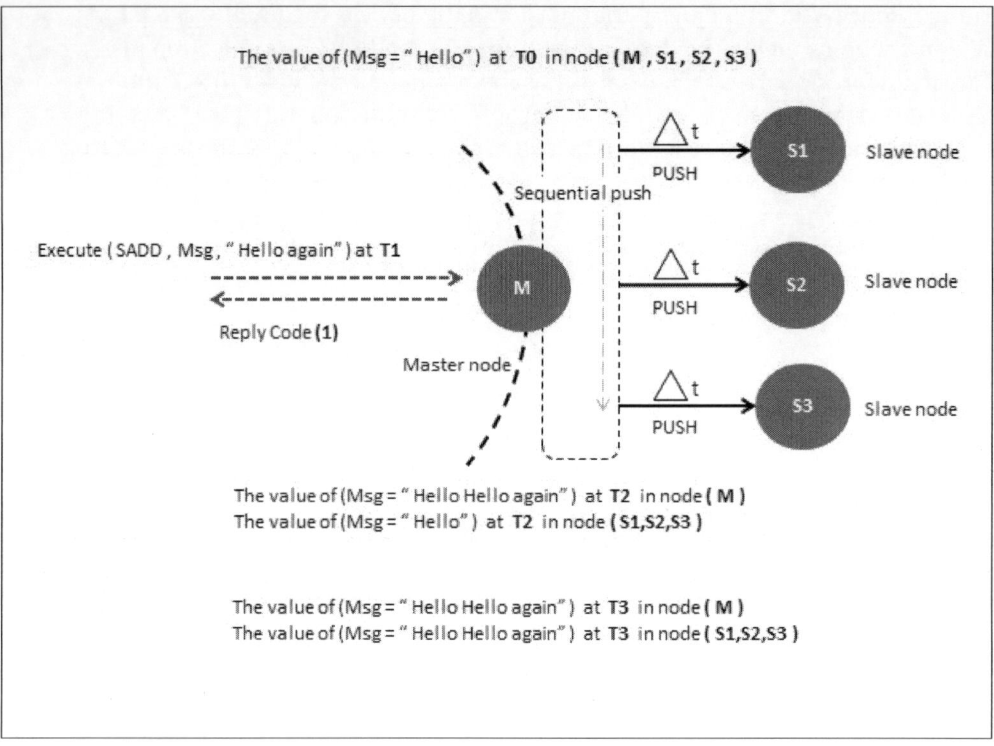

Data replication in master-slave

So what happens when a slave is down and an update happens in the master? Well, in that case, the particular slave misses the update and still carries the older value. However, when the slave again connects back to the master, the first thing it does is fire a `SYNC` command to the master. This command sends the data to the slave nodes wherein it can update itself.

Setting master and slave nodes

Setting up master slave nodes is pretty simple in Redis. What we will do here is set up a master and a slave node for Redis in our local machine. The first thing we do here is to copy the Redis folder (in our case `redis 2.6`) to a suitable location. So now we have Redis distribution in two separate locations.

redis-2.6.slave	File folder	28-05-2015 11:38
redis-2.6	File folder	28-05-2015 11:38

Master node folder and slave node folder

For the sake of better understanding, we will refer to **Redis-2.6** as the master node and **Redis-2.6.slave** as the slave node. Now open the master node and go to the `bin/release`" folder and start the Redis-server. This will start the Redis server in the localhost and with port address 6379. Now open the slave node and open the `Redis.conf` file in a suitable text editor. There are at least two properties that need to be changed in order to start our slave node. The first property which needs to be edited is `port`. In our case, let's change the value from 6379 to 6380. Since the master node is going to listen for requests at 6379, the slave has to listen at a different port (we are going to launch both the master and the slave from the same machine). The second property change that needs to be done is `slaveof`, the value of which is going to be `127.0.0.1 6379`. This is basically telling the slave where and what port the master is running. This is helpful since the slave is going to use this address to send `SYNC` and other commands to the master. With these minimal changes we are good to go. Now go to the `bin/release` folder of the slave node and start the Redis-server.

When you start the Redis-server, provide the path of `Redis.conf` of the slave node, that is Redis-server `F:\path\to\config-file\Redis.conf`.

The first thing we would see when we fire the slave node is that it will try to connect to the master. From its `Redis.conf`, the slave node will figure out the host and port of the master node. One thing again which is different in Redis as compared to other datastores is that it uses one port for catering to business requests as well as catering to `SYNC` and other ports for similar request from slave nodes. This is primarily because Redis is a single threaded server and the thread only listens to the messages coming to the socket.

The following figure represents how your command prompt might look when the slave node starts (please make sure your master node is up and running):

```
[2356] 04 Feb 12:14:48.560 # Warning: 32 bit instance detected but no memory limit set.

                                  Redis 2.6.12 (00000000/0) 32 bit

                                  Running in stand alone mode
                                  Port: 6380
                                  PID: 2356

                                        http://redis.io

[2356] 04 Feb 12:14:48.576 # Server started, Redis version 2.6.12
[2356] 04 Feb 12:14:48.591 * The server is now ready to accept connections on port 6380
[2356] 04 Feb 12:14:49.559 * Connecting to MASTER...
[2356] 04 Feb 12:14:49.559 * MASTER <-> SLAVE sync started
[2356] 04 Feb 12:14:49.559 * Non blocking connect for SYNC fired the event.
[2356] 04 Feb 12:14:49.559 * Master replied to PING, replication can continue...
[2356] 04 Feb 12:14:51.010 * MASTER <-> SLAVE sync: receiving 5222918 bytes from master
[2356] 04 Feb 12:14:51.104 * MASTER <-> SLAVE sync: Loading DB in memory
```

Slave node starting at port 6380

There are a couple of things that need to be noted here. The first thing is that the moment the slave node starts, it fires a `SYNC` command to the master. The command is a nonblocking command which means that the single thread will not hold other requests in order to cater to this request. What basically the master does is put it in a request stack for that connection and time slices it with the other connections, and when the activity is complete for that command of that connection (in our case `SYNC` for slave) it sends it to slave. In this case, what it sends back is the command and the data that the slave needs to have to become at par with the master. This command is executed with the data and it is then subsequently loaded in the slave's database. All the commands that the master sends are the commands which alter the data and not the data `getter` commands. The protocol used by the master to connect to the slaves is the **Redis protocol**.

Let's look into some scenarios and see how Redis behaves in the master slave mode:

- Master is up and a telnet session connects to the master:
    1. Make sure Redis master node is up.
    2. Make sure Redis client for the master is running.
    3. Open your command prompt and connect to the master using the command `telnet 127.0.0.1  6379`.
    4. Type the command `SYNC` in the telnet client. The following text should appear in the command prompt:

```
PING
*1
$4
PING
*1
$4
PING
```

Master pinging telnet client

    5. Go to your master client prompt and type the command `SET MSG "Learning Redis master slave replication"` and execute it. Immediately shift to the telnet command prompt and you will see the following output:

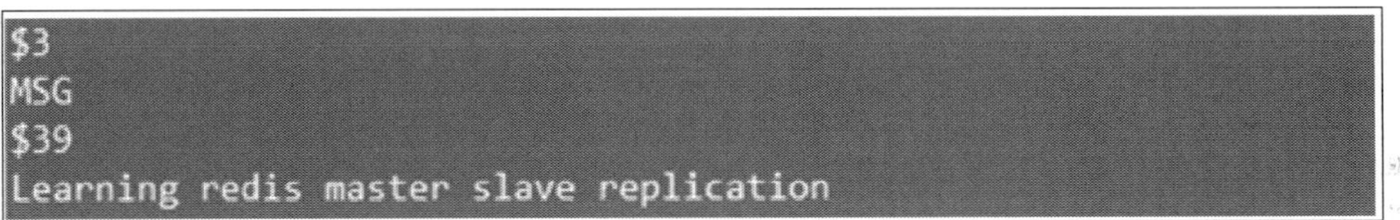

Master sending the data to telnet client

    6. Now execute the `GET MSG` command at the client prompt of the master node

- Master is up and the slave connects for the first time:
    1. The slave console is similar to the previous figure.
    2. Fire a command from master Redis-cli as `SET MSG "Learning Redis"`.
    3. Fire a command from slave Redis-cli as `GET MSG`.

4. Make sure you give the host and port addresses; in our case since we have configured it in localhost and port is configured at 6380, the command would look like `Redis-cli.exe -h localhost -p 6380`.
5. The result should be `"Learning Redis"`.

- Master is up and slave comes up again after being disconnected for a while:
    1. Kill the slave node and the client.
    2. Go to the master's client command prompt and write the command `SET MSG "Slave node is down"`.
    3. Now start the slave node and its client (provide host and port information).
    4. Execute the command `GET MSG` from slave's client command prompt and the result should be `"Slave node is down"`.
- Master is up and is executing a pipeline command and we are reading the value from slave:
    1. Make sure master and slave are up and running.
    2. Write the `SCARD MSG` command in slave client's command prompt but do not execute it. We are going to get the number of members in the set `MSG`.
    3. Open you Java client and write the following program:

```
package org.learningRedis.chapter.five;
import Redis.clients.jedis.Jedis;
import Redis.clients.jedis.Pipeline;
public class PushDataMaster {
        public static void main(String[] args) {
          PushDataMaster test = new PushDataMaster();
          test.pushData();
        }
        private void pushData() {
          Jedis jedis = new Jedis("localhost",6379);
          Pipeline pipeline = jedis.pipelined();
for(int nv=0;nv<900000;nv++){
            pipeline.sadd("MSG", ",data-"+nv);
          }
          pipeline.sync();
        }
}
```

4. Execute this command and immediately switch to your slave client command prompt and execute the command you had written. The result will be similar to the figure shown next. What it tells us is that the moment a command is executed in the master node which changes the dataset, the master starts buffering these commands and sends them to the slave. In our case, when we did a `SCARD` on the set, we saw results in an incremental way.

```
redis localhost:6380> scard  MSG
(integer) 0
redis localhost:6380> scard  MSG
(integer) 30000
redis localhost:6380> scard  MSG
(integer) 145050
redis localhost:6380> scard  MSG
(integer) 300000
redis localhost:6380> scard  MSG
(integer) 148733
redis localhost:6380> scard  MSG
(integer) 247218
redis localhost:6380> scard  MSG
(integer) 318259
redis localhost:6380> scard  MSG
(integer) 396970
redis localhost:6380> scard  MSG
(integer) 474631
redis localhost:6380> scard  MSG
(integer) 555770
redis localhost:6380> scard  MSG
(integer) 616139
redis localhost:6380> scard  MSG
(integer) 706251
redis localhost:6380> scard  MSG
(integer) 900000
```

Result of SCARD command on slave node

5. Master is up and is executing a transaction command and we are reading the value from slave.

- Promoting slave as master when the master goes down and restarting master as slave:
    1. Start master and slave Redis servers.
    2. Execute the following Java program from your IDE:

```
package org.learningRedis.chapter.five.masterslave;
import Redis.clients.jedis.Jedis;
public class MasterSlaveTest {
  public static void main(String[] args) throws
InterruptedException {
    MasterSlaveTest test = new MasterSlaveTest();
    test.masterslave();
  }
  private void masterslave() throws InterruptedException {
    Jedis master = new Jedis("localhost",6379);
    Jedis slave = new Jedis("localhost",6380);
    master.append("msg", "Learning Redis");
    System.out.println("Getting message from master: " +
master.get("msg"));
    System.out.println("Getting message from slave : " +
slave.get("msg"));
    master.shutdown();
    slave.slaveofNoOne();
    slave.append("msg", " slave becomes the master");
    System.out.println("Getting message from slave turned
master : " + slave.get("msg"));
    Thread.currentThread().sleep(20000);
    master = new Jedis("localhost",6379);
    master.slaveof("localhost", 6380);
    Thread.currentThread().sleep(20000);
    System.out.println("Getting message from master turned
slave : " + master.get("msg"));
    master.append("msg", "throw some exceptions !!");
  }
}
```

    3. When the program goes to sleep for the first time, quickly go to the command prompt of the master and restart it (don't touch the slave node). Allow the program to finish and the output is going to be similar to the following image:

```
Getting message from master: Learning RedisLearning Redis
Getting message from slave :  slave becomes the master
Getting message from slave turned master :  slave becomes the master slave becomes
the master
Exception in thread "main" redis.clients.jedis.exceptions.JedisConnectionException:
java.net.ConnectException: Connection refused: connect
	at redis.clients.jedis.Connection.connect(Connection.java:134)
	at redis.clients.jedis.BinaryClient.connect(BinaryClient.java:69)
	at redis.clients.jedis.Connection.sendCommand(Connection.java:79)
	at redis.clients.jedis.Connection.sendCommand(Connection.java:75)
	at redis.clients.jedis.BinaryClient.slaveof(BinaryClient.java:657)
	at redis.clients.jedis.BinaryJedis.slaveof(BinaryJedis.java:2825)
	at MasterSlaveTest.masterslave(MasterSlaveTest.java:24)
	at MasterSlaveTest.main(MasterSlaveTest.java:8)
Caused by: java.net.ConnectException: Connection refused: connect
	at java.net.DualStackPlainSocketImpl.waitForConnect(Native Method)
	at java.net.DualStackPlainSocketImpl.socketConnect(Unknown Source)
	at java.net.AbstractPlainSocketImpl.doConnect(Unknown Source)
	at java.net.AbstractPlainSocketImpl.connectToAddress(Unknown Source)
	at java.net.AbstractPlainSocketImpl.connect(Unknown Source)
	at java.net.PlainSocketImpl.connect(Unknown Source)
	at java.net.SocksSocketImpl.connect(Unknown Source)
	at java.net.Socket.connect(Unknown Source)
	at redis.clients.jedis.Connection.connect(Connection.java:129)
	... 7 more
```

Master becomes slave and slave becomes master

4. The second sleep in the program is meant for the master to sync up with the new master.
5. When the old master attempts to write against the key, it fails since slaves cannot write.
6. Server messages when the old slave became new master.

```
[3892] 09 Feb 19:15:57.421 # Server started, Redis version 2.6.12
[3892] 09 Feb 19:15:57.421 * DB loaded from disk: 0.000 seconds
[3892] 09 Feb 19:15:57.421 * The server is now ready to accept connections on port 6380
[3892] 09 Feb 19:15:58.406 * Connecting to MASTER...
[3892] 09 Feb 19:15:58.406 * MASTER <-> SLAVE sync started
[3892] 09 Feb 19:15:58.406 * Non blocking connect for SYNC fired the event.
[3892] 09 Feb 19:15:58.406 * Master replied to PING, replication can continue...
[3892] 09 Feb 19:15:58.500 * MASTER <-> SLAVE sync: receiving 18 bytes from master
[3892] 09 Feb 19:15:58.546 * MASTER <-> SLAVE sync: Loading DB in memory
[3892] 09 Feb 19:15:58.546 * MASTER <-> SLAVE sync: Finished with success
[3892] 09 Feb 19:16:29.437 * MASTER MODE enabled (user request)
[3892] 09 Feb 19:16:49.515 * Slave ask for synchronization
[3892] 09 Feb 19:16:49.531 * Starting BGSAVE for SYNC
[3892] 09 Feb 19:16:49.531 * cowBkgdSaveReset deleting 0 SDS and 0 obj items
[3892] 09 Feb 19:16:49.578 * DB saved on disk
[3892] 09 Feb 19:16:49.671 * Background saving terminated with success
[3892] 09 Feb 19:16:49.671 * cowBkgdSaveReset deleting 0 SDS and 0 obj items
[3892] 09 Feb 19:16:49.703 * Synchronization with slave succeeded
```

Slave becomes master

7. Server messages when the old master is started as a new slave. We can also see that the moment the old master restarts, the first thing it does as a slave is to sync with the new master and update its datasets.

```
[5064] 09 Feb 19:16:36.500 # Server started, Redis version 2.6.12
[5064] 09 Feb 19:16:36.500 * DB loaded from disk: 0.000 seconds
[5064] 09 Feb 19:16:36.500 * The server is now ready to accept connections on port 6379
[5064] 09 Feb 19:16:49.437 * SLAVE OF localhost:6380 enabled (user request)
[5064] 09 Feb 19:16:49.515 * Connecting to MASTER...
[5064] 09 Feb 19:16:49.515 * MASTER <-> SLAVE sync started
[5064] 09 Feb 19:16:49.515 * Non blocking connect for SYNC fired the event.
[5064] 09 Feb 19:16:49.515 * Master replied to PING, replication can continue...
[5064] 09 Feb 19:16:49.703 * MASTER <-> SLAVE sync: receiving 65 bytes from master
[5064] 09 Feb 19:16:49.718 * MASTER <-> SLAVE sync: Loading DB in memory
[5064] 09 Feb 19:16:49.718 * MASTER <-> SLAVE sync: Finished with success
```

Master becomes slave

8. If we don't give the second sleep in the program, the old master will not get time to sync with the new master and if there is a client request for a key then it will end up showing the old value for the key

Until now we have learnt the master-slave capabilities of Redis and how it behaves in cases where master goes down or slave goes down. We also discussed that master sends data to slave and replicates the dataset. But still the question is what does Redis master send when it has to send data to the slaves? To find out, let's run a small experiment which will clarify the behind the scene activities.

Performance pattern – high reads

In a production environment, it becomes important to have some kind of a strategy when the concurrency is high. Having a replication pattern surely helps to distribute the load across the environment. The replication pattern followed in this pattern is to write to the master and read from the slaves.

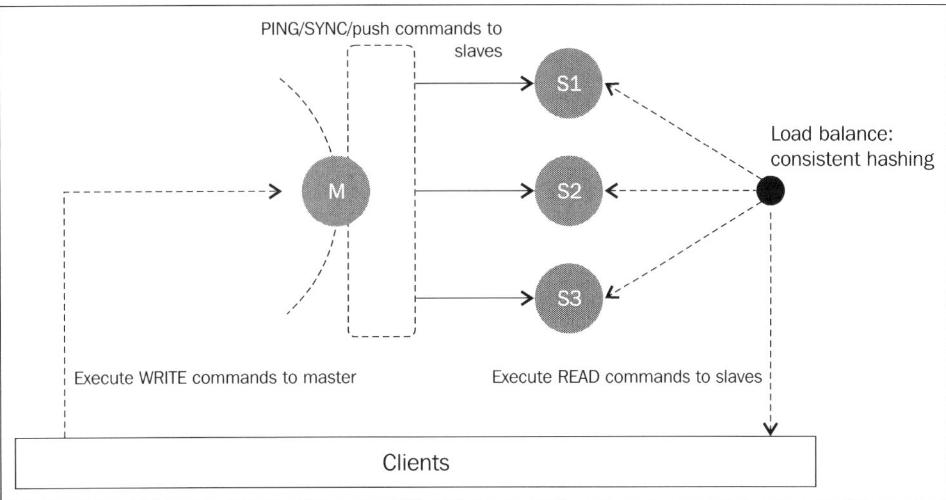

Replication strategy in master and slaves

The sample we will run will not be a proper replication of the previous mentioned solution since the master and the slave will run from the same machine (my laptop). By running the master and the slave nodes in the same machine, we are utilizing common memory and processing power. On top of it, the client program also uses the same resources. But still the difference will be observed because of server I/O happenings at two different ports, which means that at least a separate socket memory bound to two separate server threads (Redis is a single thread server) are processing the read requests.

In a production environment, it is better if every node works out of its own core since Redis cannot make use of multi-core.

In this sample, we will use one master and two slave nodes. In the first use case, we will use the master to write data into and the slaves to read data from. We will take the total time taken for the reads only and compare it with a scenario where the reads will be done entirely on the master node.

To prepare for the sample we need to prepare for the environment and the following diagram depicts in brief what the setup shall be for this sample. Here note that all the resources are from a single machine:

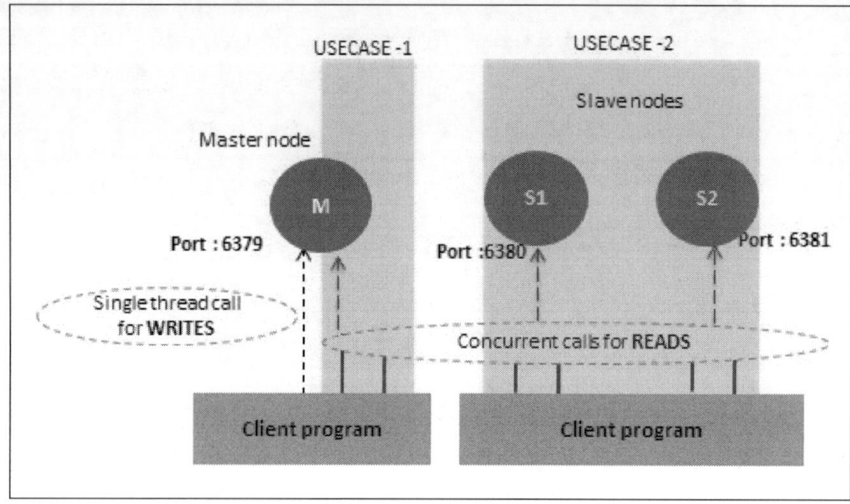

Setup for the sample

The following written program can accommodate both the scenarios discussed earlier. To work in the **USECASE-1** mode (write to master and read from master node), call the following functions:

1. Call `test.setup()` in the first run.
2. Call `test.readFromMasterNode()` in the second run
3. Please comment the following function call this will not allow **USECASE-2** to run `// test.readFromSlaveNodes();`.

To work in the **USECASE-2** mode (write to master and read from two slaves), call the following functions, but before that, execute `FLUSHDB` command to clean up the data or don't execute the `test.setup();` function:

1. Call `test.setup();` in the first run (optional).
2. Call `test.readFromSlaveNodes();` in the second run.
3. Please comment the following function call this will not allow **USECASE-1** to run `// test.readFromMasterNode();`.

The code has three simple classes and a brief description of the classes is as follows:

- `MasterSlaveLoadTest`: This class has the following characteristics:
    - This is the main class
    - This class coordinates the flow for **USECASE-1** and **USECASE-2**
    - This class is responsible for creating threads for **USECASE-1** and **USECASE-2**
    - Following is the code for `MasterSlaveLoadTest`:

```
package org.learningRedis.chapter.five.highreads;
import java.util.ArrayList;
import java.util.List;
import Redis.clients.jedis.Jedis;
public class MasterSlaveLoadTest {
  private List<Thread> threadList = new ArrayList<Thread>();
  public static void main(String[] args) throws
InterruptedException {
    MasterSlaveLoadTest test = new MasterSlaveLoadTest();
    test.setup();
//make it sleep so that the master finishes writing the //
values in the datastore otherwise reads will have either //
null values
//Or old values.
    Thread.currentThread().sleep(40000);
    test.readFromMasterNode();
    test.readFromSlaveNodes();
  }
  private void setup() {
    Thread pumpData = new Thread(new PumpData());
    pumpData.start();
  }
  private void readFromMasterNode() {
    long starttime = System.currentTimeMillis();
    for(int number=1;number<11;number++){
      Thread thread = new Thread(new FetchData(number,startt
ime,"localhost",6379));
      threadList.add(thread);
    }
    for(int number=0;number<10;number++){
      Thread thread =threadList.get(number);
      thread.start();
    }
  }
```

```
    private void readFromSlaveNodes() {
      long starttime0 = System.currentTimeMillis();
      for(int number=1;number<6;number++){
        Thread thread = new Thread(new FetchData(number,startt
ime0,"localhost",6381));
        threadList.add(thread);
      }
      long starttime1 = System.currentTimeMillis();
      for(int number=6;number<11;number++){
        Thread thread = new Thread(new FetchData(number,startt
ime1,"localhost",6380));
        threadList.add(thread);
      }
      for(int number=0;number<10;number++){
        Thread thread =threadList.get(number);
        thread.start();
      }
    }
}
```

- `PumpData`: This class has the following characteristics:
    - This is the class responsible for pushing the data into the main node
    - The data pushing is single threaded
    - The code for `PumpData` is as follows:

```
package org.learningRedis.chapter.five.highreads;
import Redis.clients.jedis.Jedis;
public class PumpData implements Runnable {
  @Override
  public void run() {
    Jedis jedis = new Jedis("localhost",6379);
    for(int index=1;index<1000000;index++){
      jedis.append("mesasge-"+index, "my dumb value "+
index);
    }
  }
}
```

- `FetchData`: This class has the following characteristics:
    - This is the class responsible for fetching the data from the Redis nodes
    - This class is called in a multi-threaded mode

- This class is passed at start time so the last result returned will indicate the total time the execution has taken place
- The code for `FetchData` is as follows:

```
package org.learningRedis.chapter.five.highreads;
import Redis.clients.jedis.Jedis;
import Redis.clients.jedis.JedisPool;
public class FetchData implements Runnable {
  int endnumber  = 0;
  int startnumber= 0;
  JedisPool jedisPool = null;
  long starttime=0;
  public FetchData(int number, long starttime, String
localhost, int port) {
    endnumber   = number*100000;
    startnumber = endnumber-100000;
    this.starttime = starttime;
    jedisPool = new JedisPool(localhost,port);
  }
  @Override
  public void run() {
    Jedis jedis = jedisPool.getResource();
    for(int index=startnumber;index<endnumber;index++){
      System.out.println("printing values for index =
message"+index+" = "+jedis.get("mesasge-"+index));
      long endtime = System.currentTimeMillis();
      System.out.println("TOTAL TIME" + (endtime-
starttime));
    }
  }
}
```

- Run the preceding program for a few iterations and take out the best and worst record, and then take out the average result. For the iterations that I ran, I got the following results:
- For USECASE-1, the average time was 95609 milliseconds
- For USECASE-2, the average time was 72622 milliseconds
- Though the results in your machines will be different in terms of number, but the results will be similar. This clearly shows that reading from slave nodes and writing to master node clearly is better performing.

Performance pattern – high writes

In a production environment, it becomes important to have some kind of a strategy when the demand for concurrency is high for writes. Having a replication pattern surely helps to distribute the load across the environment but replication pattern alone is not helpful when the need for concurrency in writes is high. Also, in Redis the slave nodes cannot have write capability. In order to make the data write highly concurrent in the database, it is important to shard the dataset across many database nodes in the environment. Many databases come with the in-built capability to shard the data accordingly across nodes. The advantage of having the dataset sharded, apart from high concurrency in writes, is to provide mechanism of partial failure tolerance. In other words, even if one of the nodes goes down, it will make the dataset contained in it unavailable but the other nodes can still cater to the requests for the data they hold.

Redis as a database lacks the capability to shard the data across many nodes. But it is possible to have some sort of intelligence built on top of Redis which can do the work of sharding, thus enabling high concurrent writes for Redis. The whole idea here is to take the responsibility out of the Redis nodes and keep it in a separate location.

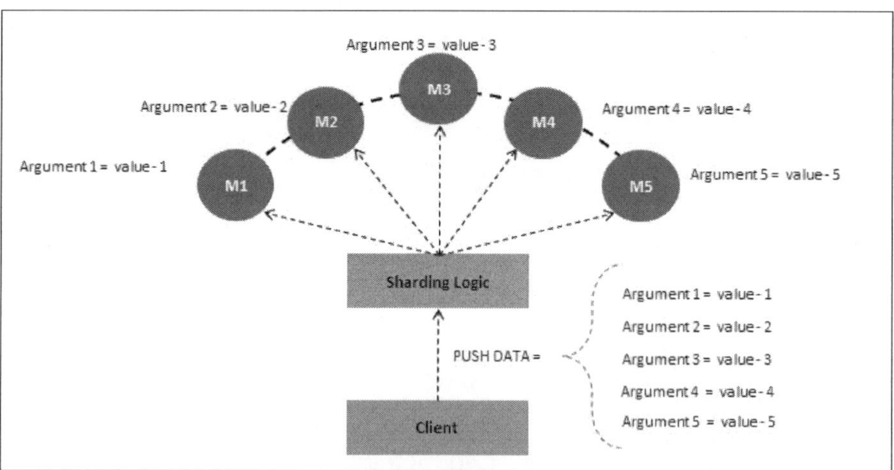

Distributing the data across nodes based on sharding logic

There are various logics that can be built on top of Redis which can be used to distribute the write load. Logic can be based on a round robin where the data can be distributed on sequentially arranged nodes; for example, data will go to **M1**, then **M2**, then **M3**, and so on and so forth. But the problem in this mechanism is that if one of the nodes were to go down, the round robin logic cannot factor in the lost node and it will continue to send data to the defective node which will end up in data loss. Even if we build logic to skip the defective node and put the data in the subsequent node, this strategy will result in that node having its own share of data, and the data of the defective node thus fills up its memory resources very fast.

Consistent Hashing is one of the algorithms which can come in handy when equally distributing data amongst the nodes. What basically we do here is that based on algorithms we generate, a Hash which distributes the key equally amongst the entire set of available Redis server.

The Redis client for Java already has the algorithm for consistent Hashing built into it to distribute the writes. This is as follows:

```
package org.learningRedis.chapter.five.sharding;
import java.util.ArrayList;
import java.util.List;
import org.apache.commons.pool.impl.GenericObjectPool.Config;
import Redis.clients.jedis.Jedis;
import Redis.clients.jedis.JedisSentinelPool;
import Redis.clients.jedis.JedisShardInfo;
import Redis.clients.jedis.ShardedJedis;
import Redis.clients.jedis.ShardedJedisPool;
public class MyShards {
  List<JedisShardInfo> shards = new ArrayList<JedisShardInfo>();
  public static void main(String[] args) {
    MyShards test = new MyShards();
    test.setup();
    test.putdata();
  }
  private void setup() {
    JedisShardInfo master0 = new JedisShardInfo("localhost", 6379);
    JedisShardInfo master1 = new JedisShardInfo("localhost", 6369);
    shards.add(master0);
    shards.add(master1);
  }
  private void putdata() {
    ShardedJedisPool pool = new ShardedJedisPool(new Config(),
shards);
    for(int index=0;index<10;index++){
      ShardedJedis jedis = pool.getResource();
      jedis.set("mykey"+index, "my value is " + index);
      pool.returnResource(jedis);
    }
    for(int index=0;index<10;index++){
      ShardedJedis jedis = pool.getResource();
      System.out.println("The value for the key is "+ jedis.
get("mykey"+index));
```

```
        System.out.println("The following information is from master
running on port : " + jedis.getShardInfo("mykey"+index).getPort());
        pool.returnResource(jedis);
      }
    }
  }
```

Persistence handling in Redis

Redis provides a wide range of options for persisting data. These mechanisms help in deciding what kind of persistence model we need for our data, and that solely depends on the kind of data we want to store in Redis. The four options that we have in Redis are as follows:

- Persisting via the RDB option
- Persisting via the AOF option
- Persisting via combination of AOF and RDB option
- Not persisting at all

Let's run a simple program and see the importance of persistence mechanism, because then only we can appreciate the importance of persistence. Follow the steps and see for yourself how lack of persistence can cause data loss:

1. Start your Redis server.
2. Open a Redis client command prompt.
3. Execute the command `SET msg 'temporary value'`.
4. Quickly kill the Redis server manually, either by **Kill-9** option in Linux or through **close** option in Command Prompt in windows.
5. Restart your Redis server.
6. Execute the command `get msg`.

```
redis 127.0.0.1:6379> get msg
(nil)
```

Get msg without persistence handling

Persisting via the RDB option

Redis database file (**RDB**) is an option where the Redis server persists the dataset at regular interval or in other words, snapshots the data in memory at regular intervals. The format is a single, very compact file which is useful for keeping data as backups. This file can act as a saving grace in case of a disaster and thus is very important. The Redis server can be configured to take snapshots at various intervals. From a performance perspective, this way of persisting data will result in higher performance since the Redis server will fork a child process to do this in a nonblocking manner. Another advantage is that since it is the dataset only that is stored in the RDB files, the server start-ups are very fast in case of RDB files. But storing dataset in RDB comes with its own disadvantage since chances of data loss is possible if Redis were to fail in between two snapshots. Another problem might crop up if the dataset is very high in volume because in that case the Redis server's forked child process will take time to load up the data and this time taken can block client requests for that duration. This problem will not come in production scenarios as there is always a time lag between the servers to restart and for the server to process the client request. From a hardware perspective, a machine with a faster processor will always do the trick.

Configuring Redis for RDB persistence

Here we will learn how to persist data on a RDB file. Well in Redis, the RDB persistence mechanism can be configured by editing the `Redis.conf` file or through the client prompt. When we open our `Redis.conf` file and go to the `snapshotting` section, we see the following options:

- `Save 900 1`: Save in 15 minutes if one key has changed
- `Save 300 10`: Save in 5 minutes if 10 keys have changed
- `Save 60 10000`: Save in 1 minute if 10,000 keys have changed

Apart from these preconfigured options, we can add our own options by tweaking the value in the `Redis.conf` file. Clients can also be used to add configurations at runtime for dataset snapshotting. For example, `CONFIG SET SAVE "900 2 300 10"` will set snapshotting as `Save in 15 minutes if 2 keys have changed` and `Save in 10 minutes if one key has changed`, and this will override the previous values.

Let's run a simple program like the previous program wherein we see data loss due to lack of persistence and we will configure the Redis to have persistence mechanism:

1. Start your Redis server.
2. Open a Redis client command prompt.

3. Execute the command `Set msg 'temp value'`.
4. Quickly kill the Redis server manually, either by **Kill-9** option in Linux or through **close** option in command prompt in windows.
5. Restart your Redis server.
6. Execute the command `get msg`.

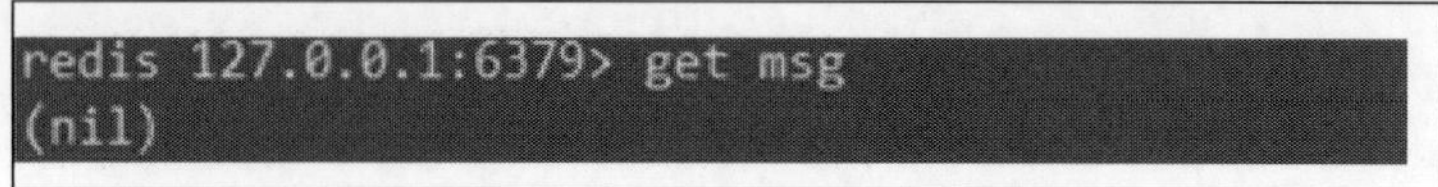

Get msg without persistence handling

7. Now execute the command `CONFIG SET SAVE "60 1"`, which tells the Redis server to save the data in one minute if one key has changed.
8. Execute the command `Set msg 'temp value'`.
9. Wait for a minute or go and grab a cup of your favorite beverage.
10. Kill the server.
11. Restart your Redis server.
12. Open a new client connection and execute the command `get msg`, which would result in the following display:

Get msg RDB persistence handling

13. Instead of waiting for one minute, you can also use the `save` command which will immediately push the data in memory into the RDB file.
14. The parameters that you need to give attention to for persisting your data into a RDB file are as follows:
    - `dbfilename`: Give the name of you RDB file
    - `dir`: Give the path of the RDB file only
    - `rdbchecksum yes`: This is default value which adds CRC64 checksum placed at the end of the file to make it resistant to corruption but has a minor performance penalty on server restarts

Use case for using RDB persistence

Redis can be configured to have RDB persistence mechanism in cases where data is stateless. What I want to convey here is that if the data is a piece of information that has no relation to the data stored before or the next piece of data it is going to store, then it becomes a perfect candidate for RDB persistence. Moreover, the relation can be in terms of sequence, time, rank, and so on, or the data itself can contain information of state. Take for example where the data stored is `START`, `PAUSE`, `RESUME`, and `STOP`. In this case, if we were to lose data such as `PAUSE` or `RESUME` during snapshotting, then it might bring the entire system to an unstable mode.

Let's take a use case where the website records the URLs the user visits in a browsing session. This data is analyzed for profiling the user behavior in order to give the user a better service. In this case, the data, that is the URL of the page visited, is not related to the data stored previously or the data to be stored in future, so it does not have a state. So even in a case of failure between two snapshots, if some amount of data is lost it is not going to impact the overall analysis.

Another use case where RDB persistence can be used is when we want to use Redis as a caching engine where there will be fewer data writes and data reads are going to be very frequent.

Persisting via the AOF option

Append only file (**AOF**) is a durable mechanism of storing data in the Redis datastore. When AOF is enabled, Redis will append all the commands (that write into the dataset) and the associated data, so that when the Redis server is restarted it will rebuild the dataset to the correct state. This mode of persistence is useful when we are storing data that have states. This is because when we are doing state management or have a state associated with a dataset in the eventuality of a server shutdown the information (the state information stored in the memory) will be lost. This in turn would result in some sort of state mismatch. Let's say that we have a piece of information at state A and subsequent activities on that information change its state from A to B and from B to C, and so on and so forth. Now from a user's perspective, the last state change brought the information in the D state, which in principle would be in memory, and in the case of a server shutdown (crash), the information will be lost, so the state change information D will be lost. So when the server restarts, and if the user changes the state of that information to E, the state change history will look like A to B, B to C, and C to E. This in certain scenarios would result in corrupt data. The AOF way of persisting takes care of the problems that may arise due to this.

Configuring Redis for AOF persistence

AOF can be enabled by making a change in the `Redis.conf` file. The property `appendonly` needs to be set to `yes`. By setting it to true, we signal Redis to record the write commands and the data into a file which will reply itself when the server restarts, bringing it to the same state in which it was before shutdown.

Redis provides three flavors or strategies to mitigate problems arising due to inconsistent states. The first strategy is to record every write event in the AOF file. This mechanism is the safest but not very good in performance. The way this can be achieved is via `appendfsync always`.

The second mechanism is time-based wherein we instruct the Redis server to buffer every write command and schedule an AOF append every second. This technique is more efficient since this is happening in every second and not on every write. The way it can be achieved is by telling Redis to `appendfsync everysec`. Here in this mechanism, there is a miniscule chance of state loss.

The third mechanism is more like a delegation where the control to append is given to the underlying operating server to flush the write commands from the buffer to the AOF file. The frequency of append is once every few seconds (in a Linux-based machine, the frequency is close to once every 30 seconds). The performance is the fastest in this technique since this is happening every 30 seconds. However, the chances and amount of data loss is also high in this mechanism. This way of appending can be achieved by telling Redis to `appendfsync no`.

Let's run a simple program like the previous program wherein we see data loss due to a lack of persistence and we will configure the Redis to have AOF persistence mechanism:

1. Start your Redis server.
2. Open a Redis client command prompt.
3. Execute the command `Set msg 'temp value'`.
4. Quickly kill the Redis server manually, either by **Kill-9** option in Linux or through **close** option in command prompt in windows.
5. Restart your Redis server.
6. Execute the command `get msg`.

```
redis 127.0.0.1:6379> get msg
(nil)
```

Get msg without persistence handling

7. Open your `Redis.conf` file and go to the section `APPEND ONLY MODE` and change the `appendonly no` to `appendonly yes`.
8. Uncomment the `appendfilename appendonly.aof` property. Here, you can choose to provide your own name but the default name is `appendonly.aof`.
9. Change the append mechanism to `appendfsync always`.
10. Start your Redis server with the following argument `--appendonly yes --appendfilename C:\appendonly.aof` (use this technique if you do not want to make the change in the `Redis.conf` file).
11. Execute the command `Set msg 'temp value'`.
12. Quickly kill the Redis server manually, either by **Kill-9** option in Linux or through **close** option in Command Prompt in windows.
13. Restart your Redis server with the following argument `--appendonly yes --appendfilename C:\appendonly.aof` (use this technique if you do not want to make the change in the `Redis.conf` file).
14. Execute the command `get msg`.

```
redis 127.0.0.1:6379> get msg
"temp value"
```

Get msg with AOF persistence handling

15. Open file from `C:\appendonly.aof` and see the following:

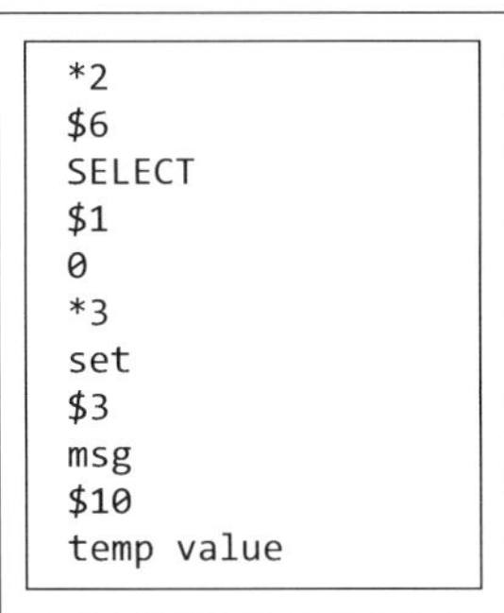

```
*2
$6
SELECT
$1
0
*3
set
$3
msg
$10
temp value
```

Opening the appendonly.aof

One thing that can be observed here is that there is no `get` command which gets recorded since they do not change the dataset. A problem that should be kept in mind is that if the writes are very frequent then AOF file will get bigger and bigger and the server restarts are going to take longer.

Use case for using AOF persistence

Redis can be configured to have AOF persistence mechanism in cases where data is state full. What I want to convey here is that if the data is a piece of information that has relation to the data stored before, or the next piece of data it is going to store, then it becomes a perfect candidate for AOF persistence. Suppose we are building a workflow engine where every state is responsible for the next state; in this kind of situation, using a AOF persistence is the best option.

Dataset handling commands in Redis

We have seen commands used by the client program to either set data or get data in Redis but there are some useful commands that are needed to handle Redis as a datastore. These commands help in maintaining Redis in the production environment and are usually the domain of the Redis administration. Since these commands have an impact on the data stored in Redis, one should be careful in executing them. Following are some of the commands:

- `FLUSHDB`: This command deletes all the keys (and their held data) in the chosen database. As we have seen, in Redis we can create a database which is more like a SILO wherein we can store data in a segregated manner (more like separation of concern). This command never fails.
- `FLUSHALL`: This command deletes all of the keys in all the databases in Redis node. This command never fails.
- `MONITOR`: This command is a debugging command that relays all the commands that the Redis server is processing. You can either use the Redis-cli or the telnet to monitor what the server is doing.

```
+OK
+1391880161.796875 [0 127.0.0.1:3983] "SET" "MSG" "this command is being monitored"
+1391880174.015625 [0 127.0.0.1:3983] "GET" "MSG"
+1391880255.937500 [0 127.0.0.1:3983] "SET" "MSG" "monitoring commands helps in debugging while development"
+1391880272.250000 [0 127.0.0.1:3983] "SET" "MSG" "monitoring commands has a massive performance penalty"
quit
+OK


Connection to host lost.
```

Using telnet to monitor commands

Here we have used telnet to monitor the Redis server and whatever command is issued in the client is replicated here. Monitoring commands gives an inside look into the working of Redis but has a performance penalty. You can use this command to even monitor the slave nodes.

- `SAVE`: This is a synchronous blocking call save to snapshot all the data in the memory to a RDB file. This command in a production environment should be used carefully because this will block every client command and perform this task.
- `BGSAVE`: This command is more like a background save. The previous command `SAVE` is a blocking call but this command does not block the client calls. By issuing this command, Redis forks another process which starts to persist the data to a RDB file in the background. Issuing this command immediately returns the `OK` code but the client can check the result by issuing the `LASTSAVE` command. Let's try a small example and see if it's working:
    1. Start the Redis server and a client.
    2. Execute `LASTSAVE` command from the client; in my case the value it showed was an integer **1391918354** but in your case it might show a different time.
    3. Open your telnet prompt and execute `MONITOR` command (this is done on purpose to retard the performance of your Redis server).
    4. Open your Java editor and type in the following program which will insert lots of values into the Redis server:

    ```
    package org.learningRedis.chapter.five;
    import Redis.clients.jedis.Jedis;
    public class PushLotsOfData {
      public static void main(String[] args) {
        PushLotsOfData test = new PushLotsOfData();
        test.pushData();
      }
      private void pushData() {
        Jedis jedis = new Jedis("localhost",6379);
        for(int nv=0;nv<900000;nv++){
          jedis.sadd("MSG-0", ",data-"+nv);
        }
      }
    }
    ```

5. In the client prompt I issued the following commands and the result is as follows:

```
redis 127.0.0.1:6379> lastsave
(integer) 1391920035
redis 127.0.0.1:6379> bgsave
Background saving started
redis 127.0.0.1:6379> time
1) "1391920077"
2) "859375"
redis 127.0.0.1:6379> lastsave
(integer) 1391920077
redis 127.0.0.1:6379> lastsave
(integer) 1391920077
redis 127.0.0.1:6379> flushall
OK
(1.58s)
redis 127.0.0.1:6379> lastsave
(integer) 1391920265
```

Checking nonblocking nature of BGSAVE

I issued the `TIME` command after the `BGSAVE` command but when I issued `LASTSAVE`, the time I got was later to `BGSAVE` command. So we can conclude that `BGSAVE` is a nonblocking way of saving data. Since the command `FLUSHALL` manipulates the entire dataset, it automatically calls the `SAVE` command after execution. See the `LASTSAVE` command which shows time as **1391920265** and the previous `LASTSAVE` before `FLUSHALL`, which shows time as **1391920077** prove that `FLUSHALL` does as save.

- `LASTSAVE`: This command is similar to `BGSAVE` command, and it shows when the last time the data was persisted to the RDB file.
- `SHUTDOWN SAVE/NOSAVE`: This command basically quits the server but before doing that it closes the connection of the entire set of clients and performs a blocking save, and then flushes the AOF if it is enabled.
- `DBSIZE`: This returns the number of keys in the database.
- `BGREWRITEAOF`: This instructs the Redis server to start a back ground write to an AOF. If this instruction fails, the old AOF file is retained.

- `CLIENT SETNAME`: This sets the name of a client and we can see the name set when we do a `CLIENT LIST`. Execute the following command in the client prompt `CLIENT SETNAME "myclient"`, and you should see something thing similar to the following image:

```
addr=127.0.0.1:1481 fd=1932 name=myclient age=336 idle=0 flags=N db=0
```

Naming a client

- `CLIENT LIST`: This gets the list of clients connected to the IP address and the `PORT` address. Let's do a simple experiment:
    1. Open a telnet client to a Redis server with `telnet localhost 6379` and execute the `MONITOR` command.
    2. Open a Redis server master node client prompt and execute the command `CLIENT LIST`. The command prompt should look similar to the following image:

```
redis 127.0.0.1:6379> client list
addr=127.0.0.1:1478 fd=1892 name= age=42 idle=35 flags=O db=0 sub=0 psub=0 multi=-1 qbuf=0
addr=127.0.0.1:1481 fd=1932 name= age=5 idle=0 flags=N db=0 sub=0 psub=0 multi=-1 qbuf=0 qb
```

Getting client list

- `CLIENTKILL`: This kills the client. Now, to the previous experiment, issue the following command in the client that we have opened up:
    1. Execute the command `CLIENT KILL 127.0.0.1:1478`.
    2. Execute the command `CLIENT LIST` we will see the number of lines displayed to go down by one.
- `DEBUG sEGFAULT`: This crashes the Redis server. The utility can be used to simulate bugs during development. This command can be used to simulate the scenario where we want to check the fault tolerance of the system by purposefully bringing the Redis server down. It would be interesting to see how the slave node behaves, how fault tolerance is handled by the clients, and so on.

- `SLOWLOG`: This command shows which commands took time during execution. Execute the program that you wrote in the *Performance pattern – high reads* section, and after the execution open a client for the master and execute this command. The result seen in the following image is a snapshot and is not the full result of what you might get in your command prompt:

```
redis 127.0.0.1:6379> slowlog GET
 1) 1) (integer) 374
    2) (integer) 1392265888
    3) (integer) 15608
    4) 1) "GET"
       2) "mesasge-897245"
 2) 1) (integer) 373
    2) (integer) 1392265887
    3) (integer) 15609
    4) 1) "GET"
       2) "mesasge-695227"
 3) 1) (integer) 372
    2) (integer) 1392265887
    3) (integer) 15608
    4) 1) "GET"
       2) "mesasge-294313"
 4) 1) (integer) 371
    2) (integer) 1392265887
    3) (integer) 15608
    4) 1) "GET"
       2) "mesasge-599726"
```

Slowlog command

Summary

In this chapter, we saw and learnt how to handle the entire dataset in Redis. Apart from that, we learnt patterns for performance in a production environment. We also learnt commands to manage the Redis server ecosystem.

In the next chapter, we will apply the knowledge we have learnt until now to develop common components in web programming and see how Redis fits as a great tool to take care of some of the problems in this space.

6
Redis in Web Applications

Web in the present scenario is the ubiquitous platform through which the world today communicates. From a simple portal to massively scalable e-commerce, collaborative web sites, banking, social media, web applications over mobile networks, and so on, everyone uses web protocols as an interface to interact with the outside world. What we normally see as web platform is just a small part of the application that is under web operations, backend web applications, such as supply chain management, order management, online, offline analytics, and so on, are also web applications or use web protocols to integrate for example HTTP, SOAP, REST and so on.

One of the reasons for the web's success is its effective simplicity, open standards, and multiple channels through which it can operate. The fact that it's popular is forcing people and companies to come out with solutions that are simple, cost effective, high performing, and easy to maintain and develop. This new breed of software should have intrinsic or extrinsic capabilities to scale and perform well.

Redis, the datastore that is more like a Swiss army knife, is multi-faceted and a proof to those capabilities we saw in previous chapters. In this chapter, we will extend and map the capabilities of Redis for components used in web domain and a create few proof of concept for components which form an inherent part of any web application.

To understand the concepts of Redis better, let's make a sample web application and use Redis as a datastore. This sample web application is no way a complete end-to-end web application but intends to highlight the areas where Redis can come in handy. The solution itself is not complete in terms of functionality but intends to be a demo which practitioners can take forward and extend.

Simple E-Commerce, as we intend to call this demo website, is a Redis backed website which does not have a web page but communicates via simple services. The idea is to expose simple services and not bring in webpages (containing HTML, CSS and so on) to decouple services from the presentation layer. As we are moving more towards the era of single page application, it becomes imperative that we take an approach where the application residing in the client browser memory does all the coordination and the traditional web server does the job of serving the request via services it exposes. The advantage of this mechanism is that development and testing becomes easy as every service is independent of other service and there is no tight coupling with the presentation aspect of a web app. As we all have been involved in web development at one time or another, we can understand the frustration we face when we see a bug and when a considerable amount of time is spent in debugging whether the problem arose because of the client side code or the business methods it was calling. With the rising capabilities of single page application, this problem can be taken care of to a large extent since the business methods are exposed as independent services and can be tested separately from the presentation component. One of the salient features of a single page application is that it takes away a lot of compute activity from the server side to the client side (browser) which results in more compute resource for the server.

Simple e-commerce – a Redis backed e-commerce site

This sample e-commerce site, like other e-commerce sites, has products which the registered user can browse, purchase, and so on. The website also recommends products based on the users' browsing and purchasing habits. In parallel, the website gives real time statistics of the activities happening in the website and provides you with capabilities to do real-time and soft-real-time analytics. So, let's get cracking and build this website, and like in any design, let's divide the requirement into commands, which are listed as follows:

- **Session and catalogue management**: The following commands are offered as service:
    - **Register user**: Command name is `register`; this command will register the user to the system.
    - **See my data**: Command name is `mydata`; this command will allow the user to see his/her data.
    - **Edit my data**: Command name is `editmydata`; this command will allow the user to edit his data.

- **Login user**: Command name is `login`; this command will log in the user and generates a session-ID for the user to communicate with the server.
- **Relogin user**: Command name is `relogin`; this command will again log the user but the session-ID will remain the same. All the session or profile data of the user will also remain the same.
- **Logout user**: Command name is `logout`; this command will log out the user and kill his session or profile data.
- **Add to cart**: Command name is `add2cart`; this command will add the item to the shopping cart.
- **See my shopping cart**: Command name is `showmycart`; this command will show the items in the shopping cart.
- **Edit my shopping cart**: Command name is `editcart`; this command will edit user preference in the shopping cart.
- **Buy products**: Command name is `buy`; this command will buy the items in the shopping cart of the user. For the current application, we will not take you to some merchant's site but instead we will generate a sample receipt for you. The idea is to have analysis, so when somebody buys the product we give credit points for that product which will help us for our recommendation service. The credit point for buying is `10`.
- **Commission product**: Command name is `commission`; this command will commission the product and create its profile in the system.
- **Display product**: Command name is `display`; this command will display the product.
- **Browse products**: Command name is `browse`; this command will log the product the user is currently browsing. The idea is that when somebody browses the product, we give credit points for the product which will help us for our recommendation service. The credit point for browsing is `1`.

* **Online Analytics**: Following commands come under this:
    - **Recommend**: Command name is `recommendbyproduct`; this command will recommend other products similar to the current product based on their popularity which the user is browsing.
    - **User's statistics**: Command name is `stats`; this command will show the user's statistics.

  - **Display by category**: Command name is `displaytag`; this command will display the products under a category.
  - **Display by category history**: Command name is `taghistory`; this command will display the history by category.
  - **Visits for a book**: Command name is `visittoday`; this will give total number of unique visitors in a day.
  - **Purchases for a book**: Command name is `purchasestoday`; this will give the total number of unique visitors who purchased the item in a day.

The design is kept very simple for this simple e-commerce site. To understand the entire application, have a look at the following figure:

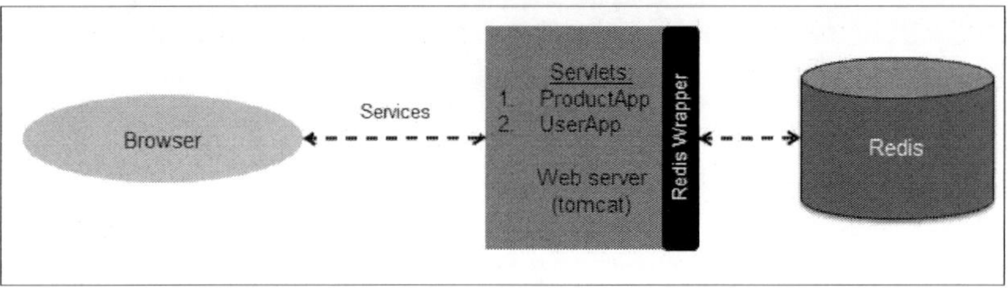

Simple design for out simple e-commerce site

The prerequisites for this exercise are as follows:

- **Client**: Any browser with a `REST` plugin or HTTP client plugin. I will be using Chrome browser with a `REST` client plugin called `POSTMAN`. If you are comfortable with any other plugin then be my guest. The application would work without any problem if we replace this client with a pure Java program, for example Apache HTTP Client. The services in this simple e-commerce application are `Get` based. In production system, we should have `POST` but for display purposes, `Get` is chosen here.

- **Server**: Any web application server. We will be using Tomcat. You can use any web application server of your choice but creation of servlets should be done accordingly. If you want to use something like Node.js, then code will change accordingly but design philosophy would remain the same.
- **Datastore**: Needless to say that Redis will be the datastore here.

Before we dive into the code, it is important to understand the evolution process that led to a state wherein we are using Redis. As discussed earlier, the two categories on the basis of which this web application is segregated are stated as follows:

- Session and catalogue management
- Online analytics

Let's spend some time and understand how they have evolved over a period of time and how Redis comes into picture. We will understand the code for this application thereafter.

Session management

Every web application has session in one way or another. Session management captures information of user activity which can be used for the user and by the user. Information for the shopping cart or the wish list can be used by the user, and the same information can be used by the back-end systems to analyze user preferences and pass promotional and campaign management schemes back to the user. This is one of the common use cases in the e-commerce platform. Information stored in session management is always the recent information and the end user expects performance around it, or in other words, the user outsources his recent memory to the system and expects the system to take care of it. The end user might not know the level of detailing and activity that happens behind the scene but expects the information stored in a session to be acted upon fast and as efficiently as his brain.

In some cases, the user expects even more than what his brain can process; be it shopping cart purchases, or putting things in a wish list, or reminding him of a certain activity which he might have forgotten. In other words, the end users are closest to this data as compared to any other data. They remember this data and expect the system to match it, which results in more personalized involvement of the user with the system or the website.

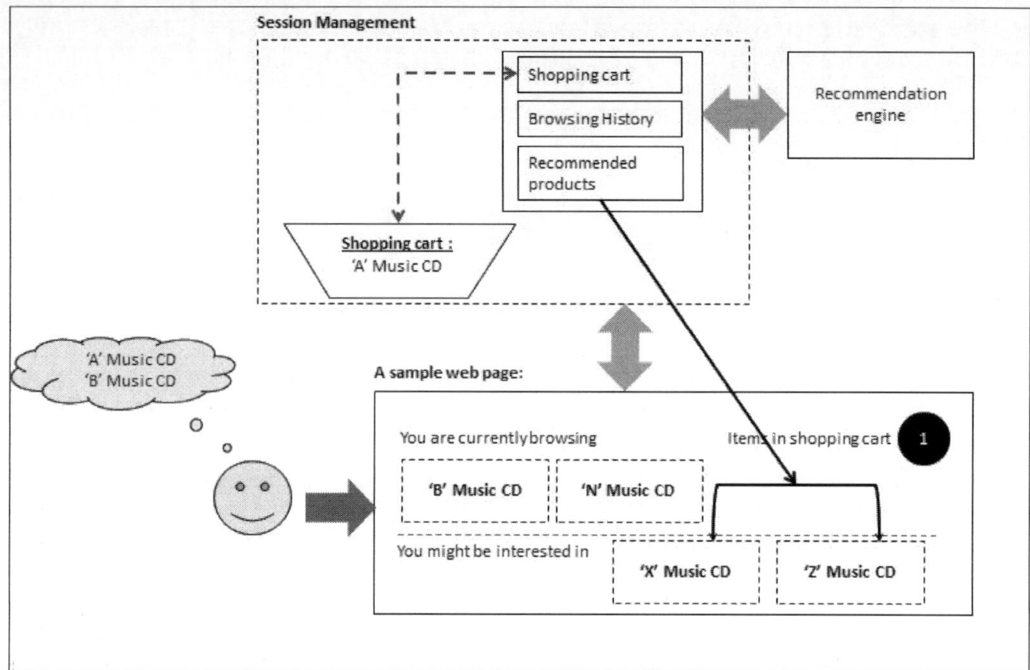

User and his interaction with an e-commerce platform

The previous diagram is a representation of how the user interacts with the system (website). When the user browses a website, he/she has an idea of what he is looking for. Let's say in our case it's some music he is looking for and after searching for the music, the user will put the music tracks in the shopping cart. It is also possible that the user might be interested in some other music CD of the same genre or interested in the comments of the other buyers in the *comments section*. At this point, the user might be interested in buying his/her music CD in the shopping cart or keeping it in the shopping cart to buy it in near future. One thing the user expects here is that when he logs into the system again, the system should remember the products that he had put in the shopping cart.

There are couple of things that are happening here. Firstly, the user is interacting with the system and the system is responding by storing the user's choices, recording the user's activities, and so on. Secondly, the user has pushed information which he might find interesting, thus offering him wide choices as well as educating him about what people are commenting about the product, thereby helping him take a decision. In this section, we will be talking more about the part where the user is storing his information, and call it session management.

Session data has high importance and stays in the users' mind, but the lifespan of this data is short (until the time the product is delivered or until the attention shifts to another product). This is where session management comes into picture and in this section we are going to go a bit deeper as to how Redis can help us in solving this highly critical problem.

To handle session data, the earliest and easiest option has been using the memory of the application server itself. Back in the day the web application had limited capability and offered limited services. Usage of application server memory was the order of the day. But as the web became more accessible, and people started to use web more in their daily lives, websites grew rapidly and to survive competition between web applications had to exist. This required the web application to have more compute and memory resources.

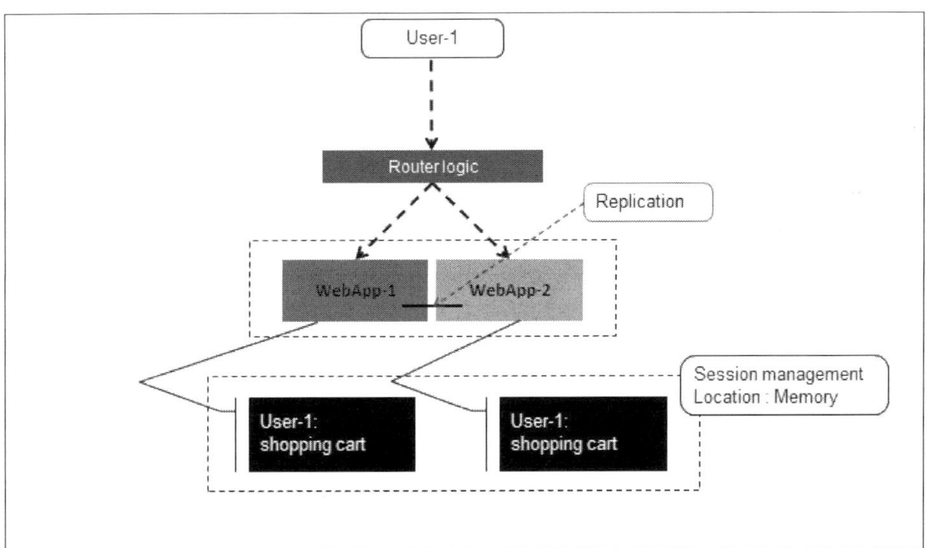

Scaling web application with memory to store session data

The common technique was to replicate the data and load balance the system so that all the web servers were in the same state and requests could be catered from any of the web applications. This technique had some issues as the session management was tightly coupled with the web servers, it provided limited scalability, and when concurrency increased this pattern became an anti-pattern. Another limitation this technique had was that as data in session management grew, this pattern proved problematic since session data was stored in the memory and the amount of memory that could be allocated for session management was contested by the memory requirement of business logic.

The next logical step was to decouple the session management from the web application servers executing business logic. This step was in the right direction since now it provided more scalability as the web servers were free from doing the session management which required syncing up state with peers frequently.

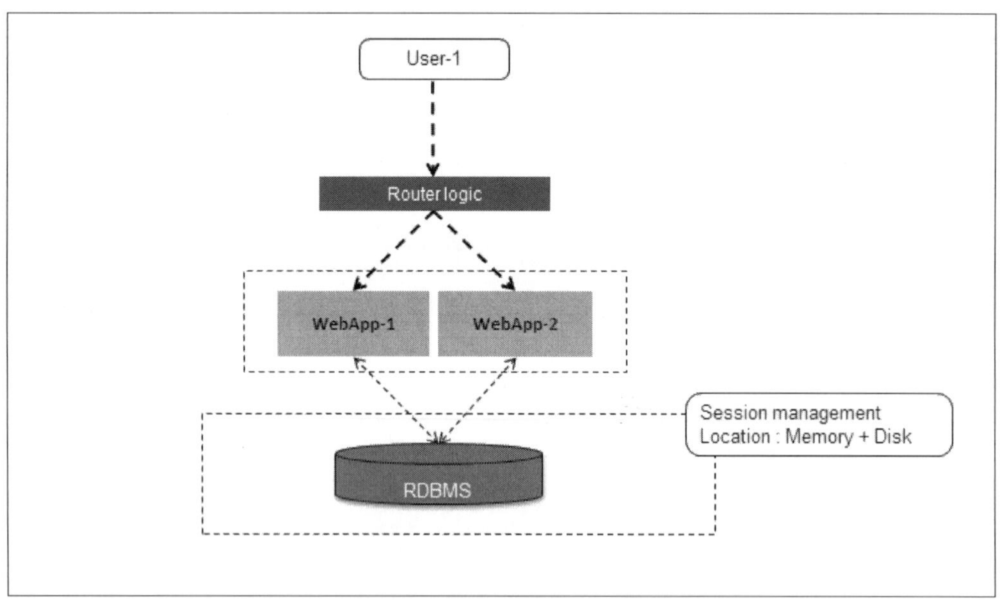

Scaling web application with RDBMS to store session data

This approach, though in the right direction, had some problems—mainly with the choice of datastore used. RDBMS are used to store relational data and are very efficient in dealing with those types of data. Session data on the other hand is more like key value pair and does not have the kind of relationship that is expected out of transactional data. The problem with storing session data in RDBMS was that performance took a hit since RDBMS was never engineered for this kind of data though scaling out of web application server was much easier.

The next step in this evolution process was using a datastore which provided the scalability and also performance. The obvious choice was to use a cache engine which stores information in the memory so that performance becomes faster and the scalability remains good, because session data decoupled from web application server.

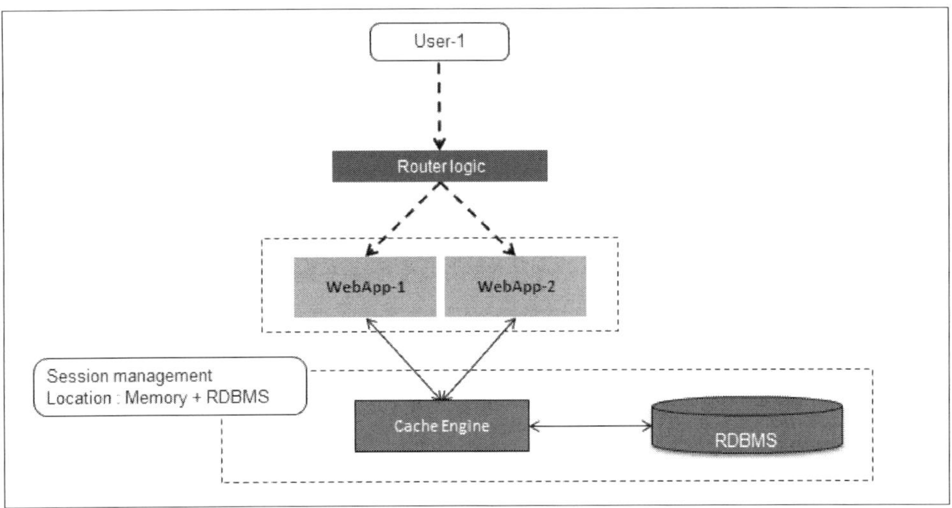

Scaling web application with cache as front end over RDBMS to store session data

The problem with this approach is from functional requirements and from maintainability perspective. From a maintainability perspective, the cache engine depends upon RDBMS for data persistence since most of the caching engines do not have disk persistence and depend upon RDBMS for fault management. There are some cache engines that provide persistence mechanisms, but the big problem comes from a functional perspective since they store everything as a key value where value is a string. It is the responsibility of the program to convert the data in string to the information pattern they are interested in and then take the value out. Take for example the value stored for a user profile which has hundreds of attributes stored in the session data. If the user were to take few attributes out, then in that case the user has to fetch the entire dataset, construct the object, and then fetch the required attributes. Another problem is that many a times we need session data for a fixed duration of time and after that the usability of the data is not there. In those cases, cache engines and RDBMS do not prove beneficial since they do not have a in-built mechanism of *time to live* for data then to store. To achieve this feature, we have to write a trigger to clean the data from RDBMS and then from the cache.

Redis comes in handy in these cases, where we store information the way we want to use, as it provides data structures to hold values. In case of session management, we can have a map to logically group attributes under it. If we need to take values out, we can select the values that we want to change or add more attributes to it. Moreover, the performance aspect in Redis also makes it suitable for session management. Redis also has features called **time to live** (**TTL**) feature to clean the data after the time is over. This way we can have separate TTL for the keys we require depending upon the requirement and also change the TTL at runtime. Redis can be used to have scalable and high performing session management.

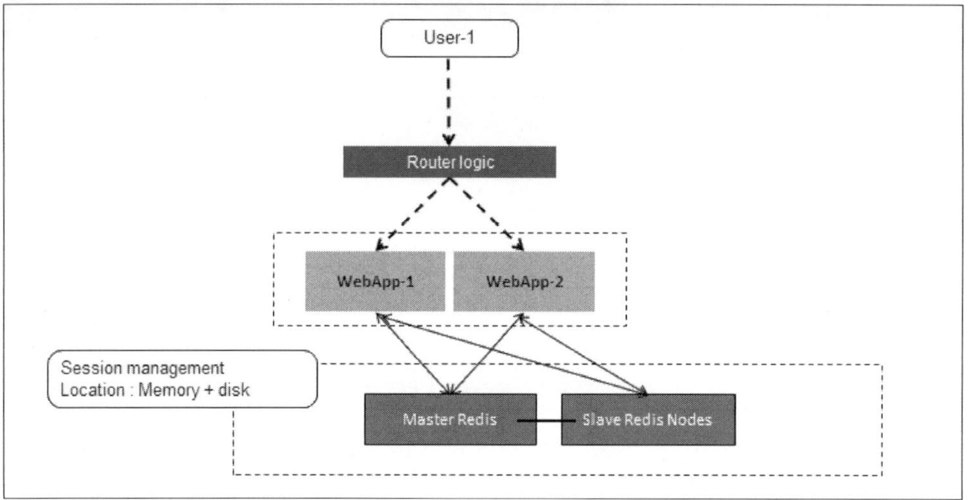

Scaling web application with cache as front end over RDBMS to store session data

Catalogue management

Catalogue management is the information about the products and items which the website is keen to offer. The information stored under catalogue management can be a product's cost, dimension, color, and so on, that is meta information of a product. This information, unlike session information, is read centric. But like session data, catalogue data has seen evolution starting with RDBMS systems which were the natural choice back then because of lack of choices to store data. The problem with RDBMS system was that it did not offer performance. Also, the fixed schema centric systems added to the problems since the meta information of products changed with the products themselves. Some products had color, length, breadth, and height whereas some had author, number of pages, and ISBN. Creating schemas to accommodate this requirement was always cumbersome and, at some point or another we have faced this problem.

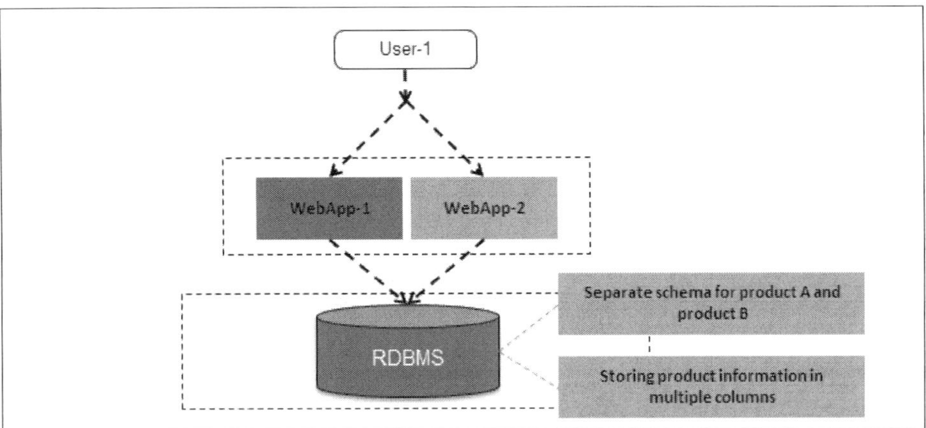

Catalogue management with RDBMS as datastore

The natural evolution process to overcome this fixed schema problem was to store the information in XML format and to cache this information in some caching engine. This mechanism helped the designers and architects to overcome the problem of fixed schema and performance. But this technique came with its own share of problems; the data which was in XML had to be converted to a programming language object before usage. The other problem was that if a property value had to be changed, then either the value was changed in the XML first and then changed in the RDBMS, or the value was changed in the RDBMS first and then in the cache. These techniques had problems in maintaining consistent state across RDBMS and the cache engines, and it required special attention especially if the property was related to the cost of the product.

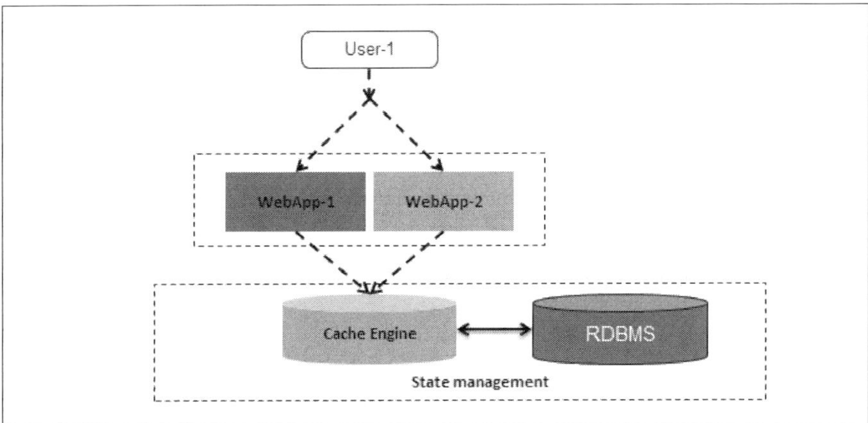

Handling state management between cache engine and RDBMS

Redis once again comes in handy to store catalogue data. Redis being schema less and as a datastore provides data structures, such as maps which can be used to store as many properties as the product requires. Apart from that, it also provides capability to change, add, and read the properties without bringing the entire dataset to work upon. Another advantage of having Redis is that we need not do *object to data* conversions, and vice versa, as this does away the very need to have hundreds of data objects in the system; thus making the code base smaller and development faster.

Online analytics

Online analytics or real-time analytics is a relatively new requirement that is gaining popularity. The whole idea behind online analytics is to provide a richer and engaging user experience to the user. Online analytics works in a way where data is collected, analyzed, and crunched in real-time.

In good old early days of web revolution, analytics had only one principle stake holder which was the website management team. They used to collect the data and do analysis in the offline mode, and then used to apply it for business usage. This technique of offline analysis is still needed. However, in today's world when everything is connected to social media, it is imperative that the user's views, his/her social group, and his/her opinion should be reflecting in his/her shopping experience. For example, let's say a user and his social group are talking favorably about some music or book. When the user checks into his favorite e-commerce site, the home page of that site has this product in the recommendation section. This gives high probability that the user might end up buying the product. This degree of personalization is very important for the website to be successful.

The kind of analysis that is happening in this case is in soft real-time, that is when the user is interacting with his social group, data in parallel is getting crunched and the context is getting created which is used by the website to create a personalized shopping experience for the user.

Another kind of analysis that happens is based on the context the user creates while browsing products in the website. This context creation is collaborative in nature though the users might be unaware of this fact. The higher the number of users searching for a product or buying the product, the more popular the product becomes. The complexity in this type of analytics is that it's real-time and performance is paramount.

In a way, if we compare the offline analytics engine with real-time analytics, the difference is that the analytics engine which was outside the realm of business logic becomes a part of the business logic, practically sharing the same compute resource. Another difference is that the amount of data is relatively small in case of real-time analytics but its contextual data from a user's shopping perspective is what makes it important from a business perspective. The following figure explains the difference between offline and online (real-time) analytics in a concise manner:

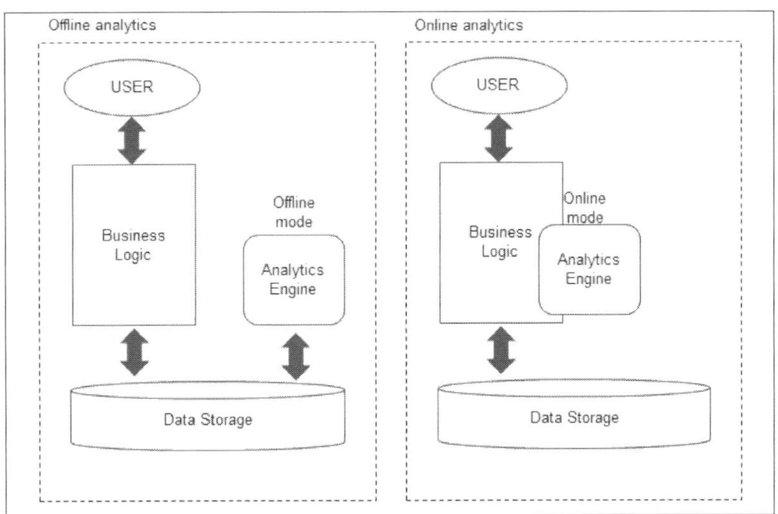

Offline and online analytics in web application

Now if the same real-time were to be done using a datastore such as RDBMS, the problem would be in performance because this kind of crunching will consume a lot of computing resources, and other business use cases executing in parallel might take a hit because of this. RDBMS such as Oracle, can provide the capability of scaling but they come with a price, that is they are pretty expensive.

Redis can be a very good datastore which can be used for online analytics. As Redis is memory-based, it's very fast and achieving scalability in Redis is much easier. On top of it, Redis provides data structures such as Set and Sorted set, which can be very helpful for segregating and aggregating data for real-time analytics.

Another advantage Redis has to offer is that it's open source and runtime resource requirement of Redis is very less. Moreover, the concurrent calls handling capability in Redis is pretty impressive.

In the sample application that we will develop, we will see some real-time analytics in form of a recommendation engine which will recommend products based on its popularity.

Implementation – simple e-commerce

Let's begin with some code to get a clear understanding of how to use Redis for our session, catalogue management, and online analytics. But before we do that, let's finalize on the buckets which we will be creating to store data:

- **Bucket name "<username>@userdata"**: This bucket will store user profile data such as name, email, phone number, address, and so on. From the application's perspective, this bucket will be `sessionID` of the user which will bind this bucket to `"<sessionID>@sessiondata"`. The data structure used here is Map.
- **Bucket name "<sessionID>@sessiondata"**: This bucket will store session data of the user such as lastlogin and loginstatus. Apart from session data, this will also store the user name as this is the key which will bind `"<username>@userdata"` bucket to this bucket. The data structure used here is Map.
- **Bucket name "<sessionID>@browsinghistory"**: This bucket will store the browsing history of the user based on his session ID. Data structure used here is Sorted Set.
- **Bucket name "<name>@purchasehistory"**: This will give the purchase history of the user. Data structure used here is Sorted Set.
- **Bucket name "<sessionID>@shoppingcart"**: This bucket will store the shopping cart items of the user. Data structure used here is Map.
- **Bucket name "sessionIdTracker"**: This will track the total number of users in the system. Data structure used here is Bitmap.
- **Bucket name "<productname>"**: This will store the product attributes. Being schemaless, it can store any number of attributes for the product. Data structure used here is Map.
- **Bucket name "<tags>"**: This will store the product mapped to this tag. For example, `"Learning Redis"` can be tagged under tags such as Redis, NoSQL, database, and so on. Data structure used here is Sorted Set.
- **Bucket name "<productname>@visit"**: This will store the number of unique visitors. In production system, this can be made on a daily basis to give a statistics of how many people visited this product on a day-to-day basis and help calculate how many people visited the site on a monthly basis. Data structure used here is Bitmap.
- **Bucket name "<productname>@purchase"**: This will store the number of unique visitors who purchased the product. Like the previous bucket, this bucket can be made on a daily basis to give an aggregate count for a week or month. Data structure used here is Bitmap.

Now that we have a hang of how our database is going to look like, let's get to the servlets which are going to accept service request from the browser and send a HTTP response back to the client.

There are two servlets in this simple e-commerce website. They will be accepting all the commands and are listed as follows:

- **UserApp servlet**: This will cater to all the commands pertaining to the user
- **ProductApp servlet**: This will cater to all the commands pertaining to the user

One thing that we have to keep in mind is that the order of execution is not dependent upon the order in which the servlets or the command within the servlet is listed. For example, there is no point in registering or logging in unless we have provisioned a few products in the system, or there is no point seeing recommendation unless we have browsed or bought few products as this will create the graph data for the recommendation.

Let's get a hang of all the utility class that will be used in the code listing in the rest of the chapter. The list of all such classes is as follows:

- **Commands**: This is the parent and abstract class for all the commands that will be implemented in the application:

  ```
  package org.learningRedis.web;
  import org.learningRedis.web.util.Argument;
  public abstract class Commands {
    private Argument argument;
    public Commands(Argument argument) {
      this.argument = argument;
    }
    public abstract String execute();
    public Argument getArgument() {
      return argument;
    }
  }
  ```

- **Default command**: This is default command which will get into action if the command passed in the URL is not recognized by the application:

  ```
  package org.learningRedis.web;
  import org.learningRedis.web.util.Argument;
  public class DefaultCommand extends Commands {
    public DefaultCommand(Argument argument) {
      super(argument);
    }
  ```

```
    @Override
    public String execute() {
      return "Command Not Recognized !!";
    }
  }
```

- **Argument**: The primary goal of this class is to wrap all the name value attributes coming in the request and to put it in a map which can be used in the program later on:

```
package org.learningRedis.web.util;
import java.util.HashMap;
import java.util.Map;
public class Argument {
  Map<String, String> argumentMap = new HashMap<String, String>();
  public Argument(String args) {
    String[] arguments = args.split(":");
    for (String argument : arguments) {
      String key = argument.split("=")[0];
      String value = argument.split("=")[1];
      argumentMap.put(key, value);
    }
  }
  public String getValue(String key) {
    return argumentMap.get(key);
  }
  public Map<String, String> getAttributes() {
    return argumentMap;
  }
}
```

Now that we have covered the utility classes across the application, let's get to the classes which will be instrumental in giving a shape to the application.

ProductApp

ProductApp servlet will contain commands around product management. The code for ProductApp servlet is as follows:

```
package org.learningRedis.web;
import java.io.IOException;
import java.io.PrintWriter;
import javax.servlet.ServletException;
import javax.servlet.http.HttpServlet;
import javax.servlet.http.HttpServletRequest;
```

```
import javax.servlet.http.HttpServletResponse;
import org.learningRedis.web.analytics.commands.PurchasesCommand;
import org.learningRedis.web.analytics.commands.VisitTodayCommand;
import org.learningRedis.web.productmgmt.commands.
CommissionProductCommand;
import org.learningRedis.web.productmgmt.commands.DisplayTagCommand;
import org.learningRedis.web.productmgmt.commands.DisplayCommand;
import org.learningRedis.web.productmgmt.commands.TagHistoryCommand;
import org.learningRedis.web.productmgmt.commands.UpdateTagCommand;
import org.learningRedis.web.util.Argument;
public class ProductApp extends HttpServlet {
  public ProductApp() {
    super();
  }
  protected void doGet(HttpServletRequest request, HttpServletResponse
response) throws ServletException, IOException {
    String command = request.getParameter("command");
    Argument argument = new Argument(request.getParameter("args"));
    PrintWriter out = response.getWriter();
    switch (command.toLowerCase()) {
    case "commission":
      Commands commission = new CommissionProductCommand(argument);
      out.println(commission.execute());
      break;
    case "display":
      Commands display = new DisplayCommand(argument);
      out.println(display.execute());
      break;
    case "displaytag":
      Commands displaytag = new DisplayTagCommand(argument);
      out.println(displaytag.execute());
      break;
    case "updatetag":
      Commands updatetag = new UpdateTagCommand(argument);
      out.println(updatetag.execute());
      break;
    case "visitstoday":
      Commands visittoday = new VisitTodayCommand(argument);
      out.println(visittoday.execute());
      break;
    case "purchasestoday":
      Commands purchasestoday = new PurchasesTodayCommand (argument);
      out.println(purchasestoday.execute());
      break;
```

```
        case "taghistory":
          Commands taghistory = new TagHistoryCommand(argument);
          out.println(taghistory.execute());
          break;
        default:
          Commands defaultUC = new DefaultCommand(argument);
          out.println(defaultUC.execute());
          break;
        }
      }
    }
```

Now that we have the first servlet ready, let's look into the commands which we are implementing for this:

- `CommisionProductCommand`: This will implement the `commission` command. The implementation of the command is as follows:

```
package org.learningRedis.web.productmgmt.commands;
import java.util.Map;
import org.learningRedis.web.Commands;
import org.learningRedis.web.util.Argument;
import org.learningRedis.web.util.ProductDBManager;
public class CommissionProductCommand extends Commands {
    public CommissionProductCommand(Argument argument) {
    super(argument);
  }
  @Override
  public String execute() {
    System.out.println(this.getClass().getSimpleName() + ":  " + "
Entering the execute function");
    Map<String, String> productAttributes = this.getArgument().
getAttributes();
    boolean commisioning_result = ProductDBManager.singleton.commi
sionProduct(productAttributes);
    boolean tagging_result = ProductDBManager.singleton.enterTagEn
tries(productAttributes.get("name"),
        productAttributes.get("tags"));
    if (commisioning_result & tagging_result) {
      return "commisioning successful";
    } else {
      return "commisioning not successful";
    }
  }
}
```

Test URL: `http://localhost:8080/simple-ecom/productApp?command=commission&args=name=Redisbook-1:cost=10:catagory=book:author=vinoo:tags=Redis@5,NoSql@3,database@2,technology@1`.

Description: This, for all reasons, is the first command that should get called since this command is going to provision products into the system. The two parts in the URL that need to be focused on are the `command` which is equal to `commission`, and the argument part, that is `args`. Here `args` contains the attributes of the book, for example `name=Redisbook-1`. The attribute `tags` represents the words the book will be associated with. The tags for this book are `Redis@5`, `NoSQl@3`, `database@2`, and `technology@1`. The tags are associated with the weights that will come into play whenever recommendation engine kicks in. Whenever a user is browsing for `Redisbook-1`, he will be shown more recommendations for Redis books. Here the user will be shown five books on Redis, three books on NoSQL, and so on and so forth. For the sake of simplicity in this application, the sum total of weights should be 10.

Screenshot for successful product commissioning

To create test data, commission few test books with different weights, few with the same tags, and few with slightly different tags. Make sure that the sum total of weights is equal to 10.

- `Display command`: This will implement the `display` command. The implementation of the command is as follows:

```
package org.learningRedis.web.productmgmt.commands;
import org.learningRedis.web.Commands;
import org.learningRedis.web.util.Argument;
import org.learningRedis.web.util.ProductDBManager;
public class DisplayCommand extends Commands {
  public DisplayCommand(Argument argument) {
```

```
        super(argument);
    }
    @Override
    public String execute() {
        String display = ProductDBManager.singleton.
getProductInfo(this.getArgument().getValue("name"));
        return display;
    }
}
```

Test URL: `http://localhost:8080/simple-ecom/productApp?command=display&args=name=Redisbook-1`.

Description: This program will display the attributes of the book. The two parts in the URL that need to be focused on are the command which is equal to display, and the argument part, that is args. Here, args contains a single attribute called name.

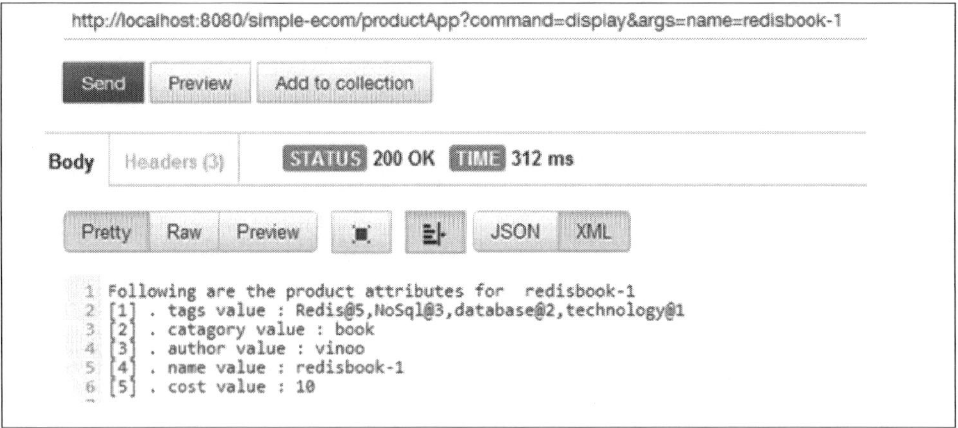

Screenshot for successful displaying of a product attributes

- `DisplayTagCommand`: This will implement the `browse` command. The implementation of the command is as follows:

```
package org.learningRedis.web.productmgmt.commands;
import org.learningRedis.web.Commands;
import org.learningRedis.web.util.Argument;
import org.learningRedis.web.util.ProductDBManager;
public class DisplayTagCommand extends Commands {
    public DisplayTagCommand(Argument argument) {
        super(argument);
    }
    @Override
```

```
  public String execute() {
    System.out.println(this.getClass().getSimpleName() + ":  " + "
Entering the execute function");
    String tagName = this.getArgument().getValue("tagname");
    String details = ProductDBManager.singleton.
getTagValues(tagName);
    return details;
  }
}
```

Test URL: `http://localhost:8080/simple-com/productApp?command=displaytag&args=tagname=nosql`.

Description: This program will display books on the basis of hits for a book. The two parts in the URL that need to be focused on are the `command`, which is equal to `displaytag`, and the argument part, that is `args`. Here `args` contains a single attribute called `tagname`. Since I have already commissioned a book into the system, the output is as shown in the next image. Visit this tag later when a user starts browsing for products; the order will change when you fire the same command.

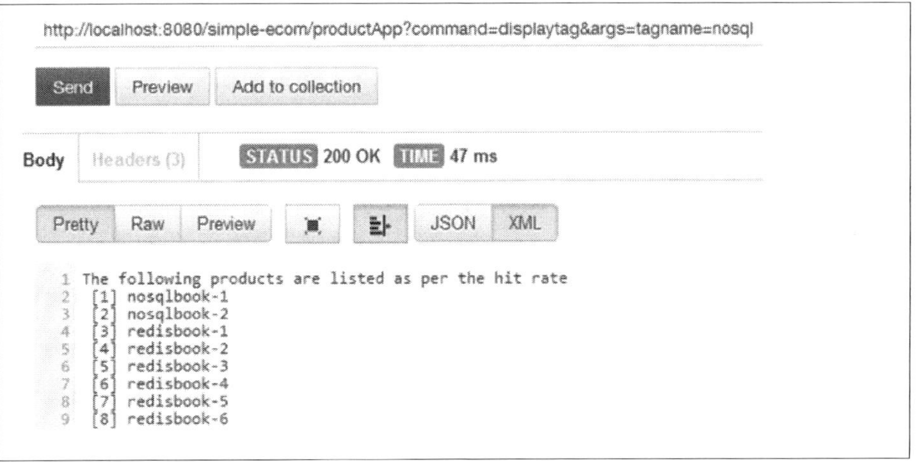

Screenshot for successful displaying of a products belonging to a tag that is NoSQL

- `UpdateTag`: This will implement the `UpdateTagCommand` command. The implementation of the command is as follows:

```
package org.learningRedis.web.productmgmt.commands;
import org.learningRedis.web.Commands;
import org.learningRedis.web.util.AnalyticsDBManager;
import org.learningRedis.web.util.Argument;
```

```
import org.learningRedis.web.util.ProductDBManager;
public class UpdateTagCommand extends Commands {
  public UpdateTagCommand(Argument argument) {
    super(argument);
  }
  @Override
  public String execute() {
    System.out.println(this.getClass().getSimpleName() + ":  " + "
Entering the execute function");
    String sessionid = this.getArgument().getValue("sessionid");
    String productname = this.getArgument().
getValue("productname");
    String details = this.getArgument().getValue("details");
    String actionType = this.getArgument().getValue("action");
    switch (actionType.toLowerCase()) {
    case "browse":
      if (productname != null & ProductDBManager.singleton.
keyExist(productname)) {
        AnalyticsDBManager.singleton.
updateRatingInTag(productname, 1);
        AnalyticsDBManager.singleton.updateProductVisit(sessionid,
productname);
      }
      break;
    case "buy":
      System.out.println("Buying the products in the shopping cart
!! ");
      String[] products = details.split(",");
      for (String product : products) {
        if (product != null & !product.trim().equals("")) {
          AnalyticsDBManager.singleton.updateRatingInTag(product,
10);
          AnalyticsDBManager.singleton.updateProductPurchase(sessi
onid, product);
        }
      }
      break;
    default:
      System.out.println("The URL cannot be acted uppon  ");
      break;
    }
    return "";
  }
}
```

Test URL: http://localhost:8080/simple-ecom/productAp p?command=updatetag&args=sessionid=<sessionID of the user>:productname=<product name which the user is browsing or has bought>:action=<browse or buy>.

Description: This command is called when a user is browsing a product or purchasing a product. The idea behind this command is that when a user is browsing a product or purchasing a product, it is gaining popularity, and so proportionally, the popularity of the product should increase among other products in the same tag. So in short, it helps calculate the most popular product in its category (tags). To test this command, make sure you create some dummy users and make them log into the system and then hit the browse command URL or buy command URL.

- VisitTodayCommand: This will implement the browse command. The implementation of the command is as follows:

```
package org.learningRedis.web.analytics.commands;
import org.learningRedis.web.Commands;
import org.learningRedis.web.util.AnalyticsDBManager;
import org.learningRedis.web.util.Argument;
public class VisitTodayCommand extends Commands {
  public VisitTodayCommand(Argument argument) {
    super(argument);
  }
  @Override
  public String execute() {
    System.out.println(this.getClass().getSimpleName() + ":  " +
"Entering the execute function");
    String productName = this.getArgument().
getValue("productname");
    Integer visitCount = AnalyticsDBManager.singleton.
getVisitToday(productName);
    System.out.println(this.getClass().getSimpleName() + ":  " +
"Printing the result for execute function");
    System.out.println("Result = " + "Total Unique Visitors are: "
+ visitCount.toString());
    return "Total Unique Visitors are: " + visitCount.toString();
  }
}
```

Test URL: http://localhost:8080/simple-ecom/productApp?command=v isitstoday&args=productname=Redisbook-1.

Description: This command can be executed if we want to check how many unique users visited the product. The data structure implementing this use case is a Bitmap. Bitmap in Redis has a consistent performance irrespective of the data it holds.

Screenshot for displaying total number of viewers in a day for the product redisbook-1

- `PurchasesTodayCommand`: This will implement the `purchasestoday` command. The implementation of the command is as follows:

```
package org.learningRedis.web.analytics.commands;
import org.learningRedis.web.Commands;
import org.learningRedis.web.util.Argument;
import org.learningRedis.web.util.ProductDBManager;
public class PurchasesTodayCommand extends Commands {
  public PurchasesTodayCommand(Argument argument) {
    super(argument);
  }
  @Override
  public String execute() {
    System.out.println(this.getClass().getSimpleName() + ":  " +
"Entering the execute function");
    String productName = this.getArgument().
getValue("productname");
    Integer purchaseCount = ProductDBManager.singleton.
getPurchaseToday(productName);
    System.out.println(this.getClass().getSimpleName() + ":  " +
"Printing the result for execute function");
    System.out.println("Result = " + "Total Unique Customers are:
" + purchaseCount.toString());
    return "Total Unique Customers are: " + purchaseCount.
toString();
  }
}
```

Test URL: `http://localhost:8080/simple-ecom/productApp?command=purchasestoday&args=productname=Redisbook-1`.

Description: This command can be executed if we want to check how many unique users purchased the given product. The data structure implementing this use case is a Bitmap. Bitmap in Redis has a consistent performance irrespective of the data it holds.

Screenshot for displaying total number of buyers in a day for the product redisbook-1

- `TagHistoryCommand`: This will implement the `browse` command. The implementation of the command is as follows:

```
package org.learningRedis.web.productmgmt.commands;
import org.learningRedis.web.Commands;
import org.learningRedis.web.util.AnalyticsDBManager;
import org.learningRedis.web.util.Argument;
public class TagHistoryCommand extends Commands {
  public TagHistoryCommand(Argument argument) {
    super(argument);
  }
  @Override
  public String execute() {
    String tagname = this.getArgument().getValue("tagname");
    String tagHistory = AnalyticsDBManager.singleton.
getTagHistory(tagname);
    return tagHistory;
    }
    }
```

Test URL: `http://localhost:8080/simple-ecom/productApp?command=taghistory&args=tagname=Redis`.

Description: This command can be executed if we want to see the tag history of a product. The ranking of the product is based on the points accumulated by individual products belonging to the tag. In the following sample we have shown the rankings for the tag `Redis`:

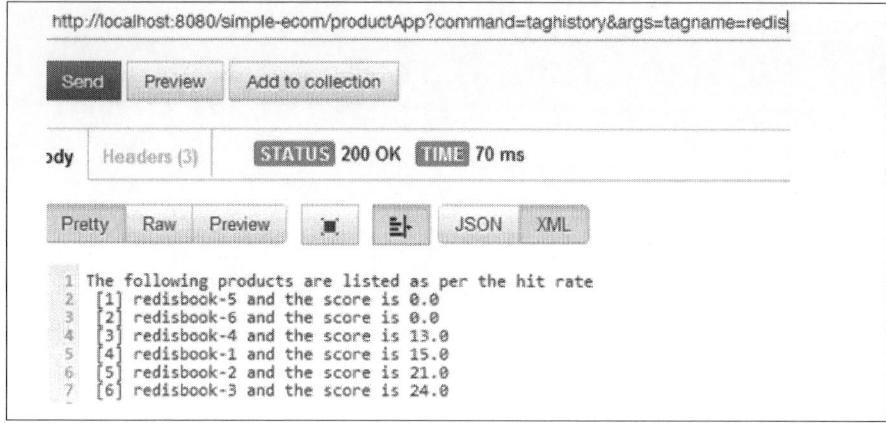

http://localhost:8080/simple-ecom/productApp?command=taghistory&args=tagname=redis
Send
Preview
Add to collection
Headers (3)
STATUS 200 OK
TIME 70 ms
Pretty
Raw
Preview
JSON
XML
The following products are listed as per the hit rate
[1] redisbook-5 and the score is 0.0
[2] redisbook-6 and the score is 0.0
[3] redisbook-4 and the score is 13.0
[4] redisbook-1 and the score is 15.0
[5] redisbook-2 and the score is 21.0
[6] redisbook-3 and the score is 24.0

Screenshot for displaying tag history for the tag redis

Test URL: `http://localhost:8080/simple-ecom/productApp?command=taghistory&args=tagname=nosql`.

Description: This command can be executed if we want to see the tag history of a product. The ranking of the product is based on the points accumulated by individual products belonging to the tag. In the following sample we have shown the rankings for the tag `nosql` to showcase the difference:

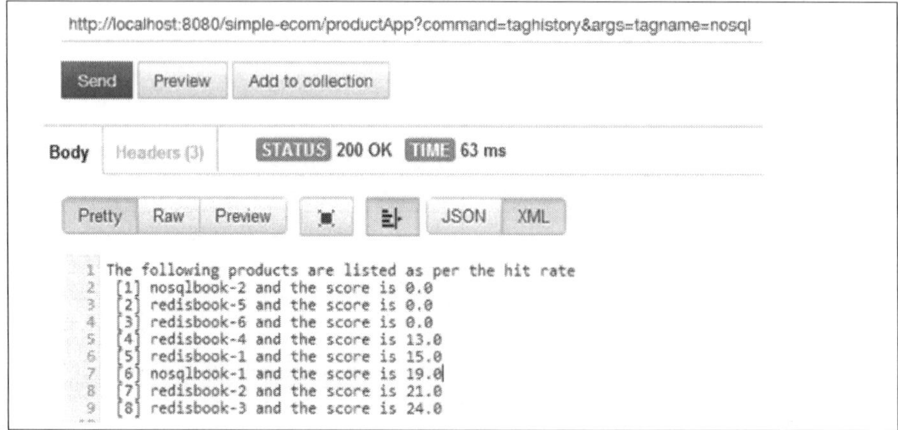

Screenshot for displaying tag history for the tag nosql

UserApp

UserApp servlet will contain commands around user management and analytics over user. The code for UserApp servlet is as follows:

```
package org.learningRedis.web;
import java.io.IOException;
import java.io.PrintWriter;
import javax.servlet.ServletException;
import javax.servlet.http.HttpServlet;
import javax.servlet.http.HttpServletRequest;
import javax.servlet.http.HttpServletResponse;
import org.learningRedis.web.analytics.commands.MyStatusCommand;
import org.learningRedis.web.analytics.commands.RecomendByProduct;
import org.learningRedis.web.sessionmgmt.commands.Add2CartCommand;
import org.learningRedis.web.sessionmgmt.commands.BrowseCommand;
import org.learningRedis.web.sessionmgmt.commands.BuyCommand;
import org.learningRedis.web.sessionmgmt.commands.EditCartCommand;
import org.learningRedis.web.sessionmgmt.commands.EditMyDataCommand;
import org.learningRedis.web.sessionmgmt.commands.LoginCommand;
import org.learningRedis.web.sessionmgmt.commands.LogoutCommand;
import org.learningRedis.web.sessionmgmt.commands.MyDataCommand;
import org.learningRedis.web.sessionmgmt.commands.MyPurchaseHistory;
import org.learningRedis.web.sessionmgmt.commands.RegistrationCommand;
import org.learningRedis.web.sessionmgmt.commands.ReloginCommand;
import org.learningRedis.web.sessionmgmt.commands.ShowMyCartCommand;
import org.learningRedis.web.util.Argument;
public class UserApp extends HttpServlet {
  private static final long serialVersionUID = 1L;
  public UserApp() {
    super();
  }
  protected void doGet(HttpServletRequest request, HttpServletResponse
response) throws ServletException, IOException {
    String command = request.getParameter("command");
    Argument argument = new Argument(request.getParameter("args"));
    PrintWriter out = response.getWriter();
    switch (command.toLowerCase()) {
    case "register":
      Commands register = new RegistrationCommand(argument);
      out.println(register.execute());
      break;
    case "login":
      Commands login = new LoginCommand(argument);
```

```
        out.println(login.execute());
        break;
      case "mydata":
        Commands mydata = new MyDataCommand(argument);
        out.println(mydata.execute());
        break;
      case "editmydata":
        Commands editMyData = new EditMyDataCommand(argument);
        out.println(editMyData.execute());
        break;
      case "recommendbyproduct":
        Commands recommendbyproduct = new RecomendByProductCommand
(argument);
        String recommendbyproducts = recommendbyproduct.execute();
        out.println(recommendbyproducts);
        break;
      case "browse":
        Commands browse = new BrowseCommand(argument);
        String result = browse.execute();
        out.println(result);
        String productname = argument.getValue("browse");
        String sessionid = argument.getValue("sessionid");
        request.getRequestDispatcher(
            "/productApp?command=updatetag&args=sessionid=" + sessionid
+ ":productname=" + productname
                + ":action=browse").include(request, response);
        break;
      case "buy":
        Commands buy = new BuyCommand(argument);
        String[] details = buy.execute().split("#");
        out.println(details[0]);
        String sessionID = argument.getValue("sessionid");
        request.getRequestDispatcher(
            "/productApp?command=updatetag&args=sessionid=" + sessionID
+ ":action=buy:details=" + details[1])
            .include(request, response);
        break;
      case "stats":
        Commands stats = new MyStatusCommand(argument);
        out.println(stats.execute());
        break;
      case "add2cart":
        Commands add2cart = new Add2CartCommand(argument);
        out.println(add2cart.execute());
```

```
        break;
      case "showmycart":
        Commands showmycart = new ShowMyCartCommand(argument);
        out.println(showmycart.execute());
        break;
      case "editcart":
        Commands editCard = new EditCartCommand(argument);
        out.println(editCard.execute());
        break;
      case "relogin":
        Commands relogin = new ReloginCommand(argument);
        out.println(relogin.execute());
        break;
      case "logout":
        Commands logout = new LogoutCommand(argument);
        out.println(logout.execute());
        break;
      case "mypurchasehistory":
        Commands mypurchasehistory = new MyPurchaseHistoryCommand
  (argument);
        out.println(mypurchasehistory.execute());
        break;
      default:
        Commands defaultUC = new DefaultCommand(argument);
        out.println(defaultUC.execute());
        break;
      }
    }
  }
```

Now that we have the first servlet ready, let's look into the commands which we are implementing for this:

- `RegistrationCommand`: This will implement the `register` command. The code for the command is as follows:

  ```
  package org.learningRedis.web.sessionmgmt.commands;
  import org.learningRedis.web.Commands;
  import org.learningRedis.web.util.Argument;
  import org.learningRedis.web.util.UserDBManager;
  public class RegistrationCommand extends Commands {
    public RegistrationCommand(Argument argument) {
      super(argument);
    }
    public String execute() {
  ```

```
    System.out.println(this.getClass().getSimpleName() + ":  " + "
Entering the execute function");
    String name = this.getArgument().getValue("name");
    if (!UserDBManager.singleton.doesUserExist(name)) {
      UserDBManager.singleton.createUser(this.getArgument().
getAttributes());
    } else {
      return "user already registered in ";
    }
    return "successful registeration  -> " + name;
  }
}
```

Test URL: `http://localhost:8080/simple-ecom/userApp?command=register&args=name=vinoo:password=******:address=test address.`

Description: This command will register the user into the system. The two parts in the URL that need to be focused on are the `command`, which is equal to `register`, and the argument part, that is `args`. This represents attributes in key value pairs. Following figure represents the success scenario if the registration is a success. The next logical step would be to log in the user.

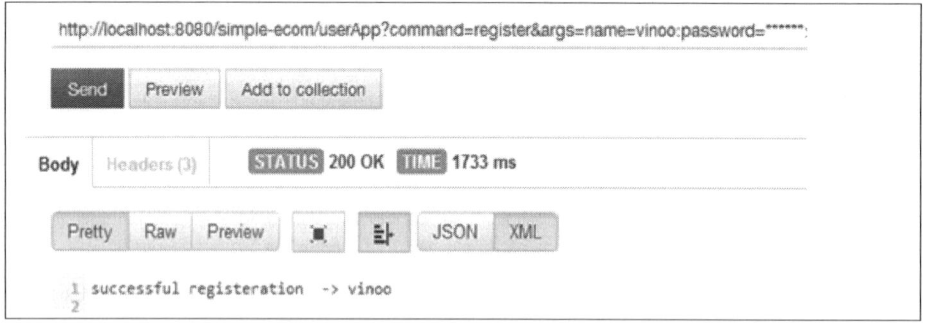

Screenshot for displaying user registration

- `LoginCommand`: This will implement the `login` command. The code for the command is as follows:

```
package org.learningRedis.web.sessionmgmt.commands;
import java.util.HashMap;
import java.util.Map;
import org.learningRedis.web.Commands;
import org.learningRedis.web.util.AnalyticsDBManager;
import org.learningRedis.web.util.Argument;
import org.learningRedis.web.util.ProductDBManager;
```

```
import org.learningRedis.web.util.UserDBManager;
public class LoginCommand extends Commands {
  public LoginCommand(Argument argument) {
    super(argument);
  }
  @Override
  public String execute() {
    System.out.println(this.getClass().getSimpleName() + ":  " + "
Entering the execute function");
    String name = this.getArgument().getValue("name");
    String password = this.getArgument().getValue("password");
    if (UserDBManager.singleton.doesUserExist(name)) {
      if (UserDBManager.singleton.getUserPassword(name).
equals(password)
          & UserDBManager.singleton.getUserSessionId(name).
equals("null")) {
        String sessionID = ProductDBManager.getRandomSessionID();
        UserDBManager.singleton.login(sessionID, name);
        Map<String, String> map = new HashMap<String, String>();
        map.put("sessionID", sessionID);
        UserDBManager.singleton.setRegistrationMap(name, map);
        System.out.println("login map : " + map);
        AnalyticsDBManager.singleton.registerInSessionTracker(sess
ionID);
        return "Login successful \n" + name + " \n use the
following session id : " + sessionID;
      } else if (UserDBManager.singleton.getUserPassword(name).
equals(password)
          & !UserDBManager.singleton.getUserSessionId(name).
equals("null")) {
        return " Login failed ...u r already logged in \n please
logout to login again \n or try relogin command ";
      } else {
        return " Login failed ...invalid password ";
      }
    } else {
      return " please register before executing command for login
";
    }
  }
}
```

Test URL: `http://localhost:8080/simple-ecom/userApp?command=login&args=name=vinoo:password=******`.

Description: This command will log in the user into the system. The two parts in the URL that need to be focused on are the `command`, which is equal to `login`, and the argument part, that is `args`. The argument will contain the name and password. The important part that needs to be focused on is that upon execution, this command will return a session ID code. This session ID is needed in most of the commands the user will execute. So if you are running a sample of this, make sure to store this number in a text pad for later use. In production system, this can be stored in the memory of the browser or client. The following figure tells me that the session ID generated for me is **26913441**. I will be using this for the rest of the samples I execute:

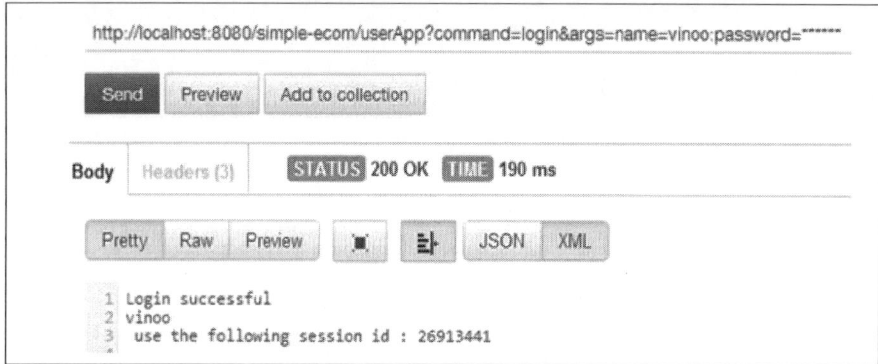

Screenshot for displaying user login and user session ID

- `MyDataCommand`: This will implement the `mydata` command. The code for the command is as follows:

```
package org.learningRedis.web.sessionmgmt.commands;
import java.util.Map;
import org.learningRedis.web.Commands;
import org.learningRedis.web.util.Argument;
import org.learningRedis.web.util.UserDBManager;
public class MyDataCommand extends Commands {
  public MyDataCommand(Argument argument) {
    super(argument);
  }
  @Override
  public String execute() {
    System.out.println(this.getClass().getSimpleName() + ":  " + "
Entering the execute function");
    String sessionid = this.getArgument().getValue("sessionid");
    String name = UserDBManager.singleton.getUserName(sessionid);
```

```
    Map<String, String> map = UserDBManager.singleton.
getRegistrationMap(name);
    return map.toString();
  }
}
```

Test URL: `http://localhost:8080/simple-ecom/userApp?command=mydata&args=sessionid=26913441`.

Description: This command will show user's data from the system. The two parts in the URL that need to be focused on are the `command`, which is equal to `mydata`, and the argument part, that is `args`. The argument has only session ID as the key value pair in the URL. The following figure shows the outcome of the command. Some of the attributes are not shown as they could not be accommodated in the figure.

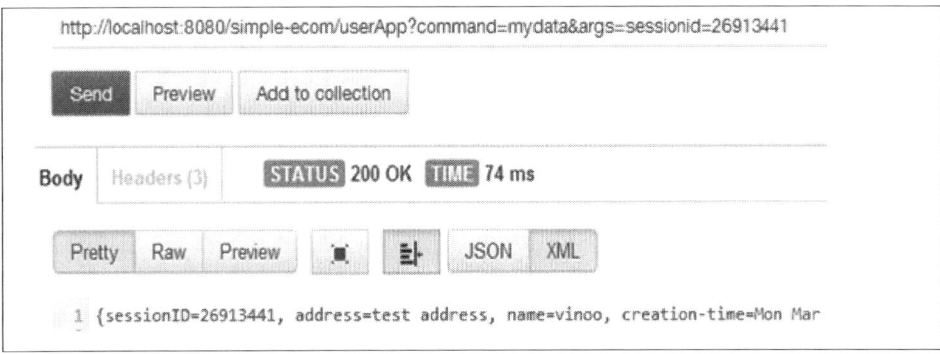

Screenshot for displaying user data

- `EditMyDataCommand`: This will implement the `editmydata` command. The code for the command is as follows:

```
package org.learningRedis.web.sessionmgmt.commands;
import java.util.Map;
import org.learningRedis.web.Commands;
import org.learningRedis.web.util.Argument;
import org.learningRedis.web.util.UserDBManager;
public class EditMyDataCommand extends Commands {
  public EditMyDataCommand(Argument argument) {
    super(argument);
  }
  @Override
  public String execute() {
    System.out.println(this.getClass().getSimpleName() + ":  " + "
Entering the execute function");
```

```
    Map<String, String> editMap = this.getArgument().
getAttributes();
    boolean result = UserDBManager.singleton.
editRegistrationMap(editMap);
    if (result) {
      return "Edit is Done....";
    } else {
      return "Edit not Done.... please check sessionid and name
combination";
    }
  }
}
```

Test URL: `http://localhost:8080/simple-ecom/userApp?command=editmydata&args=name=vinoo:password=******:address=changed address:phone=9111111119:sessionid=26913441`.

Description: This command will show user's data from the system. The two parts in the URL that need to be focused on are the `command`, which is equal to `mydata`, and the argument part, that is `args`. The argument has new and edited key value pairs. Make sure that the session ID is correct in the URL. The following figure is what you should be seeing in the output. Now you can always go back and execute the previous command `mydata` which will show the newer values.

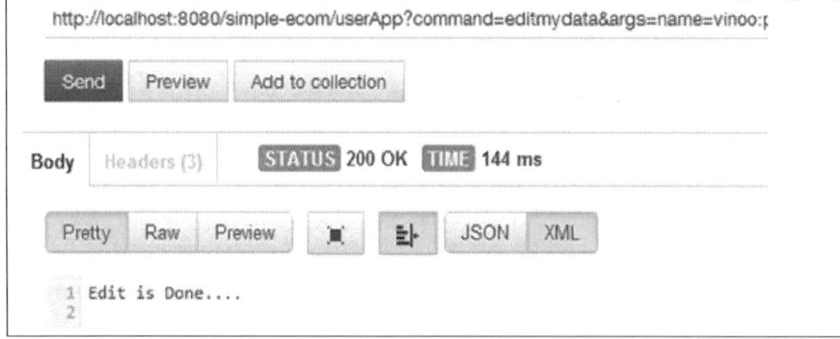

Screenshot for successful editing of user data

- `BrowseCommand`: This will implement the `browse` command. The implementation of the command is as follows:

```
package org.learningRedis.web.sessionmgmt.commands;
import org.learningRedis.web.Commands;
import org.learningRedis.web.util.AnalyticsDBManager;
import org.learningRedis.web.util.Argument;
import org.learningRedis.web.util.ProductDBManager;
public class BrowseCommand extends Commands {
  public BrowseCommand(Argument argument) {
    super(argument);
  }
  @Override
  public String execute() {
    System.out.println(this.getClass().getSimpleName() + ":  " + "
Entering the execute function");
    String productname = this.getArgument().getValue("browse");
    if (ProductDBManager.singleton.keyExist(productname)) {
      AnalyticsDBManager.singleton.updateBrowsingHistory(this.
getArgument().getValue("sessionid"), productname);
      StringBuffer stringBuffer = new StringBuffer();
      stringBuffer.append("You are browsing the following product
= " + productname + "\n");
      stringBuffer.append(ProductDBManager.singleton.
getProductInfo(productname));
      return stringBuffer.toString();
    } else {
      return "Error: The product you are trying to browse does not
exist i.e. " + productname;
    }
  }
}
```

Test URL: `http://localhost:8080/simple-ecom/userApp?command=browse&args=sessionid=26913441:browse=Redisbook-1`.

Description: This command will show the product's data from the system. The two parts in the URL that need to be focused on are the `command`, which is equal to `browse`, and the argument part, that is `args`. The argument has session ID of the user and name of the product that the user is browsing. There are a couple of things that are happening here. The user gets to see the product details and in the background a request is sent to the `updatetag` command to increase the popularity of the respective product. In our case, the product is `Redisbook-1`. For the sake of testing, browse all the products you have commissioned into the system multiple numbers of times.

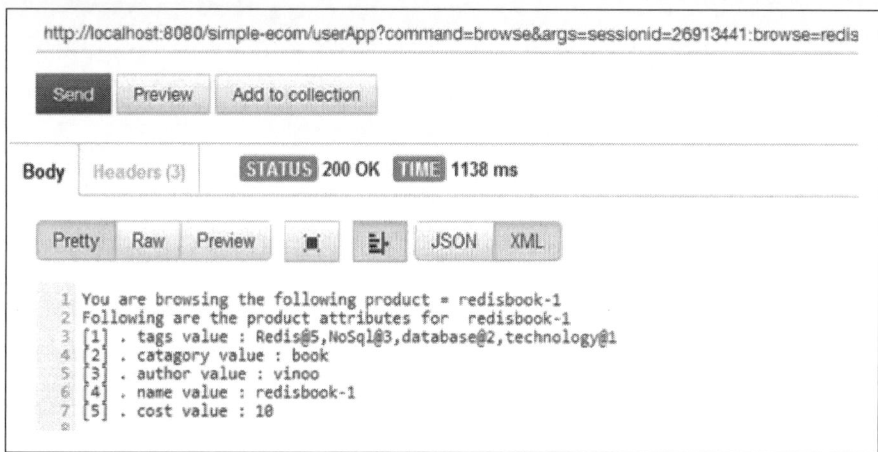

Screenshot when user wants to browse a product and see its details

- `RecommendByProductCommand`: This will implement the `recommendbyproduct` command. The code for the command is as follows:

```
package org.learningRedis.web.analytics.commands;
import java.util.List;
import java.util.Map;
import java.util.Set;
import org.learningRedis.web.Commands;
import org.learningRedis.web.util.AnalyticsDBManager;
import org.learningRedis.web.util.Argument;
import org.learningRedis.web.util.ProductDBManager;
public class RecomendByProductCommand extends Commands {
  int totalrecomendations = 10;
  public RecomendByProductCommand(Argument argument) {
    super(argument);
  }
  @Override
```

```
  public String execute() {
    System.out.println(this.getClass().getSimpleName() + ":  " + "
Entering the execute function");
    StringBuffer buffer = new StringBuffer();
    String productname = this.getArgument().
getValue("productname");
    buffer.append("If you are lookinging into " + productname + "
you might also find the following \n");
    buffer.append("products interseting... \n");
    Map<String, Integer> tags = ProductDBManager.singleton.
getProductTags(productname);
    // Lets get total sum of weights
    int totalweight = 0;
    Set<String> keys = tags.keySet();
    for (String key : keys) {
      totalweight = totalweight + tags.get(key);
    }
    for (String key : keys) {
      int slotfortag = Math.round(totalrecomendations * tags.
get(key) / totalweight);
      List<String> productnames = AnalyticsDBManager.singleton.
getTopProducts(slotfortag, key);
      for (String product : productnames) {
        if (!product.equals(productname)) {
          buffer.append("For tag = " + key + " the recomended
product is " + product);
          buffer.append("\n");
        }
      }
    }
    System.out.println(this.getClass().getSimpleName() + ":  " +
"Printing the result for execute function");
    System.out.println("Result = " + buffer.toString());
    return buffer.toString();
  }
}
```

Test URL: `http://localhost:8080/simple-ecom/userApp?command=recommendbyproduct&args=sessionid=26913441:productname=Redisbook-1`.

Description: This command will recommend products based on the product being browsed. The two parts in the URL that need to be focused on are the `command`, which is equal to `recommendbyproduct`, and the argument part, that is `args`. The argument has session ID of the user and product `Redisbook-1`.

This command will recommend top products for the user based on the purchase and browse history of the product. This will factor in what categories the product belongs to and the weight that needs to be factored for product display. This in a way is the online real-time analytics that kicks into action when the user is browsing a product. In the figure, maximum number of results are for `Redis` tag as that is the tag that has got the maximum weight. In production, some filtering needs to be done for duplicate results that might occur for similar products that share the same tags. This filtering can be done at the client side, thus saving the compute resource at the server side.

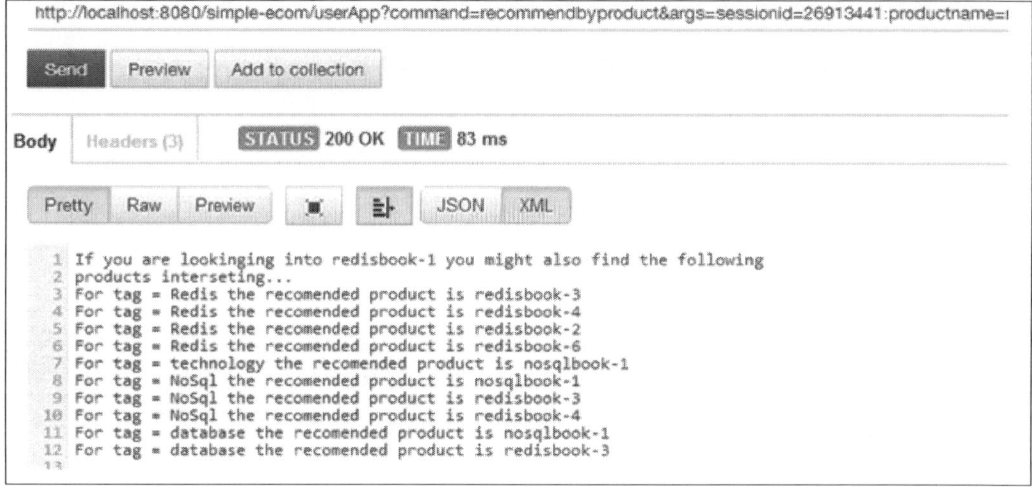
http://localhost:8080/simple-ecom/userApp?command=recommendbyproduct&args=sessionid=26913441:productname=
Send
Preview
Add to collection
Body
Headers (3)
STATUS 200 OK
TIME 83 ms
Pretty
Raw
Preview
JSON
XML
If you are lookinging into redisbook-1 you might also find the following
products interseting...
For tag = Redis the recomended product is redisbook-3
For tag = Redis the recomended product is redisbook-4
For tag = Redis the recomended product is redisbook-2
For tag = Redis the recomended product is redisbook-6
For tag = technology the recomended product is nosqlbook-1
For tag = NoSql the recomended product is nosqlbook-1
For tag = NoSql the recomended product is redisbook-3
For tag = NoSql the recomended product is redisbook-4
For tag = database the recomended product is nosqlbook-1
For tag = database the recomended product is redisbook-3

Screenshot when user wants to browse a product and see other recommended products

- `Add2CartCommand`: This will implement the `add2cart` command. The implementation of the command is as follows:

```
package org.learningRedis.web.sessionmgmt.commands;
import java.util.HashMap;
import java.util.Map;
import org.learningRedis.web.Commands;
import org.learningRedis.web.util.Argument;
import org.learningRedis.web.util.ShoppingCartDBManager;
import org.learningRedis.web.util.UserDBManager;
public class Add2CartCommand extends Commands {
  public Add2CartCommand(Argument argument) {
    super(argument);
  }
  @Override
```

```
  public String execute() {
    System.out.println(this.getClass().getSimpleName() + ":  " + "
Entering the execute function");
    String result = "did not update the shopping cart";
    String sessionid = this.getArgument().getValue("sessionid");
    String product = this.getArgument().getValue("product");
    String[] productList = product.split(",");
    Map<String, String> productQtyMap = new HashMap<String,
String>();
    for (String _product : productList) {
      String[] nameQty = _product.split("@");
      productQtyMap.put(nameQty[0], nameQty[1]);
    }
    if (UserDBManager.singleton.doesSessionExist(sessionid)) {
      result = ShoppingCartDBManager.singleton.
addToShoppingCart(sessionid, productQtyMap);
    }
    return "Result : " + result;
  }
}
```

Test URL: `http://localhost:8080/simple-ecom/userApp?command=add2cart&args=sessionid=26913441:product=Redisbook-1@2,Redisbook-4@1`.

Description: This command will put products and their quantities into the shopping cart. The two parts in the URL that need to be focused on are the `command`, which is equal to `add2cart`, and the argument part, that is `args`. The argument contains two key value pairs. First is the session ID and second is the name of the product and the quantity separated by special character `@`. The following figure shows that I have successfully added the products in my shopping cart:

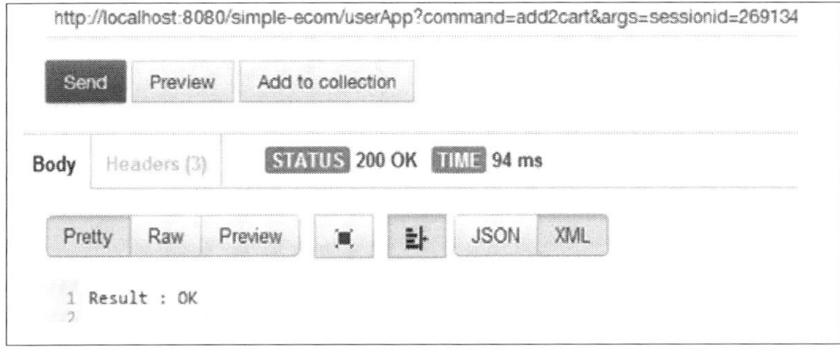

Screenshot when user wants to add products to his cart

- `ShowMyCartCommand`: This will implement the `showmycart` command. The implementation of the command is as follows:

```
package org.learningRedis.web.sessionmgmt.commands;
import java.util.Map;
import java.util.Set;
import org.learningRedis.web.Commands;
import org.learningRedis.web.util.Argument;
import org.learningRedis.web.util.ShoppingCartDBManager;
public class ShowMyCartCommand extends Commands {
  public ShowMyCartCommand(Argument argument) {
    super(argument);
  }
  @Override
  public String execute() {
    System.out.println(this.getClass().getSimpleName() + ":  " + "
Entering the execute function");
    String sessionid = this.getArgument().getValue("sessionid");
    Map<String, String> productMap = ShoppingCartDBManager.
singleton.myCartInfo(sessionid);
    StringBuffer stringBuffer = new StringBuffer();
    if (!productMap.isEmpty()) {
      stringBuffer.append("Your shopping cart contains the
following : ");
      stringBuffer.append("\n");
      Set<String> set = productMap.keySet();
      int i = 1;
      for (String str : set) {
        stringBuffer.append("[" + i + "] product name = " + str +
" Qty = " + productMap.get(str) + "\n");
        i++;
      }
      return stringBuffer.toString();
    } else {
      return " your shopping cart is empty.";
    }
  }
}
```

Test URL: `http://localhost:8080/simple-ecom/userApp?command=showmycart&args=sessionid=26913441`.

Description: This command will put products and their quantities into the shopping cart. The two parts in the URL that need to be focused on are the `command`, which is equal to `showmycart`, and the argument part, that is `args`. The argument contains the session ID only. The following figure shows my shopping cart:

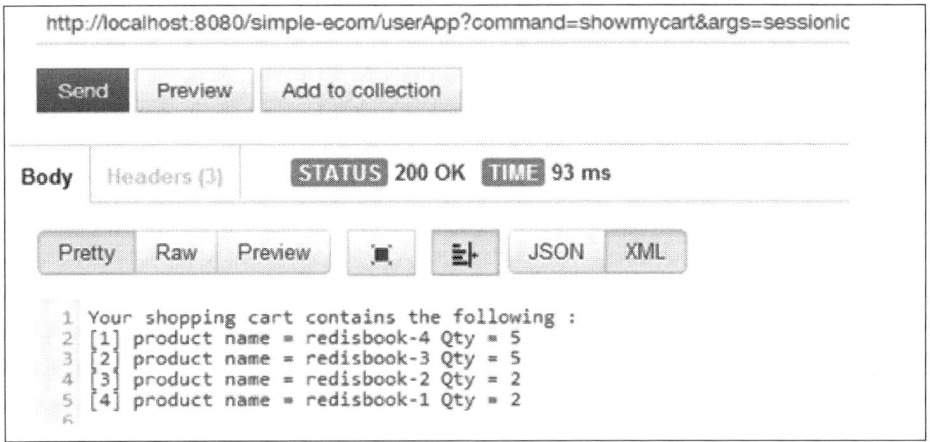
http://localhost:8080/simple-ecom/userApp?command=showmycart&args=sessionic
Send
Preview
Add to collection
Body
Headers (3)
STATUS 200 OK
TIME 93 ms
Pretty
Raw
Preview
JSON
XML
Your shopping cart contains the following :
[1] product name = redisbook-4 Qty = 5
[2] product name = redisbook-3 Qty = 5
[3] product name = redisbook-2 Qty = 2
[4] product name = redisbook-1 Qty = 2

Screenshot when user wants to see his cart

- `EditCartCommand`: This will implement the `editcart` command. The implementation of the command is as follows:

```
package org.learningRedis.web.sessionmgmt.commands;
import java.util.HashMap;
import java.util.Map;
import org.learningRedis.web.Commands;
import org.learningRedis.web.util.Argument;
import org.learningRedis.web.util.ShoppingCartDBManager;
import org.learningRedis.web.util.UserDBManager;
public class EditCartCommand extends Commands {
  public EditCartCommand(Argument argument) {
    super(argument);
  }
  @Override
  public String execute() {
    System.out.println(this.getClass().getSimpleName() + ":  " + "
Entering the execute function");
    String result = "did not edit the shopping cart";
    String sessionID = this.getArgument().getValue("sessionid");
    String product = this.getArgument().getValue("product");
    String[] productList = product.split(",");
```

```
      Map<String, String> productQtyMap = new HashMap<String,
String>();
      for (String _product : productList) {
        String[] nameQty = _product.split("@");
        productQtyMap.put(nameQty[0], nameQty[1]);
      }
      if (UserDBManager.singleton.doesSessionExist(sessionID)) {
        result = ShoppingCartDBManager.singleton.
editMyCart(sessionID, productQtyMap);
      }
      return "result : " + result;
    }
}
```

Test URL: `http://localhost:8080/simple-ecom/userApp?command=editcart&args=sessionid=26913441:product=Redisbook-4@0,Redisbook-2@1.`

Description: This command will edit the products and their quantities in the shopping cart. The two parts in the URL that need to be focused upon are the `command`, which is equal to `editcart`, and the argument part, that is `args`. The argument contains key value pairs of the products and their new quantities. If the quantity is marked as `0`, then the product will be removed from the shopping cart. On executing the `showmycart` command again, the cart should reflect the newer values. The following figure shows the newer values:

http://localhost:8080/simple-ecom/userApp?command=showmycart&args=sessionid=26913441
Send
Preview
Add to collection
Body
Headers (3)
STATUS 200 OK
TIME 85 ms
Pretty
Raw
Preview
JSON
XML
1 Your shopping cart contains the following :
2 [1] product name = redisbook-3 Qty = 5
3 [2] product name = redisbook-2 Qty = 1
4 [3] product name = redisbook-1 Qty = 2
5

Screenshot when user wants to see his cart after editing his cart

- `BuyCommand`: This will implement the `browse` command. The implementation of the command is as follows:

```
package org.learningRedis.web.sessionmgmt.commands;
import org.learningRedis.web.Commands;
import org.learningRedis.web.util.Argument;
import org.learningRedis.web.util.ShoppingCartDBManager;
public class BuyCommand extends Commands {
  public BuyCommand(Argument argument) {
    super(argument);
  }
  @Override
  public String execute() {
    System.out.println(this.getClass().getSimpleName() + ":  " + "
Entering the execute function");
    String sessionid = this.getArgument().getValue("sessionid");
    String shoppingdetails = ShoppingCartDBManager.singleton.buyIt
emsInTheShoppingCart(sessionid);
    return shoppingdetails;
  }
}
```

Test URL: `http://localhost:8080/simple-ecom/userApp?command=buy&args=sessionid=26913441`.

Description: This command will buy the products in the shopping cart. Since this is a demo website, there is no connection to the payment gateway, but the intention of having this command was to increase the `hit` counter when a purchase is made. When a product is bought, the recommendation engine increases its points by `10` as compared to `1` when the product is browsed:

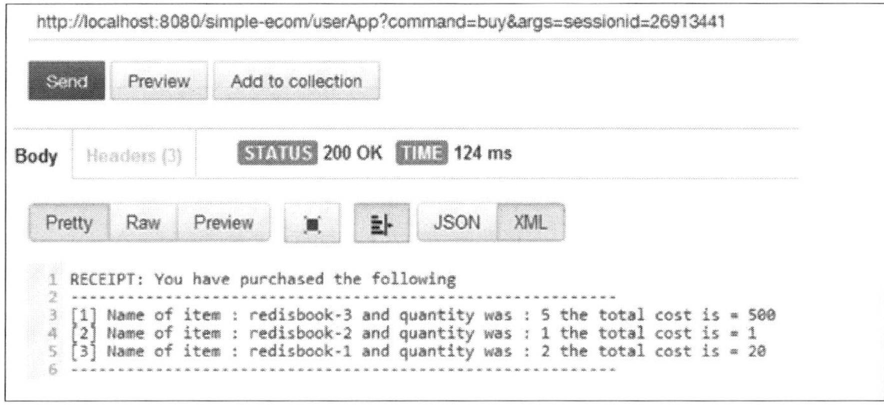

Doing dummy purchase

At this point, it would be pretty interesting to go back and revisit the `recommendbyproduct` command. The order in which the products got displayed would change, since every buy gives `10` points to the product popularity. The `recommendbyproduct` is for the product `Redisbook-1`. And the test URL is as follows: `http://localhost:8080/simple-ecom/userApp?command=recommendbyproduct&args=sessionid=26913441:productname=Redisbook-1`.

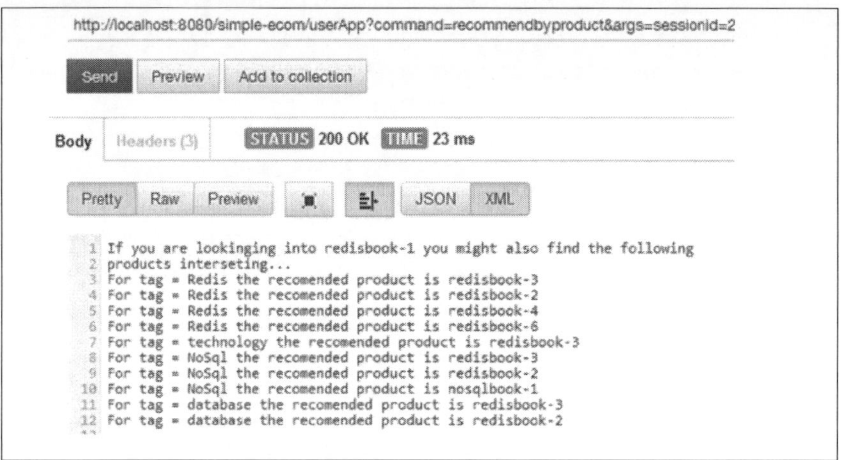
http://localhost:8080/simple-ecom/userApp?command=recommendbyproduct&args=sessionid=2
Send
Preview
Add to collection
Body
Headers (3)
STATUS 200 OK
TIME 23 ms
Pretty
Raw
Preview
JSON
XML
If you are lookinging into redisbook-1 you might also find the following
products interseting...
For tag = Redis the recomended product is redisbook-3
For tag = Redis the recomended product is redisbook-2
For tag = Redis the recomended product is redisbook-4
For tag = Redis the recomended product is redisbook-6
For tag = technology the recomended product is redisbook-3
For tag = NoSql the recomended product is redisbook-3
For tag = NoSql the recomended product is redisbook-2
For tag = NoSql the recomended product is nosqlbook-1
For tag = database the recomended product is redisbook-3
For tag = database the recomended product is redisbook-2

Screenshot for rearranged product list after successful purchase (online analytics)

- `MyStatusCommand`: This will implement the `stats` command. The implementation of the command is as follows:

```
package org.learningRedis.web.analytics.commands;
import java.util.Iterator;
import java.util.Set;
import org.learningRedis.web.Commands;
import org.learningRedis.web.util.AnalyticsDBManager;
import org.learningRedis.web.util.Argument;
import org.learningRedis.web.util.UserDBManager;
public class MyStatusCommand extends Commands {
  public MyStatusCommand(Argument argument) {
    super(argument);
  }
  @Override
  public String execute() {
    System.out.println(this.getClass().getSimpleName() + ":  " +
"Entering the execute function");
```

```
    String sessionID = this.getArgument().getValue("sessionid");
    if (UserDBManager.singleton.doesSessionExist(sessionID)) {
      Set<String> browsingHistory = AnalyticsDBManager.singleton.
getBrowsingHistory(sessionID);
      StringBuffer buffer = new StringBuffer();
      buffer.append(" View your browsing history where the one on
top is the least visited product");
      buffer.append("\n and the product at the bottom is the most
frequented product ");
      buffer.append("\n");
      Iterator<String> iterator = browsingHistory.iterator();
      int i = 1;
      while (iterator.hasNext()) {
        buffer.append("[" + i + "] " + iterator.next() + "\n");
        i++;
      }
      System.out.println(this.getClass().getSimpleName() + ":  " +
"Printing the result for execute function");
      System.out.println("Result = " + buffer.toString());
      return buffer.toString();
    } else {
      return "history is not available";
    }
  }
}
```

Test URL: `http://localhost:8080/simple-ecom/userApp?command=stats&args=sessionid=26913441`.

Description: This command will give the browsing history of the user. Here the result will be listed on the basis of frequency at which the user is revisiting a particular product. The two parts in the URL that need to be focused on are the `command`, which is equal to `stats`, and the argument part, that is `args`. The argument contains the session ID of the user. The following figure represents the browsing history of the user with session ID **26913441**:

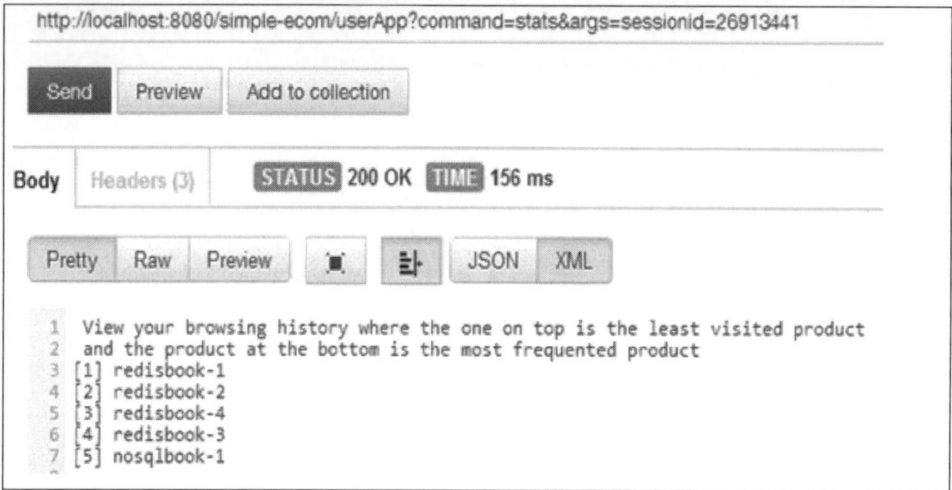

Screenshot for viewing browsing history of a user

- `MyPurchaseHistoryCommand`: This will implement the `mypurchasehistory` command. The implementation of the command is as follows:

```
package org.learningRedis.web.sessionmgmt.commands;
import java.util.List;
import org.learningRedis.web.Commands;
import org.learningRedis.web.util.AnalyticsDBManager;
import org.learningRedis.web.util.Argument;
public class MyPurchaseHistoryCommand extends Commands {
  public MyPurchaseHistoryCommand(Argument argument) {
    super(argument);
  }
  @Override
  public String execute() {
    System.out.println(this.getClass().getSimpleName() + ":  " + "
Entering the execute function");
    StringBuffer report = new StringBuffer();
```

```
    String sessionid = this.getArgument().getValue("sessionid");
    List<String> purchasehistory = AnalyticsDBManager.singleton.ge
tMyPurchaseHistory(sessionid);
    report.append("Your purchase history is as follows : \n");
    int i = 0;
    for (String purchase : purchasehistory) {
      report.append("[" + i + "] You purchased " + purchase);
      report.append("\n");
      i++;
    }
    return report.toString();
  }
}
```

Test URL: `http://localhost:8080/simple-ecom/userApp?command=mypurchasehistory&args=sessionid=26913441.`

Description: This command will give the purchasing history of the user. Here the result will be listed on the basis of dates on which the user bought particular products. The two parts in the URL that need to be focused on are the `command`, which is equal to `stats`, and the argument part, that is `args`. The argument is session ID of the user:

Screenshot for viewing purchase history of a user

- `ReloginCommand`: This will implement the `relogin` command. The implementation of the command is as follows:

```
package org.learningRedis.web.sessionmgmt.commands;
import org.learningRedis.web.Commands;
import org.learningRedis.web.util.Argument;
import org.learningRedis.web.util.UserDBManager;
public class ReloginCommand extends Commands {
  public ReloginCommand(Argument argument) {
    super(argument);
  }
  @Override
  public String execute() {
    System.out.println(this.getClass().getSimpleName() + ":  " + "
Entering the execute function");
    String name = this.getArgument().getValue("name");
    String password = this.getArgument().getValue("password");
    if (UserDBManager.singleton.doesUserExist(name)) {
      if (UserDBManager.singleton.getUserPassword(name).
equals(password)) {
        String sessionID = UserDBManager.singleton.
getUserSessionId(name);
        return "ReLogin successful \n" + name + " \n use the
following session id : " + sessionID;
      } else {
        return " ReLogin failed ...invalid password ";
      }
    } else {
      return " please register before executing command for login
";
    }
  }
}
```

Test URL: `http://localhost:8080/simple-ecom/userApp?command=relogin&args=name=vinoo:password=******`.

Description: This command will again check the user and password of the user and return back the associated session ID of the user. The idea is to have session which can exist many shopping and browsing sessions of a user.

- `LogoutCommand`: This will implement the `logout` command. The implementation of the command is as follows:

```
package org.learningRedis.web.sessionmgmt.commands;
import org.learningRedis.web.Commands;
import org.learningRedis.web.util.Argument;
```

```
import org.learningRedis.web.util.UserDBManager;
public class LogoutCommand extends Commands {
  public LogoutCommand(Argument argument) {
    super(argument);
  }
  @Override
  public String execute() {
    System.out.println(this.getClass().getSimpleName() + ":  " + "
Entering the execute function");
    String sessionid = this.getArgument().getValue("sessionid");
    if (UserDBManager.singleton.expireSession(sessionid)) {
      return "logout was clean";
    } else {
      return "logout was not clean";
    }
  }
}
```

Test URL: `http://localhost:8080/simple-ecom/userApp?command=logout&args=sessionid=26913441`.

Description: This command will log out the user from the system, and based on the session ID, delete all the datastore of the user, such as purchase history, shopping cart, and browsing history.

Now that we have a hang of the commands, let's look into the package which will take care of the connection management and other functional calls with Redis.

RedisDBManager

This class is the backbone of this application; it is responsible for connecting with the database and managing the connection pool. It also has some utility functions. The implementation is explained by the following code snippet:

```
package org.learningRedis.web.util;
import java.text.DateFormat;
import java.text.SimpleDateFormat;
import java.util.Date;
import Redis.clients.jedis.Jedis;
import Redis.clients.jedis.JedisPool;
public class RedisDBManager {
  private static Date date = new Date();
  private static int minimum = 1;
  private static int maximum = 100000000;
  // going with the default pool.
```

```
  private static JedisPool connectionPool = new JedisPool("localhost",
6379);
  public Jedis getConnection() {
    return connectionPool.getResource();
  }
  public void returnConnection(Jedis jedis) {
    connectionPool.returnResource(jedis);
  }
  public static String getDate() {
    DateFormat dateFormat = new SimpleDateFormat("dd-MM-yyyy");
    String dateValue = dateFormat.format(date);
    return dateValue;
  }
  public static String getRandomSessionID() {
    int randomNum = minimum + (int) (Math.random() * maximum);
    return new Integer(randomNum).toString();
  }
}
```

ProductDBManager

This class extends the `RedisDBManager` and is responsible for product related functional calls to the data base. This class is implemented as follows:

```
package org.learningRedis.web.util;
import java.util.ArrayList;
import java.util.BitSet;
import java.util.HashMap;
import java.util.List;
import java.util.Map;
import java.util.Set;
import Redis.clients.jedis.Jedis;
public class ProductDBManager extends RedisDBManager {
  private ProductDBManager() {
  }
  public static ProductDBManager singleton = new ProductDBManager();
  public boolean commisionProduct(Map<String, String>
productAttributes) {
    Jedis jedis = this.getConnection();
    String productCreationResult = jedis.hmset(productAttributes.
get("name"), productAttributes);
    if (productCreationResult.toLowerCase().equals("ok")) {
      this.returnConnection(jedis);
      return true;
```

```
    } else {
      this.returnConnection(jedis);
      return false;
    }
  }
  public boolean enterTagEntries(String name, String string) {
    Jedis jedis = this.getConnection();
    String[] tags = string.split(",");
    boolean boolResult = false;
    List<String> tagList = new ArrayList<String>();
    for (String tag : tags) {
      String[] tagAndRating = tag.split("@");
      tagList.add(tagAndRating[0]);
    }
    for (String tag : tagList) {
      long result = jedis.zadd(tag.toLowerCase(), 0, name);
      if (result == 0) {
        break;
      } else {
        boolResult = true;
      }
    }
    this.returnConnection(jedis);
    return boolResult;
  }
  public String getProductInfo(String name) {
    Jedis jedis = this.getConnection();
    Map<String, String> map = jedis.hgetAll(name);
    StringBuffer stringBuffer = new StringBuffer();
    stringBuffer.append("Following are the product attributes for  " +
name);
    stringBuffer.append("\n");
    Set<String> keys = map.keySet();
    int i = 1;
    for (String key : keys) {
      stringBuffer.append("[" + i + "] . " + key + " value : " + map.
get(key));
      stringBuffer.append("\n");
      i++;
    }
    this.returnConnection(jedis);
    return stringBuffer.toString();
  }
```

```
  public String getTagValues(String tagName) {
    Jedis jedis = this.getConnection();
    StringBuffer stringBuffer = new StringBuffer();
    Set<String> sortedTagList = jedis.zrange(tagName.toLowerCase(), 0,
10000);
    stringBuffer.append("The following products are listed as per the
hit rate \n");
    int i = 1;
    for (String tagname : sortedTagList) {
      stringBuffer.append(" [" + i + "] " + tagname + "\n");
      i++;
    }
    this.returnConnection(jedis);
    return stringBuffer.toString();
  }
  public boolean keyExist(String keyName) {
    Jedis jedis = this.getConnection();
    boolean result = jedis.exists(keyName);
    this.returnConnection(jedis);
    return result;
  }
  public int getPurchaseToday(String productName) {
    Jedis jedis = this.getConnection();
    if (jedis.get(productName + "@purchase:" + getDate()) != null) {
      BitSet users = BitSet.valueOf(jedis.get(productName + "@
purchase:" + getDate()).getBytes());
      this.returnConnection(jedis);
      return users.cardinality();
    } else {
      this.returnConnection(jedis);
      return 0;
    }
  }
  public Map<String, Integer> getProductTags(String productname) {
    Jedis jedis = this.getConnection();
    String producttags = jedis.hget(productname, "tags");
    Map<String, Integer> map = new HashMap<String, Integer>();
    String[] tagAndweights = producttags.split(",");
    for (String tagAndWeight : tagAndweights) {
      map.put(tagAndWeight.split("@")[0], new Integer(tagAndWeight.
split("@")[1]));
    }
    this.returnConnection(jedis);
    return map;
  }
}
```

AnalyticsDBManager

This class extends the `RedisDBManager` and is responsible for analytics-related functional calls to the data base. The class is implemented as follows:

```
package org.learningRedis.web.util;
import java.util.ArrayList;
import java.util.BitSet;
import java.util.Iterator;
import java.util.List;
import java.util.Set;
import Redis.clients.jedis.Jedis;
public class AnalyticsDBManager extends RedisDBManager {
  private AnalyticsDBManager() {
  }
  public static AnalyticsDBManager singleton = new
AnalyticsDBManager();
  public void registerInSessionTracker(String sessionID) {
    Jedis jedis = this.getConnection();
    Long sessionvalue = new Long(sessionID);
    jedis.setbit("sessionIdTracker", sessionvalue, true);
    this.returnConnection(jedis);
  }
  public void updateBrowsingHistory(String sessionID, String
productname) {
    Jedis jedis = this.getConnection();
    jedis.zincrby(sessionID + "@browsinghistory", 1.0, productname);
    this.returnConnection(jedis);
  }
  public Set<String> getBrowsingHistory(String sessionID) {
    Jedis jedis = this.getConnection();
    Set<String> range = jedis.zrange(sessionID + "@browsinghistory",
0, 1000000);
    this.returnConnection(jedis);
    return range;
  }
  public int getVisitToday(String productName) {
    Jedis jedis = this.getConnection();
    if (jedis.get(productName + "@visit:" + getDate()) != null) {
      BitSet users = BitSet.valueOf(jedis.get(productName + "@visit:"
+ getDate()).getBytes());
      this.returnConnection(jedis);
      return users.cardinality();
    } else {
      this.returnConnection(jedis);
```

```
        return 0;
      }
    }
    public void updateProductVisit(String sessionid, String productName)
  {
      Jedis jedis = this.getConnection();
      jedis.setbit(productName + "@visit:" + getDate(), new
  Long(sessionid), true);
      this.returnConnection(jedis);
    }
    public void updateProductPurchase(String sessionid, String
  productName) {
      Jedis jedis = this.getConnection();
      jedis.setbit(productName + "@purchase:" + getDate(), new
  Long(sessionid), true);
      this.returnConnection(jedis);
    }
    public void updateRatingInTag(String productname, double rating) {
      Jedis jedis = this.getConnection();
      String string = jedis.hget(productname, "tags");
      String[] tags = string.split(",");
      List<String> tagList = new ArrayList<String>();
      for (String tag : tags) {
        String[] tagAndRating = tag.split("@");
        tagList.add(tagAndRating[0]);
      }
      for (String tag : tagList) {
        jedis.zincrby(tag.toLowerCase(), rating, productname);
      }
      this.returnConnection(jedis);
    }
    public List<String> getMyPurchaseHistory(String sessionid) {
      Jedis jedis = this.getConnection();
      String name = jedis.hget(sessionid + "@sessiondata", "name");
      List<String> purchaseHistory = jedis.lrange(name + "@
  purchasehistory", 0, 100);
      this.returnConnection(jedis);
      return purchaseHistory;
    }
    public String getTagHistory(String tagname) {
      Jedis jedis = this.getConnection();
      Set<String> sortedProductList = jedis.zrange(tagname.
  toLowerCase(), 0, 10000);
      StringBuffer stringBuffer = new StringBuffer();
```

```
    stringBuffer.append("The following products are listed as per the
hit rate \n");
    int i = 1;
    for (String productname : sortedProductList) {
      stringBuffer.append(" [" + i + "] " + productname + " and the
score is "
          + jedis.zscore(tagname.toLowerCase(), productname) + "\n");
      i++;
    }
    this.returnConnection(jedis);
    return stringBuffer.toString();
  }
  public List<String> getTopProducts(int slotfortag, String tag) {
    Jedis jedis = this.getConnection();
    Set<String> sortedProductList = jedis.zrevrange(tag.toLowerCase(),
0, 100000000);
    List<String> topproducts = new ArrayList<String>();
    Iterator<String> iterator = sortedProductList.iterator();
    int index = 0;
    while (iterator.hasNext()) {
      if (index <= slotfortag) {
        topproducts.add(iterator.next());
        index++;
      } else {
        break;
      }
    }
    this.returnConnection(jedis);
    return topproducts;
  }
}
```

ShoppingCartDBManager

This class extends the `RedisDBManager` and is responsible for shopping cart-related functional calls to the data base. The implementation is as follows:

```
package org.learningRedis.web.util;
import java.util.Map;
import java.util.Set;
import Redis.clients.jedis.Jedis;
public class ShoppingCartDBManager extends RedisDBManager {
  private ShoppingCartDBManager() {
  }
```

```
  public static ShoppingCartDBManager singleton = new
ShoppingCartDBManager();
  public String addToShoppingCart(String sessionid, Map<String,
String> productQtyMap) {
    Jedis jedis = this.getConnection();
    String result = jedis.hmset(sessionid + "@shoppingcart",
productQtyMap);
    this.returnConnection(jedis);
    return result;
  }
  public Map<String, String> myCartInfo(String sessionid) {
    Jedis jedis = this.getConnection();
    Map<String, String> shoppingcart = jedis.hgetAll(sessionid + "@
shoppingcart");
    this.returnConnection(jedis);
    return shoppingcart;
  }
  public String editMyCart(String sessionID, Map<String, String>
productQtyMap) {
    Jedis jedis = this.getConnection();
    String result = "";
    if (jedis.exists(sessionID + "@shoppingcart")) {
      Set<String> keySet = productQtyMap.keySet();
      for (String key : keySet) {
        if (jedis.hexists(sessionID + "@shoppingcart", key)) {
          Integer intValue = new Integer(productQtyMap.get(key)).
intValue();
          if (intValue == 0) {
            jedis.hdel(sessionID + "@shoppingcart", key);
          } else if (intValue > 0) {
            jedis.hset(sessionID + "@shoppingcart", key,
productQtyMap.get(key));
          }
        }
      }
      result = "Updated the shopping cart for user";
    } else {
      result = "Could not update the shopping cart for the user !! ";
    }
    this.returnConnection(jedis);
    return result;
  }
  public String buyItemsInTheShoppingCart(String sessionid) {
    Jedis jedis = this.getConnection();
```

```
    Map<String, String> cartInfo = jedis.hgetAll(sessionid + "@
shoppingcart");
    Set<String> procductNameList = cartInfo.keySet();
    StringBuffer stringBuffer = new StringBuffer();
    stringBuffer.append("RECEIPT: You have purchased the following
\n");
    stringBuffer.append("-----------------------------------" + "\n");
    int i = 1;
    for (String productname : procductNameList) {
      String unitCost = jedis.hget(productname, "cost");
      int unitCostValue = new Integer(unitCost).intValue();
      String quantity = cartInfo.get(productname);
      int quantityValue = new Integer(quantity).intValue();
      stringBuffer.append("[" + i + "] Name of item : " + productname
+ " and quantity was : " + quantity
          + " the total cost is = " + quantityValue * unitCostValue +
"\n");
      i++;
    }
    stringBuffer.append("-----------------------------------------");
    stringBuffer.append("#");
    for (String productname : procductNameList) {
      stringBuffer.append(productname);
      stringBuffer.append(",");
    }
    // Update the user purchase history:
    String name = jedis.hget(sessionid + "@sessiondata", "name");
    for (String productname : procductNameList) {
      jedis.lpush(name + "@purchasehistory", productname + " on " +
getDate());
    }
    this.returnConnection(jedis);
    return stringBuffer.toString();
  }
}
```

UserCartDBManager

This class extends the `RedisDBManager` and is responsible for user related functional calls to the data base. The implementation is as follows:

```
package org.learningRedis.web.util;
import java.util.Date;
import java.util.HashMap;
import java.util.Map;
```

```
import Redis.clients.jedis.Jedis;
public class UserDBManager extends RedisDBManager {
  private UserDBManager() {
  }
  public static UserDBManager singleton = new UserDBManager();
  public String getUserName(String sessionID) {
    Jedis jedis = this.getConnection();
    String name = jedis.hget(sessionID + "@sessiondata", "name");
    this.returnConnection(jedis);
    return name;
  }
  public void createUser(Map<String, String> attriuteMap) {
    Jedis jedis = this.getConnection();
    Map<String, String> map = attriuteMap;
    map.put("creation-time", new Date().toString());
    map.put("sessionID", "null");
    jedis.hmset(attriuteMap.get("name") + "@userdata", map);
    this.returnConnection(jedis);
  }
  public Map<String, String> getRegistrationMap(String name) {
    Jedis jedis = this.getConnection();
    Map<String, String> attributeMap = new HashMap<String, String>();
    attributeMap = jedis.hgetAll(name + "@userdata");
    this.returnConnection(jedis);
    return attributeMap;
  }
  public boolean doesUserExist(String name) {
    Jedis jedis = this.getConnection();
    String value = jedis.hget(name + "@userdata", "name");
    this.returnConnection(jedis);
    if (value == null) {
      return false;
    } else if (value != null & value.equals(name)) {
      return true;
    } else {
      return false;
    }
  }
  public void setRegistrationMap(String name, Map<String, String>
attributeMap) {
    Jedis jedis = this.getConnection();
    jedis.hmset(name + "@userdata", attributeMap);
    this.returnConnection(jedis);
  }
```

```
  public String getUserPassword(String name) {
    Jedis jedis = this.getConnection();
    String password = jedis.hget(name + "@userdata", "password");
    this.returnConnection(jedis);
    return password;
  }
  public void login(String sessionID, String name) {
    Jedis jedis = this.getConnection();
    Map<String, String> loginMap = new HashMap<String, String>();
    loginMap.put("LastLogin", new Date().toString());
    loginMap.put("loginstatus", "LoggedIn");
    loginMap.put("sessionID", sessionID);
    loginMap.put("name", name);
    jedis.hmset(sessionID + "@sessiondata", loginMap);
    this.returnConnection(jedis);
  }
  public boolean editRegistrationMap(Map<String, String> editMap) {
    Jedis jedis = this.getConnection();
    if (jedis.hget(editMap.get("name") + "@userdata", "sessionID").
equals(editMap.get("sessionid"))) {
      jedis.hmset(editMap.get("name") + "@userdata", editMap);
      this.returnConnection(jedis);
      return true;
    } else {
      this.returnConnection(jedis);
      return false;
    }
  }
  public String getUserSessionId(String name) {
    Jedis jedis = this.getConnection();
    String sessionID = jedis.hget(name + "@userdata", "sessionID");
    this.returnConnection(jedis);
    return sessionID;
  }
  public boolean expireSession(String sessionid) {
    // Get name from session data structure
    Jedis jedis = this.getConnection();
    String name = jedis.hget(sessionid + "@sessiondata", "name");
    // remove session id from userdata
    if (name != null) {
      Long sessionvalue = new Long(jedis.hget(name + "@userdata",
"sessionID"));
      jedis.hset(name + "@userdata", "sessionID", "null");
      // remove session data : use TTL
```

```
        if (jedis.exists(sessionid + "@sessiondata")) {
          jedis.expire(sessionid + "@sessiondata", 1);
        }
        // remove browsing history : use TTL
        if (jedis.exists(sessionid + "@browsinghistory")) {
          jedis.expire(sessionid + "@browsinghistory", 1);
        }
        // remove shopping cart : use TTL
        if (jedis.exists(sessionid + "@shoppingcart")) {
          jedis.expire(sessionid + "@shoppingcart", 1);
        }
        // make the value at offset as '0'
        jedis.setbit("sessionIdTracker", sessionvalue, false);
        this.returnConnection(jedis);
        return true;
      } else {
        this.returnConnection(jedis);
        return false;
      }
    }
    public boolean doesSessionExist(String sessionid) {
      Jedis jedis = this.getConnection();
      if (jedis.hexists(sessionid + "@sessiondata", "name")) {
        this.returnConnection(jedis);
        return true;
      } else {
        this.returnConnection(jedis);
        return false;
      }
    }
  }
```

Summary

So in this chapter, we learnt how to make a simple e-commerce site with Redis as its backbone. Also, we learnt how Redis can come handy for doing online analytics. This sample site lacked the capability for scalability which we learnt in the previous chapters. I would urge the readers to add that capability to this code base as an exercise and have fun with this awesome datastore.

In the next chapter, I will divulge how to use Redis in business applications, and make a few applications that are commonly used in all the business applications.

7
Redis in Business Applications

In *Chapter 6, Redis in Web Applications*, you saw how Redis can be useful in web applications. This usefulness of Redis can be extended to business applications. As with any enterprise, the outer layer or the boundary application usually comprises of a web application, which in a way encapsulates the core heterogeneous business applications. These business applications form the core backbone of the enterprise.

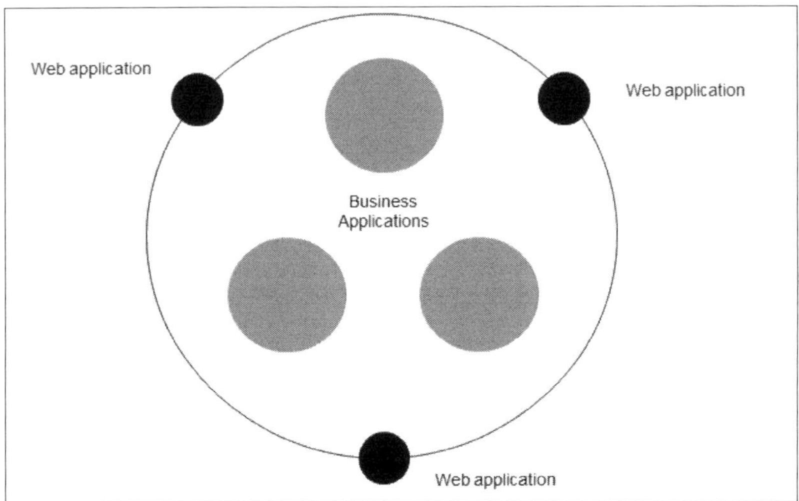

Simple representation of application in an enterprise ecosystem

As many of you will have experienced in your projects and assignments over the years, these business applications are as varied as one can imagine in their business functionality. However, they all share some features and aspects that are common to most of them. In this chapter, we will take a few of these features and see how Redis fits into the landscape of business applications. To begin with, the most common and humble feature in any application is **configuration management**.

The subsequent topic takes into consideration configuration management and puts in Redis as a core component in constructing an enterprise-level application.

Configuration management

Very often, you may have seen improper configuration management or the lack of it create problems at a later point in the development and maintenance life cycles. Another problem is when scalability comes into picture and more nodes of software are added; then, maintaining state across all the nodes becomes a challenge. Business applications have been relying on RDBMS to store configuration data. The problem with this approach is performance; if the design is **PULL**-based and the problem with **PULL**-based design is performance penalty. Another problem is if the concurrency is high (because of other business functionalities), then these RDBMS also have to cater to these requests as well as the requests for configuration data.

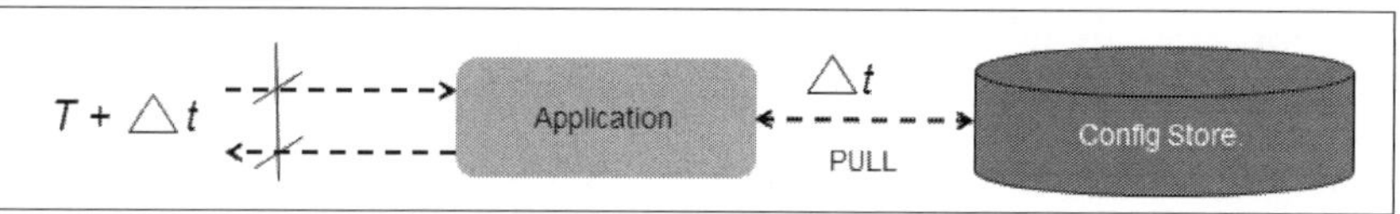

PULL-based design for config management

The idea is to convert the design from **PULL**-based to **PUSH**-based. The big advantage of this technique is performance. The state or configuration data stays close to the application, and whenever change takes place, the data is pushed to the local cache of the application. Another requirement is to have a system that is low on the compute resource footprint.

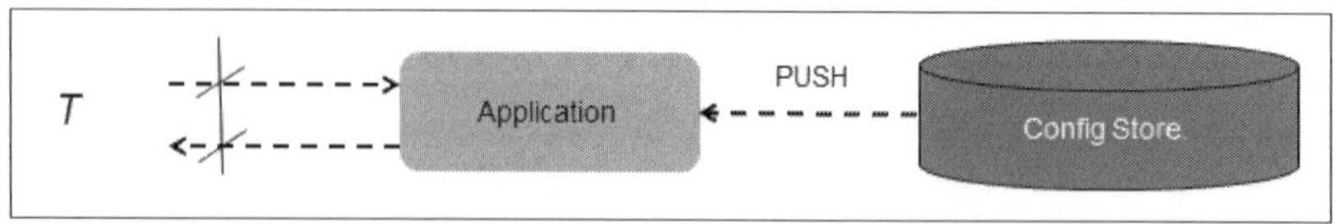

PUSH-based design for config management

Redis with its Swiss knife-like capability, low resource footprint, availability of client libraries in various languages, and capability to scale massively makes it a good candidate to be used to take care of this requirement. The sample application that we are going to discuss in subsequent topics will highlight that. This sample application is just for demo and does not take any guarantee in the production environment. So, let's have some fun developing one configuration management server with Redis as the backbone, and let's call it the **gossip server**.

Gossip server

The gossip server is a centralized node that manages configuration data and groups services in a synchronized way. The **Gossip Server** will hold data and will be managed by a node called the **Gossip Server (Admin)**. The **Gossip Server** in turn will manage all the other nodes hooked to it. The following diagram depicts that it is the responsibility of the gossip server to push configuration data to all the nodes that are connected to it:

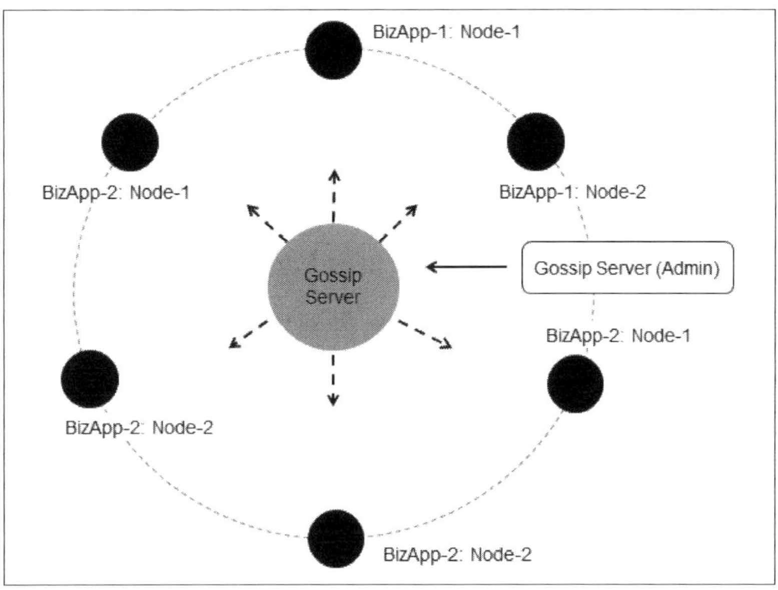

Gossip Server design overview

Internal to this gossip server is the Redis server, which provides all the capabilities that might be required by the proposed configuration management system. The nodes can be implemented in any programming language, but keeping in tradition with the examples in the book, we are going to use Java as the language of implementation in this example. The main idea of this gossip server is to keep aside a common component for configuration management the next time that you need to architect or design an enterprise grade solution, and to keep in mind Redis when doing so.

Before we get into the implementation and design specifications of our common component, let's agree upon the capabilities of this gossip server.

The following are the capabilities of the gossip server:

- The gossip server maintains all the information or configuration data
- It acts like a hub and distributes the information or configuration data to all the connected nodes
- All the nodes, including the master node, connect to the hub in order to send messages
- The master node is responsible for pushing data to a specific client node or all the client nodes
- All the client nodes are in the same position in the hierarchy
- All the client nodes can be embedded in the solutions that are to be made a part of this configuration management
- The nodes have a life cycle and they are managed by themselves
- The nodes, when they change state, inform the master and other peer client nodes
- The nodes can also send messages to other peer nodes if the business logic demands

Node

A node in the gossip server is the client component between which all the messages flow. In the current example, the node can be classified into two types, client nodes and the master node.

The client node is inherently meant to be the component that can be plugged into any solution where there is a need for configuration management. The client nodes are responsible for the application data that they store in Redis. Data in the node can come either from the application they are plugged into or from the master node, which can push the data to the client node. The whole idea behind allowing the master node to push data or rather publish data into the gossip server is to spread the control of the configuration data of the application from the application itself to another source. The benefit of doing this will be to take out the responsibility of the configuration data management from the application and have a centralized node from where data can be managed. Another advantage is that new configuration data can be introduced into the application at runtime without stopping the application.

The following diagram is a representation of the configuration data pushing capability of the gossip server:

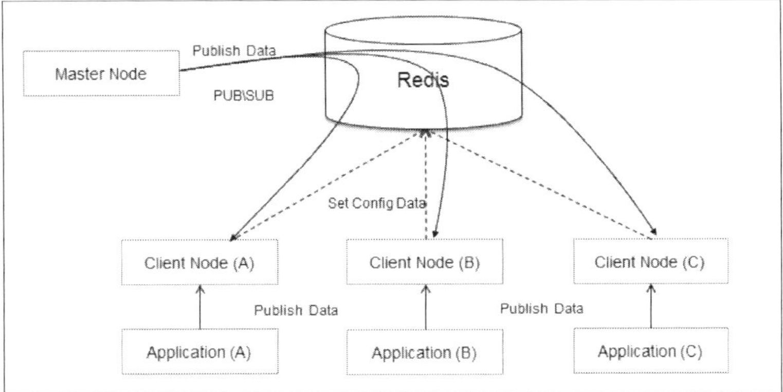

Pushing data into Gossip Server either via application or master node

Before we go further into the implementation, it's better to understand the various states that the client node can traverse in its life cycle. The following diagram is a snapshot of the various paths that the client node can take:

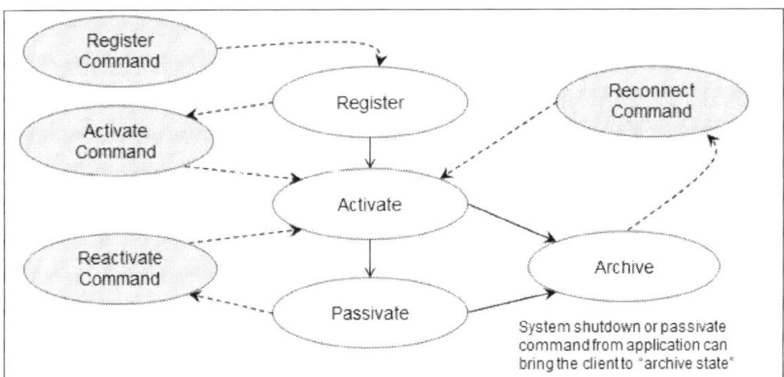

Pushing data into Gossip Server either via application or master node

The client node begins its journey with **Register**. After **Register**, the client node needs to **Activate** itself. Once the client node is activated, it can either **Passivate** itself or reach the **Archive** state. The **Archive** state can be achieved if the application is brought down or a `Kill` command is sent by the master node. Once the client node is in the **Passivate** state, it can be made **Activate** through an intermediate state of **Reactivate**. If the client node is in the **Archive** state, it can be brought to the **Activate** state via an intermediary state of **Reconnect**.

The commands for the client node are modelled around the mentioned states, and there are other commands for the management of data and for messaging data around the ecosystem. Without wasting much time, let's dive into the design of the system.

Layered design

The design for the gossip server is minimalistic and very simple to follow, but there are certain considerations to be kept in mind. As discussed, the nodes participating in the gossip server are of two types: client nodes and master nodes. Every client node is responsible for its own life cycle, and the master node has limited control over it. The nodes can communicate with each other by passing messages. The design includes four primary layers, as depicted in the following diagram:

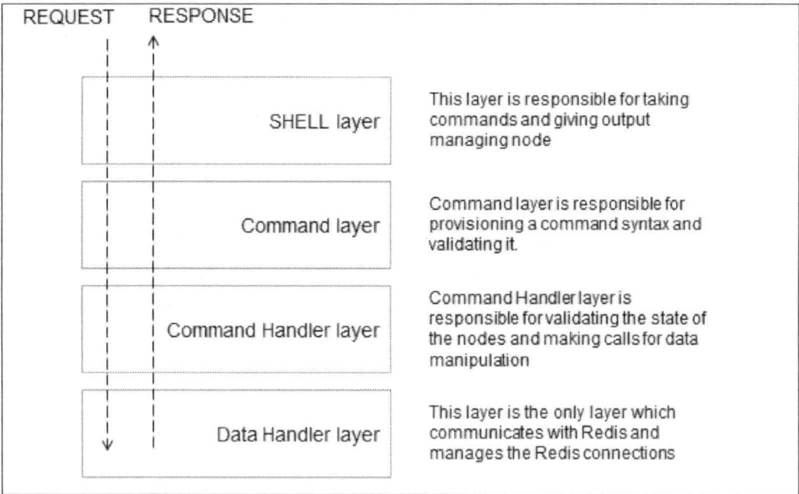

Gossip Server structural layers overview

The packages in the gossip server correspond to the layers described in the preceding diagram and include a few extra. Let's have a brief introduction of the packages and the classes they contain. Here's a list of the packages and the layers they correspond to:

- `org.redisch7.gossipserver.shell`: This corresponds to the **Shell layer**
- `org.redisch7.gossipserver.commands`: This corresponds to the **Command layer**
- `org.redisch7.gossipserver.commandhandlers`: This corresponds to the **Command Handler layer**

- `org.redisch7.gossipserver.datahandler`: This corresponds to the **Data Handler layer**
- `org.redisch7.gossipserver.util.commandparser`: This is a utility package

Shell

Shell is a program that acts like a standalone gateway to the gossip server as well as a plugin to an application that wants to use the gossip server. The shell activates the node, which in turn prepares the listeners and the command library for the node. As discussed, there are two types of nodes: client nodes and master nodes; a detailed discussion of these nodes is done in the latter portion of the chapter.

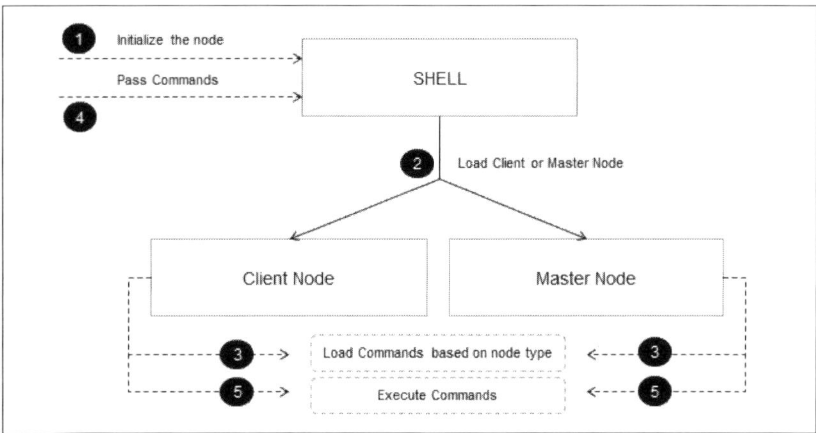

Interaction with shell

The code for the gossip server is simple and basically commands delegation to the node for processing. In the case of Shell as a standalone program, the response is displayed in Command Prompt, whereas in the case of Shell as an API plugin, the result object `CheckResult` is passed back to the program calling it. Shell is implemented as a singleton. This is the code for `Shell.java`:

```
package org.redisch7.gossipserver.shell;
/** omitting the import statements**/
public class Shell {
  private Shell() {}
  private Node      node     = null;
  private static Shell  singleton  = new Shell();
  public static Shell instance() {
    return singleton;
  }
```

```
  // : as an shell API mode.
  public Shell asClient(String nodename) {
    if (node != null && nodename != null && nodename.trim().length()
!= 0) {
      node = new ClientNode(nodename);
      return this;
    } else {
      return null;
    }
  }
  public Shell asMaster() {
    if (node != null) {
      node = new MasterNode();
      return this;
    } else {
      return null;
    }
  }
  public CheckResult execute(String commands) {
    CheckResult checkResult = new CheckResult();
    if (commands != null && commands.trim().length() == 0) {
      checkResult = node.process(commands);
    }
    return checkResult;
  }
  // : as a shell standalone mode.
  public static void main(String[] args) throws IOException {
    Shell shell = Shell.instance();
    shell.startInteracting();
  }
  private void startInteracting() throws IOException {
    System.out.println("Please enter the name of the node..");
    BufferedReader nodenameReader = new BufferedReader(new
InputStreamReader(System.in));
    String nodename = nodenameReader.readLine();
    if (nodename.equals("master")) {
      node = new MasterNode();
    } else {
      node = new ClientNode(nodename);
    }
    while (true) {
      BufferedReader commandReader = new BufferedReader(new
InputStreamReader(System.in));
      String readline = commandReader.readLine();
```

```
        if (readline == null) {
          System.out.println("Ctrl + C ");
          break;
        } else {
          CheckResult checkResult = node.process(readline);
          System.out.println(":->" + checkResult.getResult());
          System.out.println(":->" + checkResult.getReason());
          System.out.println(":->" + checkResult.getValue());
        }
      }
      System.exit(0);
    }
  }
```

Listeners

Listeners are spawned by nodes and execute independently of the thread executing the Shell. The basic job of a listener is to constantly listen for any message event coming to the node. The message is then parsed and executed accordingly. The basic idea is to provide a mechanism for the nodes to interact with each other. In the current implementation, it's the master node that interacts with the client nodes. This provides a limited remote control of the master over the client nodes. The implementation for the other way around communication is not done and can be incorporated easily if the need arises, that is, if the client nodes interact with the master node. Not all commands can be remotely executed on client nodes via this arrangement. Commands that can be executed remotely (by the master node) are `SET`, `KILL`, and `CLONE`.

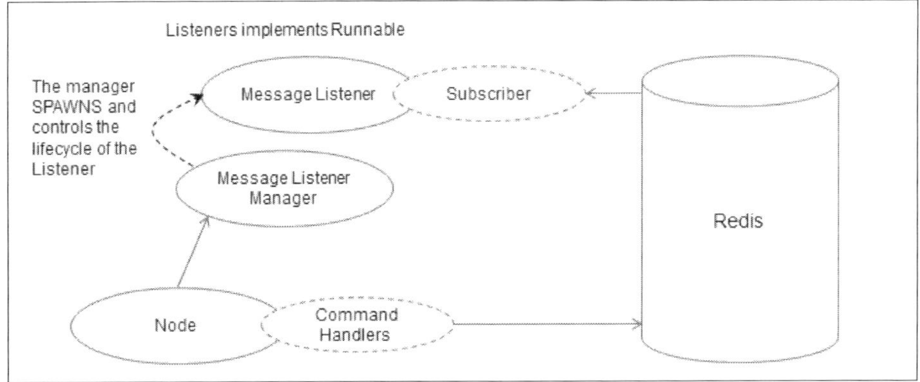

Relation between Node, Message Listener Manager, Meassage Listeners, and Subscriber

Listeners internally have a subscriber that extends the `JedisPubSub` abstract class, which is Jedis's client library's hook to Redis's messaging capability. The node maintains the life cycle of the listeners. The node activates the listeners on some commands, such as **Activate**, **Reconnect**, and so on, and deactivates on some commands, such as `Passivate`, `KILL`, and so on.

Here's the code for the client listener, which is `ClientEventMessageListener`.Java:

```
package org.redisch7.gossipserver.shell;
/** omitting the import statements **/
public class ClientEventMessageListener implements Runnable {
  private Subscriber subscriber = null;
  private Node node;
  private Jedis jedis = ConnectionManager.get();
  private Validator validator = null;
  public ClientEventMessageListener(Node node) {
    this.node = node;
    this.subscriber = new Subscriber(node);
  }
  @Override
  public void run() {
    while (!Thread.currentThread().isInterrupted()) {
      jedis.subscribe(subscriber, node.getNodename());
    }
  }
  public void unsubscribe() {
    subscriber.unsubscribe(node.getNodename());
  }
  public class Subscriber extends JedisPubSub {
    public Subscriber(Node clientNode) {
    }
    @Override
    public void onMessage(String nodename, String readmessage) {
      validator = new Validator();
      validator.configureTemplate().add(new MapListToken());
      validator.setInput(readmessage);
      CheckResult checkResult = validator.validate();
      if (checkResult.getResult()) {
        MapListToken mapListToken = (MapListToken) validator
            .getToken(0);
        if (mapListToken.containsKey("command")) {
          String commandValue = mapListToken.getNValue("command");
          if (commandValue.equals("set")) {
```

```
            MapListToken newMapListToken = mapListToken
                .removeElement("command");
            SetCommand command = new SetCommand();
            command.setName(node.getNodename());
            CheckResult result = command.execute(new CommandTokens(
                "set "
                    + newMapListToken
                        .getValueAsSantizedString()));
            System.out.println(result.getResult());
            System.out.println(result.getReason());
          } else if (commandValue.equals("kill")) {
            KillNodeCommand command = new KillNodeCommand();
            command.setName(node.getNodename());
            MapListToken newMapListToken = mapListToken
                .removeElement("command");
            CheckResult result = command.execute(new CommandTokens(
                "kill " + node.getNodename()));
            System.out.println(result.getResult());
            System.out.println(result.getReason());
          } else if (commandValue.equals("clone")) {
            CloneNodeCommand command = new CloneNodeCommand();
            command.setName(node.getNodename());
            MapListToken newMapListToken = mapListToken
                .removeElement("command");
            CheckResult result = command.execute(new CommandTokens(
                "clone "
                    + newMapListToken
                        .getValueAsSantizedString()));
            System.out.println(result.getResult());
            System.out.println(result.getReason());
          } else {
            MessageCommand messageCommand = new MessageCommand();
            messageCommand.setName(nodename);
            CommandTokens commandTokens = new CommandTokens(
                "msg master where msg=illegal_command");
            messageCommand.execute(commandTokens);
          }
        } else {
          System.out
              .println(":->"
                  + checkResult
                      .appendReason("The command sent from publisher
does not contain 'command' token"));
```

```
          }
        } else {
          System.out.println(":->" + checkResult.getReason());
        }
      }
      @Override
      public void onPMessage(String arg0, String arg1, String arg2) {
        System.out.println(arg1);
        System.out.println(arg2);
      }
      @Override
      public void onPSubscribe(String arg0, int arg1) {
      }
      @Override
      public void onPUnsubscribe(String arg0, int arg1) {
      }
      @Override
      public void onSubscribe(String arg0, int arg1) {
      }
      @Override
      public void onUnsubscribe(String arg0, int arg1) {
      }
    }
  }
```

Here's the code for the master listener, that is, `MasterEventMessageListener.java`:

```
package org.redisch7.gossipserver.shell;
/** omitting the import statements **/
public class MasterEventMessageListener implements Runnable {
  private Subscriber  subscriber  = null;
  private Node    node;
  private Jedis    jedis    = ConnectionManager.get();
  private Validator  validator  = new Validator();
  public MasterEventMessageListener(Node node) {
    this.node = node;
    this.subscriber = new Subscriber(node);
    validator.configureTemplate().add(new MapListToken());
  }
  @Override
  public void run() {
    while (!Thread.currentThread().isInterrupted()) {
      jedis.subscribe(subscriber, node.getNodename());
    }
  }
```

```
    public void unsubscribe() {
      subscriber.unsubscribe(node.getNodename());
    }
    public class Subscriber extends JedisPubSub {
      public Subscriber(Node node) {
      }
      @Override
      public void onMessage(String nodename, String readmessage) {
        System.out.println("msg: " + readmessage);
        System.out.println("Not processed further in the current 
implementation");
      }
      @Override
      public void onPMessage(String arg0, String arg1, String arg2) {
        System.out.println(arg1);
        System.out.println(arg2);
      }
      @Override
      public void onPSubscribe(String arg0, int arg1) {}
      @Override
      public void onPUnsubscribe(String arg0, int arg1) {}
      @Override
      public void onSubscribe(String arg0, int arg1) {}
      @Override
      public void onUnsubscribe(String arg0, int arg1) {}
    }
  }
```

Listener manager

Listener managers are responsible for maintaining the life cycle of the listeners. Listeners can either exist in the start mode or in the stop mode. The gossip server has an event-oriented design; therefore, on every event that the client node accepts, there is a corresponding command that gets executed.

In the system, there are two types of listener managers, one for the client node called the client node listener manager and the other for the master node called master node listener manager.

The client node listener manager is programmed to start the listeners on commands such as `Activate`, `Reactivate`, and `Reconnect` and to stop the listeners on commands such as `Passivate` and `Kill`.

The master node listener manager is programmed to start the listener on commands such as `Start` and to stop on commands such as `Stop`.

The following is the code for `ClientNodeListenerManager.java`:

```
package org.redisch7.gossipserver.shell;
/** omitting the import statements **/
public class ClientNodeListenerManager implements
NodeMessageListenerManager {
  private String              nodename;
  private ClientEventMessageListener  privateEventMessageSubscriber;
  private Thread              commonEventThread;
  private Thread              privateEventThread;
  public ClientNodeListenerManager(ClientNode clientNode) {
    this.nodename = clientNode.getNodename();
    privateEventMessageSubscriber = new ClientEventMessageListener(cl
ientNode);
  }
  @Override
  public void start() {
    System.out.println(" start the client node manager .. ");
    privateEventThread = new Thread(privateEventMessageSubscriber);
    commonEventThread.start();
    privateEventThread.start();
  }
  @Override
  public void stop() {
    System.out.println(" stop the client node manager .. ");
    privateEventMessageSubscriber.unsubscribe();
    commonEventThread.interrupt();
    privateEventThread.interrupt();
  }
  @Override
  public void passCommand(AbstractCommand command) {
    if (command instanceof ActivateCommand || command instanceof
ReactivateCommand
        || command instanceof ReConnectCommand) {
      this.start();
    } else if (command instanceof PassivateCommand || command
instanceof KillNodeCommand) {
      this.stop();
    }
  }
}
```

Here's the code for `MasterNodeListenerManager.java`:

```
package org.redisch7.gossipserver.shell;
/** omitting the import statements **/
public class MasterNodeListenerManager implements
NodeMessageListenerManager {
  private MasterEventMessageListener  masterEventMessageSubscriber;
  private Thread            privateEventThread;
  private MasterNode          masternode;
  public MasterNodeListenerManager(MasterNode masterNode) {
    this.masternode = masterNode;
    masterEventMessageSubscriber = new MasterEventMessageListener(mas
ternode);
  }
  @Override
  public void start() {
    System.out.println(" start the master node manager .. ");
    privateEventThread = new Thread(masterEventMessageSubscriber);
    privateEventThread.start();
  }
  @Override
  public void stop() {
    System.out.println(" stop the master node manager .. ");
    privateEventThread.interrupt();
    masterEventMessageSubscriber.unsubscribe();
  }
  @Override
  public void passCommand(AbstractCommand command) {
    if (command instanceof StartMasterCommand) {
      this.start();
    } else if (command instanceof StopMasterCommand) {
      this.stop();
    }
  }
}
```

The data handler layer

This layer or package is straightforward in its activity, such as interacting with the Redis server. This layer is responsible for encapsulating Redis from the rest of the application.

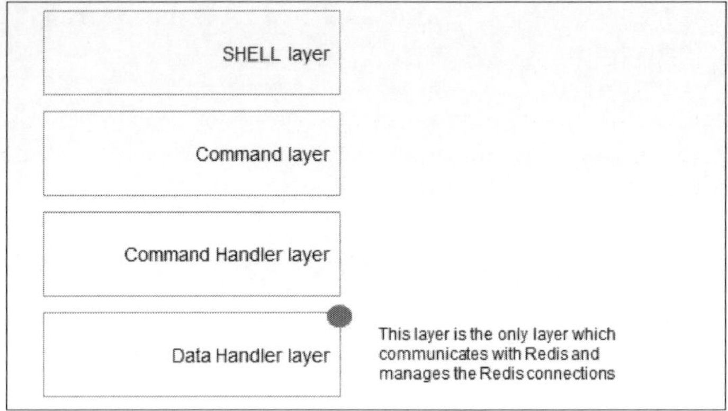

Gossip Server structural layers overview

The following are the data structures used for the current application:

- **Registration holder**: This is going to be implemented as a Set in the Redis datastore. This will hold all the nodes that are going to be registered in the system.
- **Activation holder**: This is going to be implemented as a Set in the Redis data store. This will hold all the nodes that are going to be in the `Active` state.
- **Passivation holder**: This is going to be implemented as a Set in the Redis data store. This will hold all the nodes that are going to be in the **Passive** state.
- **Configuration store**: This is going to be implemented as a Map in the Redis data store. This will hold all the configuration data pertaining to a node in the name-value format.
- **Archive store**: This is going to be implemented as a File store in the local file system of the client node. This will hold all the configuration data pertaining to a node in the name-value format that is going to be archived in the JSON format.

The most important class in this layer is `JedisUtilImpl`; let's spend some time understanding this class. The very nature of this class makes this class pretty big but easy to understand.

JedisUtil.java

This class is instrumental in conversing with the data store. All the logic around managing the account, state, and data of a node is managed here.

Note that we are using `jedis_2.1.0` as our choice of client API in order to connect to Redis. There is a bug related to using `MULTI` in `PIPELINE` functions with this version of the client library.

```
Exception in thread "main" java.lang.ClassCastException:
[B cannot be cast to java.util.List at redis.clients.
jedis.Connection.getBinaryMultiBulkReply(Connection.
java:189)
    at redis.clients.jedis.Jedis.hgetAll(Jedis.java:861)
    at com.work.jedisex.JedisFactory.main(JedisFactory.
java:59)
```

Since Redis is single-thread server, we have sacrificed the use of `MULTI` in `PIPELINE` for this application, as this will have no implications on the sanctity of the data in Redis and minimally affect the performance. We have gone ahead with sending our commands singularly and not in bulk, as in the case of `PIPELINE`. The future API of Jedis might have a solution for this, and it is up to you to change the class as you see fit if you are using a newer version of Jedis.

Client implementation in other languages or other client implementations for Redis in Java, will not have a problem as this is specific to Jedis.

Now that we have an understanding of the `JedisUtil` class, we in a way understand the working of the gossip server and the capabilities that the gossip server has to offer. So, let's focus on the commands and how they are implemented. As a rule of thumb, the flow of data can be summarized as shown in the following diagram:

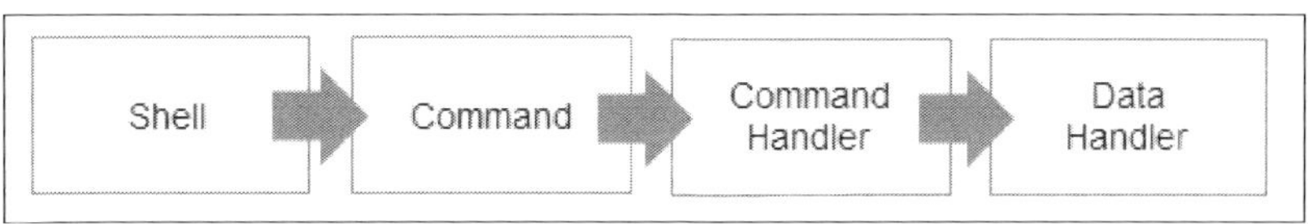

Sequence of flow of data in a command

Client node commands

The following is a list of commands that can be fired from client nodes:

- The `register` command
- The `activate` command
- The `set` command
- The `get` command
- The `status` command
- The `del` command
- The `passivate` command
- The `reacyivate` command
- The `archive` command
- The `sync` command
- The `reconnect` command

Let's take a look at each command from a design and implementation perspective.

The register command

This command will register the node into the gossip server ecosystem. The precondition for executing this command is that the node name should be unique; otherwise, a response of failure will be sent to the **Shell**. The node name will be stored in the Registration holder, which is implemented as a Set data structure in Redis. Apart from this, when the registration process takes place, an archive file is created in the local machine of the node.

Sequence of flow of data in a Register command

The syntax for this command is: `register`. The following screenshot shows the response in the Shell console:

```
register
:->true
:->Registration Successful
```

Implementation of RegisterCommand

The RegisterCommand is implemented as shown in the following code snippet:

```
package org.redisch7.gossipserver.commands;
/* OMITTING THE IMPORT STATEMENTS TO SAVE SPACE */
public class RegisterCommand extends AbstractCommand {
  private Validator validator = new Validator();
  public RegisterCommand() {
    validator.configureTemplate().add((new StringToken("register")));
  }
  @Override
  public CheckResult execute(CommandTokens commandTokens) {
    CheckResult checkResult = new CheckResult();
    validator.setInput(commandTokens);
    checkResult = validator.validate();
    if (checkResult.getResult()) {
      List<Token> tokenList = validator.getAllTokens();
      checkResult = new RegisterCommandHandler(this.getName()).
process(tokenList);
    }
    if(checkResult.getResult()){
      String path = System.getProperty("user.home") + "\\archive\\";
      File file = new File(path);
      if (!file.exists()) {
        if (file.mkdir()) {
          checkResult.appendReason("Archive folder created!");
        } else {
          checkResult.appendReason("Archive folder exists!");
        }
      }
    }
    return checkResult;
  }
}
```

Implementation of RegisterCommandHandler

The RegisterCommandHandler is implemented as shown in the following code snippet:

```
package org.redisch7.gossipserver.commandhandlers;
/* OMITTING THE IMPORT STATEMENTS TO SAVE SPACE */
public class RegisterCommandHandler extends AbstractCommandHandler {
  public RegisterCommandHandler(String nodename) {
```

```
        super(nodename);
    }
    public CheckResult process(List<Token> tokenList) {
        CheckResult checkResult = new CheckResult();
        JedisUtil jedisUtil = new JedisUtil();
        List<Boolean> result = jedisUtil
            .doesExist(this.getNodename(), Arrays
                .asList(ConstUtil.registerationHolder,
                    ConstUtil.activationHolder,
                    ConstUtil.passivationHolder, ConstUtil.
shutdownHolder));
        if ((result.get(0) == false) && (result.get(1) == false)
            && (result.get(2) == false)&& (result.get(3) == false)) {
          checkResult = jedisUtil.registerNode(this.getNodename());
        } else {
          checkResult
              .setFalse("Activation Validation :")
              .appendReason(
                  ConstUtil.registerationHolder + " = "
                      + ((Boolean) result.get(0)))
              .appendReason(
                  ConstUtil.activationHolder + " = "
                      + ((Boolean) result.get(1)))
              .appendReason(
                  ConstUtil.passivationHolder + " = "
                      + ((Boolean) result.get(2)));
        }
        return checkResult;
    }
}
```

The activate command

This command will activate the node into the gossip server ecosystem. The precondition for executing this command is that the node should be registered. When the node is activated, an entry is added to the ACTIVATION-HOLDER, which is implemented as Set in Redis. Apart from this, on activation, the client node will spawn listeners, which will be up and ready to listen to any event that can come from the master. The listeners will be basically listening for events on a separate thread.

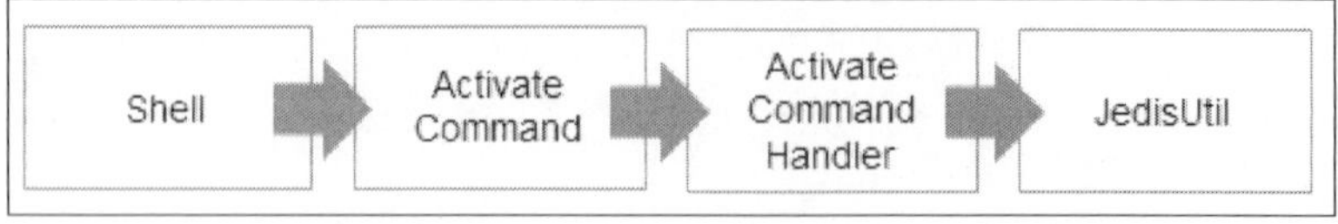

Sequence of flow of data in Activate command

The syntax for this command is: `activate`. The following screenshot shows the response in the shell console:

```
activate
:->true
:->Activation Successful
```

Implementation of ActivateCommand

The ActivateCommand is implemented as shown in the following code snippet:

```
package org.redisch7.gossipserver.commands;
/* OMITTING THE IMPORT STATEMENTS TO SAVE SPACE */
public class ActivateCommand extends AbstractCommand {
  private Validator validator = new Validator();
  public ActivateCommand() {
    validator.configureTemplate().add((new StringToken("activate")));
  }
  @Override
  public CheckResult execute(CommandTokens commandTokens) {
    CheckResult checkResult = new CheckResult();
    validator.setInput(commandTokens);
    checkResult = validator.validate();
    if (checkResult.getResult()) {
      List<Token> tokenList = validator.getAllTokens();
      checkResult = new ActivateCommandHandler(this.getName()).
process(tokenList);
    }
    return checkResult;
  }
}
```

Implementation of ActivateCommandHandler

The ActivateCommandHandler is implemented as shown in the following code snippet:

```
package org.redisch7.gossipserver.commandhandlers;
/* OMITTING THE IMPORT STATEMENTS TO SAVE SPACE */
public final class ActivateCommandHandler extends
AbstractCommandHandler {
  public ActivateCommandHandler(String nodename) {
    super(nodename);
  }
```

```
    public CheckResult process(List<Token> tokenList) {
      CheckResult checkResult = new CheckResult();
      JedisUtil jedisUtil = new JedisUtil();
      List<Boolean> result = jedisUtil.doesExist(this.getNodename(),
  Arrays
          .asList(ConstUtil.registerationHolder,
              ConstUtil.activationHolder,
              ConstUtil.passivationHolder, ConstUtil.shutdownHolder));
      if ((result.get(0) == true) && (result.get(1) == false)
          && (result.get(2) == false) && (result.get(3) == false)) {
        checkResult = jedisUtil.activateNode(this.getNodename());
      } else {
        checkResult
            .setFalse("Activation Failed :")
            .appendReason(
                ConstUtil.registerationHolder + " = "
                    + ((Boolean) result.get(0)))
            .appendReason(
                ConstUtil.activationHolder + " = "
                    + ((Boolean) result.get(1)))
            .appendReason(
                ConstUtil.passivationHolder + " = "
                    + ((Boolean) result.get(2)))
            .appendReason(
                ConstUtil.shutdownHolder + " = "
                    + ((Boolean) result.get(3)));
      }
      return checkResult;
    }
  }
```

The set command

This command will set the data in the nodes. The precondition for executing this command is that the node should be in the activated state. The command is going to insert the name values into the node's *Config-store*. The *Config store* is implemented as the Hashes data structure in Redis. As evident, multiple name-value pairs can be inserted in the *Config store*.

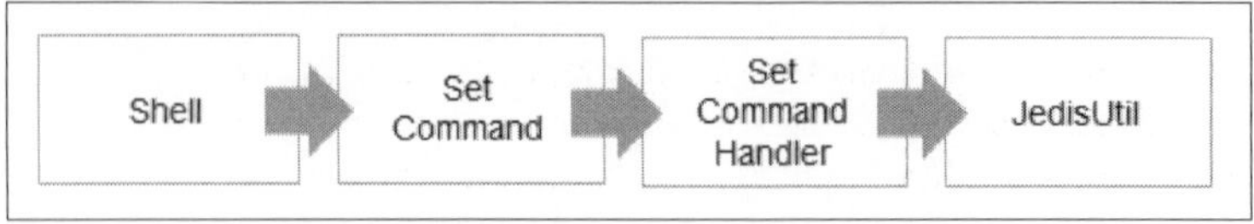

Sequence of flow of data in Set command

The syntax for this command is: `set <name=value>,<name=value>`. The following screenshot shows the response in the Shell console:

```
set x=200,y=500
:->true
:->setting done in vinoo
```

Implementation of SetCommand

The SetCommand is implemented as shown in the following lines of code:

```
package org.redisch7.gossipserver.commands;
/* OMITTING THE IMPORT STATEMENTS TO SAVE SPACE */
import org.redisch7.gossipserver.util.commandparser.Validator;
public class SetCommand extends AbstractCommand {
  Validator validator = new Validator();
  public SetCommand() {
    validator.configureTemplate().add((new StringToken("set"))).
add(new MapListToken());
  }
  @Override
  public CheckResult execute(CommandTokens commandTokens) {
    CheckResult checkResult = new CheckResult();
    validator.setInput(commandTokens);
    checkResult = validator.validate();
    if (checkResult.getResult()) {
      List<Token> tokenList = validator.getAllTokens();
      checkResult = new SetCommandHandler(this.getName()).
process(tokenList);
    }
    return checkResult;
  }
}
```

Implementation of SetCommandHandler

The `set` command handler is implemented as shown here:

```
package org.redisch7.gossipserver.commandhandlers;
/* OMITTING THE IMPORT STATEMENTS TO SAVE SPACE */
public class SetCommandHandler extends AbstractCommandHandler {
  public SetCommandHandler(String nodename) {
    super(nodename);
  }
```

```
    public CheckResult process(List<Token> tokenList) {
      CheckResult checkResult = new CheckResult();
      JedisUtil jedisUtil = new JedisUtil();
      List<Boolean> result = jedisUtil
          .doesExist(this.getNodename(), Arrays
              .asList(ConstUtil.registerationHolder,
                  ConstUtil.activationHolder,
                  ConstUtil.passivationHolder, ConstUtil.
  shutdownHolder));
      if ((result.get(0) == true) && (result.get(1) == true)
          && (result.get(2) == false)&& (result.get(3) == false)) {
        MapListToken mapListToken = (MapListToken) tokenList.get(1);
        checkResult = jedisUtil.setValuesInNode(this.getNodename(),
            mapListToken.getValueAsMap());
      } else {
        checkResult
            .setFalse("Activation Validation :")
            .appendReason(
                ConstUtil.registerationHolder + " = "
                    + ((Boolean) result.get(0)))
            .appendReason(
                ConstUtil.activationHolder + " = "
                    + ((Boolean) result.get(1)))
            .appendReason(
                ConstUtil.passivationHolder + " = "
                    + ((Boolean) result.get(2)));
      }
      return checkResult;
    }
  }
```

The get command

This command will get the data from the nodes. The precondition for executing this command is that the node should be in the activated state. The input will be a list of variables and the data needs to be picked up from the Config store. Every node will have its own Config store.

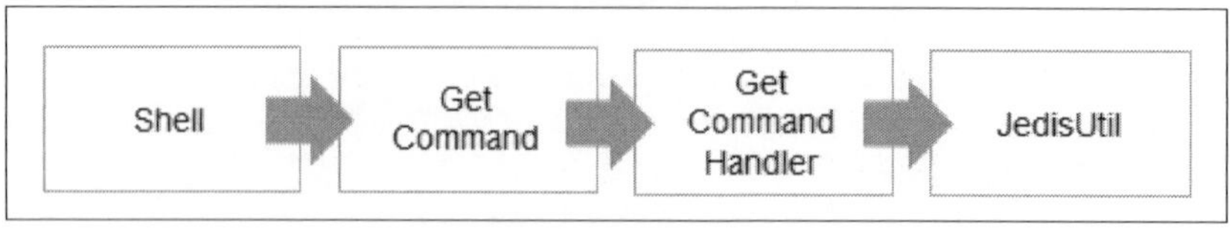

Sequence of flow of data in Get command

The syntax foe this command is: `get`. The following screenshot shows the response in the shell console:

```
get x,y
:->true
:->[200, 500]
```

Implementation of GetCommand

The GetCommand is implemented as shown in the following code snippet:

```
package org.redisch7.gossipserver.commands;
/* OMITTING THE IMPORT STATEMENTS TO SAVE SPACE */
public class GetCommand extends AbstractCommand {
  Validator validator = new Validator();
  public GetCommand() {
    validator.configureTemplate().add((new StringToken("get"))).
add(new StringListToken());
  }
  @Override
  public CheckResult execute(CommandTokens commandTokens) {
    CheckResult checkResult = new CheckResult();
    validator.setInput(commandTokens);
    checkResult = validator.validate();
    if (checkResult.getResult()) {
      List<Token> tokenList = validator.getAllTokens();
      checkResult = new GetCommandHandler(this.getName()).
process(tokenList);
    }
    return checkResult;
  }
}
```

Implementation of GetCommandHandler

The `get` command handler is implemented as shown here:

```
package org.redisch7.gossipserver.commandhandlers;
/* OMITTING THE IMPORT STATEMENTS TO SAVE SPACE */
public class GetCommandHandler extends AbstractCommandHandler {
  public GetCommandHandler(String nodename) {
    super(nodename);
  }
  public CheckResult process(List<Token> tokenList) {
```

```
        CheckResult checkResult = new CheckResult();
        JedisUtil jedisUtil = new JedisUtil();
        List<Boolean> result = jedisUtil
            .doesExist(this.getNodename(), Arrays
                .asList(ConstUtil.registerationHolder,
                    ConstUtil.activationHolder,
                    ConstUtil.passivationHolder, ConstUtil.
    shutdownHolder));
        if ((result.get(0) == true) && (result.get(1) == true)
            && (result.get(2) == false)&& (result.get(3) == false)) {
          StringListToken stringList = (StringListToken) tokenList.get(1);
          checkResult = jedisUtil.getValuesFromNode(this.getNodename(),
              stringList.getValueAsList());
        } else {
          checkResult
              .setFalse("Activation Validation :")
              .appendReason(
                  ConstUtil.registerationHolder + " = "
                      + ((Boolean) result.get(0)))
              .appendReason(
                  ConstUtil.activationHolder + " = "
                      + ((Boolean) result.get(1)))
              .appendReason(
                  ConstUtil.passivationHolder + " = "
                      + ((Boolean) result.get(2)));
        }
        return checkResult;
      }
    }
```

The del command

This command will delete the data in the nodes. The precondition for executing this command is that the node should be activated. The command will be executed by passing the name of the variable that needs to be deleted.

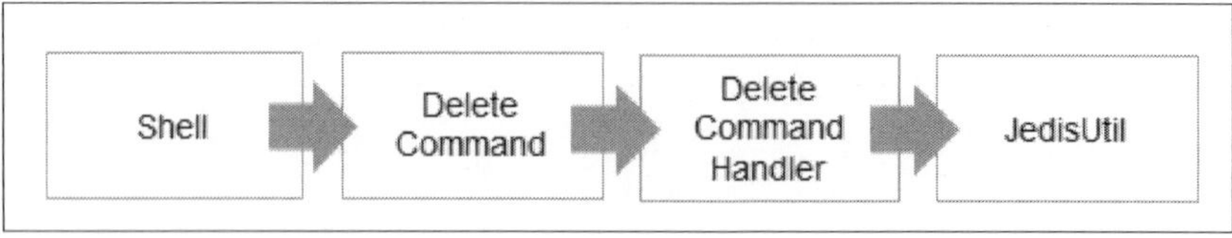

Sequence of flow of data in Delete command

The syntax for this command is: `del <parameter>`. The following screenshot shows the response in the shell console:

```
del x
:->true
:->values deleted
```

Implementation of DeleteCommand

The DeleteCommand is implemented as shown in the following code snippet:

```
package org.redisch7.gossipserver.commands;
/* OMITTING THE IMPORT STATEMENTS TO SAVE SPACE */
public class DeleteCommand extends AbstractCommand {
  Validator validator = new Validator();
       public DeleteCommand() {
    validator.configureTemplate().add((new StringToken("del"))).
add(new StringListToken());
  }
  @Override
  public CheckResult execute(CommandTokens commandTokens) {
    CheckResult checkResult = new CheckResult();
    validator.setInput(commandTokens);
    checkResult = validator.validate();
    if (checkResult.getResult()) {
      List<Token> tokenList = validator.getAllTokens();
      checkResult = new DeleteCommandHandler(this.getName()).
process(tokenList);
    }
    return checkResult;
  }
}
```

Implementation of DeleteCommandHandler

The `delete` command handler is implemented as shown here:

```
package org.redisch7.gossipserver.commandhandlers;
/* OMITTING THE IMPORT STATEMENTS TO SAVE SPACE */
public class DeleteCommandHandler extends AbstractCommandHandler {
  public DeleteCommandHandler(String nodename) {
    super(nodename);
  }
```

```
    public CheckResult process(List<Token> tokenList) {
      CheckResult checkResult = new CheckResult();
      JedisUtil jedisUtil = new JedisUtil();
      List<Boolean> result = jedisUtil
          .doesExist(this.getNodename(), Arrays
              .asList(ConstUtil.registerationHolder,
                  ConstUtil.activationHolder,
                  ConstUtil.passivationHolder, ConstUtil.
shutdownHolder));
      if ((result.get(0) == true) && (result.get(1) == true)
          && (result.get(2) == false)&& (result.get(3) == false)) {
        StringListToken stringList = (StringListToken) tokenList.get(1);
        checkResult = jedisUtil.deleteValuesFromNode(this.getNodename(),
            stringList.getValueAsList());
      } else {
        checkResult
            .setFalse("Activation Validation :")
            .appendReason(
                ConstUtil.registerationHolder + " = "
                    + ((Boolean) result.get(0)))
            .appendReason(
                ConstUtil.activationHolder + " = "
                    + ((Boolean) result.get(1)))
            .appendReason(
                ConstUtil.passivationHolder + " = "
                    + ((Boolean) result.get(2)));
      }
      return checkResult;
    }
  }
```

The status command

This command is used to get the current status of a node. The precondition for executing this command is that the node should be in some state. The command in the client focuses on the data of the client node.

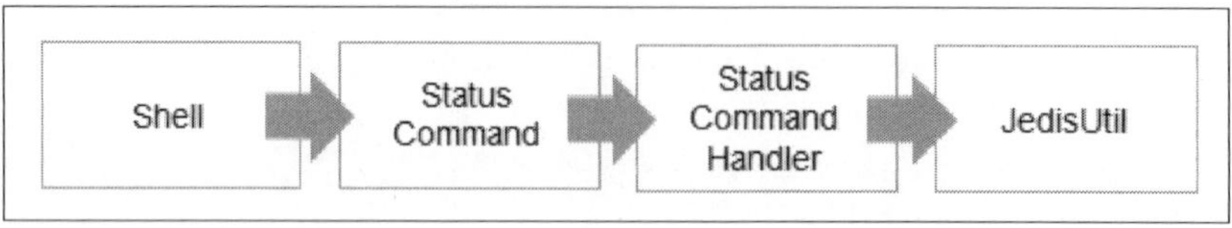

Sequence of flow of data in Passivate command

The syntax for this command is: `status`. The following screenshot shows the response in the shell console:

```
status
:->true
:->REGISTERATION-HOLDER = true
ACTIVATION-HOLDER = true
PASSIVATION-HOLDER = false
{createtime=8/19/14 1:46 PM, lastaccesstime=8/19/14 1:46 PM, y=500, x=200}
```

Implementation of StatusCommand

The `status` command is implemented as shown in the following code snippet:

```
package org.redisch7.gossipserver.commands;
/* OMITTING THE IMPORT STATEMENTS TO SAVE SPACE */
public class StatusCommand extends AbstractCommand {
  Validator validator = new Validator();
  public StatusCommand() {
    validator.configureTemplate().add((new StringToken("status")));
  }
  @Override
  public CheckResult execute(CommandTokens commandTokens) {
    CheckResult checkResult = new CheckResult();
    validator.setInput(commandTokens);
    checkResult = validator.validate();
    if (checkResult.getResult()) {
      List<Token> tokenList = validator.getAllTokens();
      checkResult = new StatusCommandHandler(this.getName()).
process(tokenList);
    }
    return checkResult;
  }
}
```

Implementation of StatusCommandHandler

The `passive` command handler is implemented as shown here:

```
package org.redisch7.gossipserver.commandhandlers;
/* OMITTING THE IMPORT STATEMENTS TO SAVE SPACE */
public class StatusCommandHandler extends AbstractCommandHandler {
  public StatusCommandHandler(String nodename) {
    super(nodename);
  }
```

```
    @Override
    public CheckResult process(List<Token> tokenList) {
      CheckResult checkResult = new CheckResult();
      JedisUtil jedisUtil = new JedisUtilImpl();
      if (this.getNodename().equals("master")) {
        List<String> registerednames = jedisUtil.
  getAllNodesFromRegistrationHolder();
        checkResult.setTrue().appendReason("The following nodes are
  registered ");
        checkResult.appendReason(registerednames.toString());
        List<String> activenodenames = jedisUtil.
  getAllNodesFromActivatedHolder();
        checkResult.setTrue().appendReason("The following nodes are
  activated ");
        checkResult.appendReason(activenodenames.toString());
        List<String> passivenodenames = jedisUtil.
  getAllNodesFromPassivatedHolder();
        checkResult.setTrue().appendReason("The following nodes are
  passivated ");
        checkResult.appendReason(passivenodenames.toString());
        List<String> inconsistentState = jedisUtil.
  getAllNodesInInconsistentState();
        checkResult.setTrue().appendReason("The following nodes are not
  in consitent state ");
        checkResult.appendReason(inconsistentState.toString());
      } else {
        checkResult = jedisUtil.getStatus(this.getNodename());
      }
      return checkResult;
    }
  }
```

The passivate command

This command will passivate the node into the gossip server ecosystem. The precondition for executing this command is that the node should be in the activated state. On passivation, the client's event listeners will be shut down and will not be in a position to take events from the master. Since the node is passivated, the data in the node's Config store will be taken and pushed into the archive file of the node.

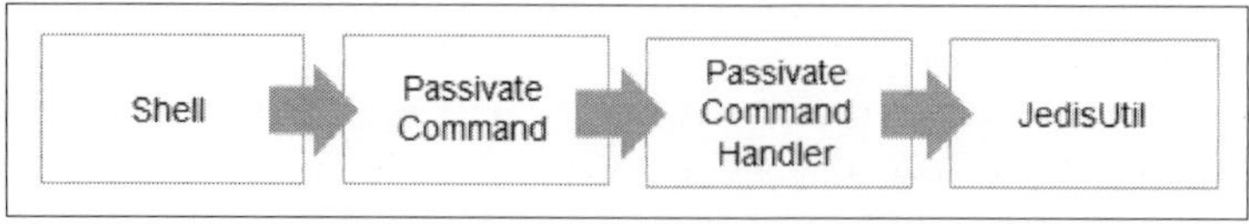

Sequence of flow of data in Passivate command

The syntax for this command is: `passivate`. The following screenshot shows the response in the shell console:

```
passivate
:->true
:->Passivation Successful
```

Implementation of PassivateCommand

The `passivate` command is implemented as shown in the following code snippet:

```
package org.redisch7.gossipserver.commands;
/* OMITTING THE IMPORT STATEMENTS TO SAVE SPACE */
public class PassivateCommand extends AbstractCommand {
  Validator validator = new Validator();
  public PassivateCommand() {
    validator.configureTemplate().add((new StringToken("passivate")));
  }
  @Override
  public CheckResult execute(CommandTokens commandTokens) {
    CheckResult checkResult = new CheckResult();
    validator.setInput(commandTokens);
    checkResult = validator.validate();
    if (checkResult.getResult()) {
      List<Token> tokenList = validator.getAllTokens();
      checkResult = new PassivateCommandHandler(this.getName()).
process(tokenList);
    }
    return checkResult;
  }
}
```

Implementation of PassivateCommandHandler

The `passivate` command handler is implemented as shown in the following code snippet:

```
package org.redisch7.gossipserver.commandhandlers;
/* OMITTING THE IMPORT STATEMENTS TO SAVE SPACE */
public class PassivateCommandHandler extends AbstractCommandHandler {
  public PassivateCommandHandler(String nodename) {
    super(nodename);
  }
  public CheckResult process(List<Token> tokenList) {
    CheckResult checkResult = new CheckResult();
```

```
        JedisUtil jedisUtil = new JedisUtil();
        List<Boolean> result = jedisUtil.doesExist(this.getNodename(),
    Arrays
            .asList(ConstUtil.registerationHolder,
                ConstUtil.activationHolder,
                ConstUtil.passivationHolder, ConstUtil.shutdownHolder));
        if ((result.get(0) == true) && (result.get(1) == true)
            && (result.get(2) == false) && (result.get(3) == false)) {
          checkResult = jedisUtil.passivateNode(this.getNodename());
        } else {
          checkResult
              .setFalse("Passivation Validation :")
              .appendReason(
                  ConstUtil.registerationHolder + " = "
                      + ((Boolean) result.get(0)))
              .appendReason(
                  ConstUtil.activationHolder + " = "
                      + ((Boolean) result.get(1)))
              .appendReason(
                  ConstUtil.passivationHolder + " = "
                      + ((Boolean) result.get(2)));
        }
        return checkResult;
      }
    }
```

The reactivate command

This command will reactivate the node. The precondition for executing this command is that the node should be in the passive mode. Upon reactivation, the client's event listener will be spawned once again. The data in the archive file will be pumped back again to the node's Config store.

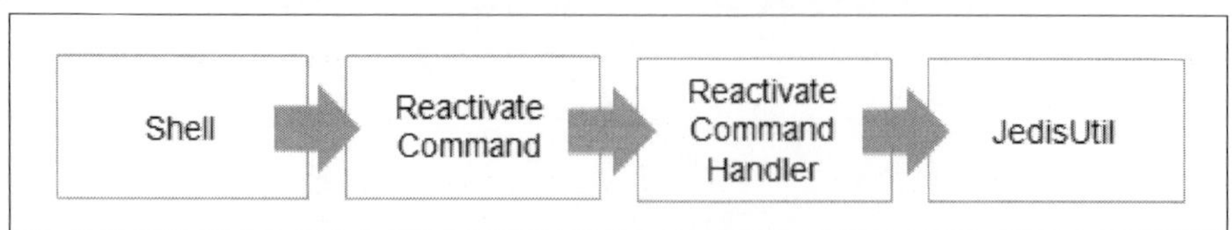

Sequence of flow of data in Reactivate command

The syntax for this command is: `reactivate`. The following screenshot shows the response in the shell console:

```
reactivate
:->true
:->Reactivation sucess ..
```

Implementation of ReactivateCommand

The `passivate` command is implemented as shown here:

```
package org.redisch7.gossipserver.commands;
/* OMITTING THE IMPORT STATEMENTS TO SAVE SPACE */
public class ReactivateCommand extends AbstractCommand {
  Validator validator = new Validator();
  public ReactivateCommand() {
    validator.configureTemplate().add((new
StringToken("reactivate")));
  }
  @Override
  public CheckResult execute(CommandTokens commandTokens) {
    CheckResult checkResult = new CheckResult();
    validator.setInput(commandTokens);
    checkResult = validator.validate();
    if (checkResult.getResult()) {
      List<Token> tokenList = validator.getAllTokens();
      checkResult = new ReactivateCommandHandler(this.getName()).
process(tokenList);
    }
    return checkResult;
  }
}
```

Implementation of ReactivateCommandHandler

The `reactivate` command handler is implemented as shown here:

```
package org.redisch7.gossipserver.commandhandlers;
/* OMITTING THE IMPORT STATEMENTS TO SAVE SPACE */
public class ReactivateCommandHandler extends AbstractCommandHandler {
  public ReactivateCommandHandler(String nodename) {
    super(nodename);
  }
```

```
    public CheckResult process(List<Token> tokenList) {
      CheckResult checkResult = new CheckResult();
      JedisUtil jedisUtil = new JedisUtil();
      List<Boolean> result = jedisUtil.doesExist(this.getNodename(),
  Arrays
          .asList(ConstUtil.registerationHolder,
              ConstUtil.activationHolder,
              ConstUtil.passivationHolder, ConstUtil.shutdownHolder));
      if ((result.get(0) == true) && (result.get(1) == false)
          && (result.get(2) == true) && (result.get(3) == false)) {
        checkResult = jedisUtil.reactivateNode(this.getNodename());
      } else {
        checkResult
            .setFalse("Passivation Validation :")
            .appendReason(
                ConstUtil.registerationHolder + " = "
                    + ((Boolean) result.get(0)))
            .appendReason(
                ConstUtil.activationHolder + " = "
                    + ((Boolean) result.get(1)))
            .appendReason(
                ConstUtil.passivationHolder + " = "
                    + ((Boolean) result.get(2)));
      }
      return checkResult;
    }
  }
```

The archive command

This command will archive the data of a node in the gossip server ecosystem. The precondition for executing this command is that the node should be in the registered mode. When this command is issued, the data in the node's Config store will be flushed and put into an archive file in the filesystem of the client node's machine.

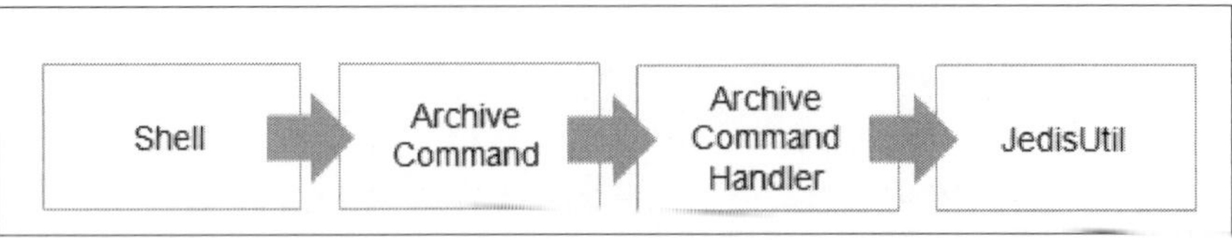

Sequence of flow of data in Archive command

The syntax for this command is: `archive`. The following screenshot shows the response in the shell console:

Implementation of ArchiveCommand

The `archive` command is implemented as shown in the following code snippet:

```
package org.redisch7.gossipserver.commands;
/* OMITTING THE IMPORT STATEMENTS TO SAVE SPACE */
public class ArchiveCommand extends AbstractCommand {
  private Validator validator = new Validator();
  public ArchiveCommand() {
    validator.configureTemplate().add((new StringToken("archive")));
  }
  @Override
  public CheckResult execute(CommandTokens commandTokens) {
    CheckResult checkResult = new CheckResult();
    validator.setInput(commandTokens);
    checkResult = validator.validate();
    if (checkResult.getResult()) {
      List<Token> tokenList = validator.getAllTokens();
      checkResult = new ArchiveCommandHandler(this.getName()).
process(tokenList);
    }
    return checkResult;
  }
}
```

Implementation of ArchiveCommandHandler

The `reactive` command handler is implemented as shown in the following code snippet:

```
package org.redisch7.gossipserver.commandhandlers;
/* OMITTING THE IMPORT STATEMENTS TO SAVE SPACE */
public final class ArchiveCommandHandler extends
AbstractCommandHandler {
  public ArchiveCommandHandler(String nodename) {
    super(nodename);
  }
```

```
    @Override
    public CheckResult process(List<Token> tokenList) {
      CheckResult checkResult = new CheckResult();
      JedisUtil jedisUtil = new JedisUtil();
      List<Boolean> result = jedisUtil
          .doesExist(this.getNodename(), Arrays
              .asList(ConstUtil.registerationHolder,
                  ConstUtil.activationHolder,
                  ConstUtil.passivationHolder, ConstUtil.
  shutdownHolder));
      if ((result.get(0) == true)
          &&  (result.get(3) == false) &&((result.get(1) == true) ||
  (result.get(2) == true))) {
        checkResult = jedisUtil.archiveNode(this.getNodename());
      } else {
        checkResult
            .setFalse("Activation Validation :")
            .appendReason(
                ConstUtil.registerationHolder + " = "
                    + (result.get(0)))
            .appendReason(
                ConstUtil.activationHolder + " = "
                    + (result.get(1)))
            .appendReason(
                ConstUtil.passivationHolder + " = "
                    + (result.get(2)));
      }
      return checkResult;
    }
  }
```

The sync command

The sync command will synchronize the data of a node in the gossip server ecosystem. The precondition for executing this command is that the node should be in the registered mode. When this command is issued, the data in the archive file is pumped back into the Config store of the user.

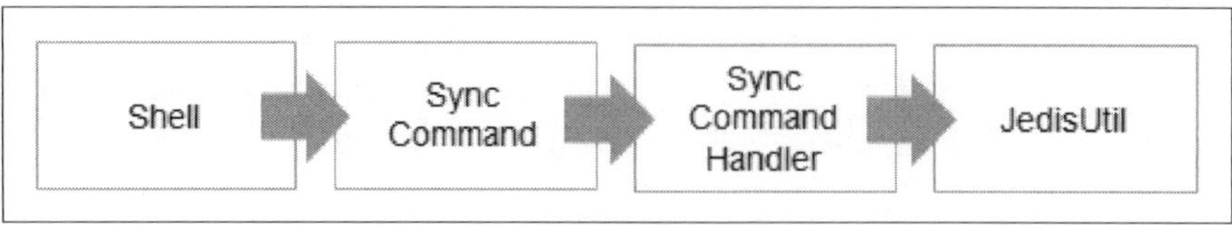

Sequence of flow of data in Sync command

The syntax of this command is: `sync`. The following screenshot shows the response in the shell console:

```
sync
:->true
:->
```

Implementation of SyncCommand

The `sync` command is implemented as shown here:

```
package org.redisch7.gossipserver.commands;
/* OMITTING THE IMPORT STATEMENTS TO SAVE SPACE */
public class SynchCommand extends AbstractCommand {
  Validator validator = new Validator();
  public SynchCommand() {
    validator.configureTemplate().add((new StringToken("sync")));
  }
  @Override
  public CheckResult execute(CommandTokens commandTokens) {
    CheckResult checkResult = new CheckResult();
    validator.setInput(commandTokens);
    checkResult = validator.validate();
    if (checkResult.getResult()) {
      List<Token> tokenList = validator.getAllTokens();
      checkResult = new SynchCommandHandler(this.getName()).
process(tokenList);
    }
    return checkResult;
  }
}
```

Implementation of SyncCommandHandler

The `sync` command handler is implemented as shown in the following code snippet:

```
package org.redisch7.gossipserver.commandhandlers;
/* OMITTING THE IMPORT STATEMENTS TO SAVE SPACE */
public class SynchCommandHandler extends AbstractCommandHandler {
  public SynchCommandHandler(String nodename) {
    super(nodename);
  }
  public CheckResult process(List<Token> tokenList) {
    CheckResult checkResult = new CheckResult();
```

```
        JedisUtil jedisUtil = new JedisUtil();
        List<Boolean> result = jedisUtil
            .doesExist(this.getNodename(), Arrays
                .asList(ConstUtil.registerationHolder,
                    ConstUtil.activationHolder,
                    ConstUtil.passivationHolder, ConstUtil.
shutdownHolder));
        if (result.get(0) && result.get(1) && (result.get(3)==false)) {
          checkResult = jedisUtil.syncNode(this.getNodename());
        } else {
          checkResult.setFalse("Synch Failed ");
        }
        return checkResult;
      }
    }
```

The reconnect command

The `reconnect` command will reconnect a node in the gossip server ecosystem. The precondition for executing this command is that the node should be in the activated state and the node should have undergone a shut down. So, when the node comes up after the shut down and this command is fired, then the listeners for the client node will get spawned and the node will be back in the activated state.

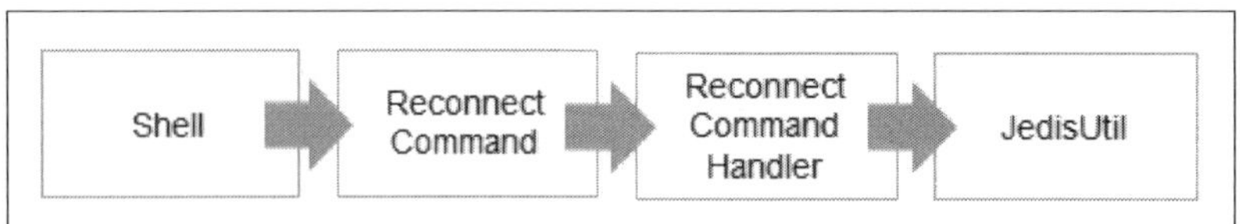

Sequence of flow of data in Reconnect command

The syntax for this command is: `reconnect`. The following screenshot shows the response in the shell console:

```
reconnect
:->true
:->
```

Implementation of ReconnectCommand

The `reconnect` command is implemented as shown here:

```
package org.redisch7.gossipserver.commands;
/* OMITTING THE IMPORT STATEMENTS TO SAVE SPACE */
public class ReConnectCommand extends AbstractCommand {
  Validator validator = new Validator();
  public ReConnectCommand() {
    validator.configureTemplate().add((new StringToken("reconnect")));
  }
  @Override
  public CheckResult execute(CommandTokens commandTokens) {
    CheckResult checkResult = new CheckResult();
    validator.setInput(commandTokens);
    checkResult = validator.validate();
    if (checkResult.getResult()) {
      List<Token> tokenList = validator.getAllTokens();
      checkResult = new ReConnectCommandHandler(this.getName()).
process(tokenList);
    }
    return checkResult;
  }
}
```

Implementation of ReconnectCommandHandler

The `reconnect` command handler is implemented as shown in the following code snippet:

```
package org.redisch7.gossipserver.commandhandlers;
/* OMITTING THE IMPORT STATEMENTS TO SAVE SPACE */
public class ReConnectCommandHandler extends AbstractCommandHandler {
  public ReConnectCommandHandler(String nodename) {
    super(nodename);
  }
  @Override
  public CheckResult process(List<Token> tokenList) {
    CheckResult checkResult = new CheckResult();
    JedisUtil jedisUtil = new JedisUtil();
    List<Boolean> result = jedisUtil.doesExist(this.getNodename(),
Arrays
        .asList(ConstUtil.registerationHolder,
            ConstUtil.activationHolder,
            ConstUtil.passivationHolder, ConstUtil.shutdownHolder));
```

```
        if ((result.get(0) == true)
            && ((result.get(1) == false) || (result.get(2) == false))
            && (result.get(3) == true)) {
          checkResult = jedisUtil.reconnectNode(this.getNodename());
        } else {
          checkResult
               .setFalse("Reconnect Failed :")
               .appendReason(
                   ConstUtil.registerationHolder + " = "
                       + (result.get(0)))
               .appendReason(
                   ConstUtil.activationHolder + " = "
                       + (result.get(1)))
               .appendReason(
                   ConstUtil.passivationHolder + " = "
                       + (result.get(2)));
        }
        return checkResult;
      }
    }
```

Master node commands

The following is a list of commands that can be fired from the master nodes:

- The `start` command
- The `status` command
- The `get` command
- The `msg` command
- The `kill` command
- The `clone` command
- The `stop` command

Let's take a look at each command from a design and implementation perspective.

The start command

The `start` command will start the master node in the gossip server ecosystem. The precondition for executing this command is that the node name should be unique.

Sequence of flow of data in Start command

The syntax for this command is: `start`. The following screenshot shows the response in the shell console:

```
start
 start the master node manager ..
:->true
:->master started..
```

Implementation of StartMasterCommand

The `start` command is implemented as shown here:

```
package org.redisch7.gossipserver.commands;
/* OMITTING THE IMPORT STATEMENTS TO SAVE SPACE */
public class StartMasterCommand extends AbstractCommand {
  private Validator validator = new Validator();
  public StartMasterCommand() {
    validator.configureTemplate().add((new StringToken("start")));
  }
  @Override
  public CheckResult execute(CommandTokens commandTokens) {
    CheckResult checkResult = new CheckResult();
    validator.setInput(commandTokens);
    return checkResult.setTrue().appendReason("master started..");
  }
}
```

The stop command

The `stop` command will stop the master node in the gossip server ecosystem. The precondition for executing this command is that the node should be in the start mode.

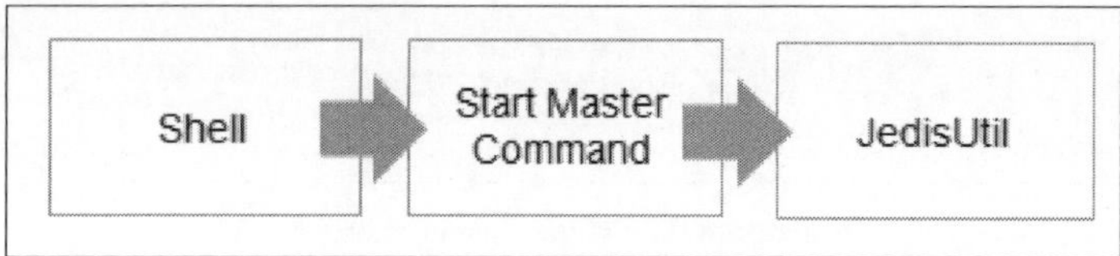

Sequence of flow of data in Start command

The syntax for this code is: `stop`. The following screenshot shows the response in the shell console:

```
stop
 stop the master node manager ..
:->true
:->master stoped..
```

Implementation of StopMasterCommand

The `stop` command is implemented as shown in the following code snippet:

```
package org.redisch7.gossipserver.commands;
/* OMITTING THE IMPORT STATEMENTS TO SAVE SPACE */
public class StopMasterCommand extends AbstractCommand {
  private Validator validator = new Validator();
  public StartMasterCommand() {
    validator.configureTemplate().add((new StringToken("stop")));
  }
  @Override
  public CheckResult execute(CommandTokens commandTokens) {
    CheckResult checkResult = new CheckResult();
    validator.setInput(commandTokens);
    return checkResult.setTrue().appendReason("master stoped..");
  }
}
```

The status command

The `status` command will show the current status of a node in the gossip server ecosystem.

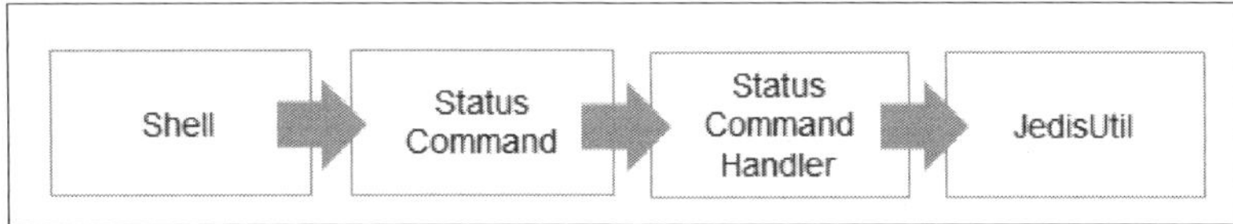

Sequence of flow of data in Status command

The syntax for this command is: `status`. The following screenshot shows the response in the shell console:

```
status
:->true
:->The following nodes are registered
[loki, vinoo]
The following nodes are activated
[loki, vinoo]
The following nodes are passivated
[]
The following nodes are not in consitent state
[]
```

Implementation of StatusCommand

The `status` command is implemented as shown here:

```
package org.redisch7.gossipserver.commands;
/* OMITTING THE IMPORT STATEMENTS TO SAVE SPACE */
public class StatusCommand extends AbstractCommand {
  Validator validator = new Validator();
  public StatusCommand() {
    validator.configureTemplate().add((new StringToken("status")));
  }
  @Override
  public CheckResult execute(CommandTokens commandTokens) {
    CheckResult checkResult = new CheckResult();
    validator.setInput(commandTokens);
    checkResult = validator.validate();
    if (checkResult.getResult()) {
      List<Token> tokenList = validator.getAllTokens();
      checkResult = new StatusCommandHandler(this.getName()).
process(tokenList);
    }
    return checkResult;
  }
}
```

Implementation of StatusCommandHandler

The `status` command handler is implemented as shown in the following code snippet:

```
package org.redisch7.gossipserver.commandhandlers;
/* OMITTING THE IMPORT STATEMENTS TO SAVE SPACE */
public class StatusCommandHandler extends AbstractCommandHandler {
  public StatusCommandHandler(String nodename) {
    super(nodename);
  }
  @Override
  public CheckResult process(List<Token> tokenList) {
    CheckResult checkResult = new CheckResult();
    JedisUtil jedisUtil = new JedisUtil();
    if (this.getNodename().equals("master")) {
      List<String> registerednames = jedisUtil.
getAllNodesFromRegistrationHolder();
      checkResult.setTrue().appendReason("The following nodes are
registered ");
      checkResult.appendReason(registerednames.toString());
      List<String> activenodenames = jedisUtil.
getAllNodesFromActivatedHolder();
      checkResult.setTrue().appendReason("The following nodes are
activated ");
      checkResult.appendReason(activenodenames.toString());
      List<String> passivenodenames = jedisUtil.
getAllNodesFromPassivatedHolder();
      checkResult.setTrue().appendReason("The following nodes are
passivated ");
      checkResult.appendReason(passivenodenames.toString());
      List<String> inconsistentState = jedisUtil.
getAllNodesInInconsistentState();
      checkResult.setTrue().appendReason("The following nodes are not
in consitent state ");
      checkResult.appendReason(inconsistentState.toString());
    } else {
      checkResult = jedisUtil.getStatus(this.getNodename());
    }
    return checkResult;
  }
}
```

The get command

The `get` command will display the state of all the nodes that are registered in the gossip server ecosystem.

The syntax for this command is: `get <field1>,<field2> where nodes are <nodename1>,<nodename2>`.

The following screenshot shows the response in the shell console:

```
get x,y where nodes are loki,vinoo
:->true
:->The results for loki :
[300, 600]

The results for vinoo :
[200, 500]
```

Implementation of GetNodeDataCommand

The `get` command is implemented as shown in the following code snippet:

```
package org.redisch7.gossipserver.commands;
/* OMITTING THE IMPORT STATEMENTS TO SAVE SPACE */
public class GetNodeDataCommand extends AbstractCommand {
  private Validator validator = new Validator();
  public GetNodeDataCommand() {
    validator.configureTemplate().add((new StringToken("get"))).
add(new StringListToken()).add(new StringToken("where"))
        .add(new StringToken("nodes")).add(new StringToken("are")).
add(new StringListToken());
  }
  @Override
  public CheckResult execute(CommandTokens commandTokens) {
    CheckResult checkResult = new CheckResult();
    validator.setInput(commandTokens);
    checkResult = validator.validate();
    if (checkResult.getResult()) {
      List<Token> tokenList = validator.getAllTokens();
      checkResult = new GetNodeDataCommandHandler(this.getName()).
process(tokenList);
    }
    return checkResult;
  }
}
```

Implementation of GetNodeDataCommandHandler

The `get` command handler is implemented as shown here:

```
package org.redisch7.gossipserver.commandhandlers;
/* OMITTING THE IMPORT STATEMENTS TO SAVE SPACE */
public class GetNodeDataCommandHandler extends AbstractCommandHandler
{
  public GetNodeDataCommandHandler(String nodename) {
    super(nodename);
  }
  @Override
  public CheckResult process(List<Token> tokenList) {
    CheckResult checkResult = new CheckResult();
    StringListToken gettersstringListToken = (StringListToken)
tokenList
        .get(1);
    StringListToken nodesstringListToken = (StringListToken) tokenList
        .get(5);
    List<String> nodeList = nodesstringListToken.getValueAsList();
    JedisUtil jedisUtil = new JedisUtil();
    for (String nodename : nodeList) {
      List<Boolean> result = jedisUtil.doesExist(nodename, Arrays.
asList(
          ConstUtil.registerationHolder, ConstUtil.activationHolder,
          ConstUtil.passivationHolder, ConstUtil.shutdownHolder));
      if ((result.get(0) == true) && (result.get(1) == true)
          && (result.get(2) == false)&& (result.get(3) == false)) {
        CheckResult chkresult = jedisUtil.getValuesFromNode(nodename,
            gettersstringListToken.getValueAsList());
        checkResult.setTrue()
            .appendReason("The results for " + nodename + " :")
            .appendReason(chkresult.getReason());
      } else {
        checkResult
            .appendReason("The node where the GET didn't work is as
follows: ");
        checkResult
            .setFalse(
                "Activation Validation for " + nodename + " :")
            .appendReason(
                ConstUtil.registerationHolder + " = "
                    + (result.get(0)))
            .appendReason(
                ConstUtil.activationHolder + " = "
```

```
                    + (result.get(1)))
            .appendReason(
                ConstUtil.passivationHolder + " = "
                    + (result.get(2)));
        }
      }
      return checkResult;
    }
  }
```

The msg command

The `msg` command is used to send messages to the nodes in the gossip server ecosystem. The precondition for executing this command is that the master node should be in the start mode.

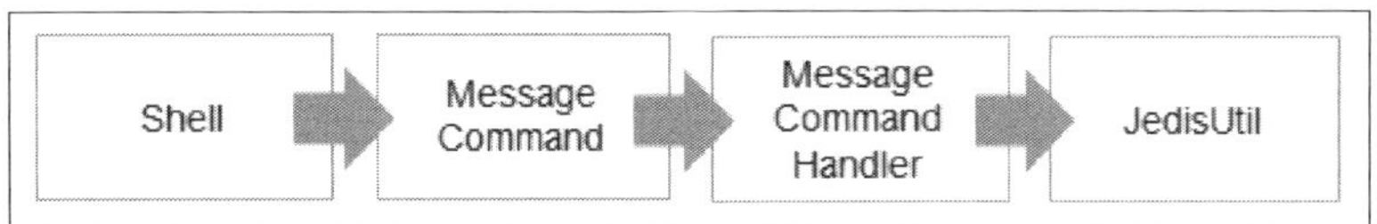

Sequence of flow of data in Message command

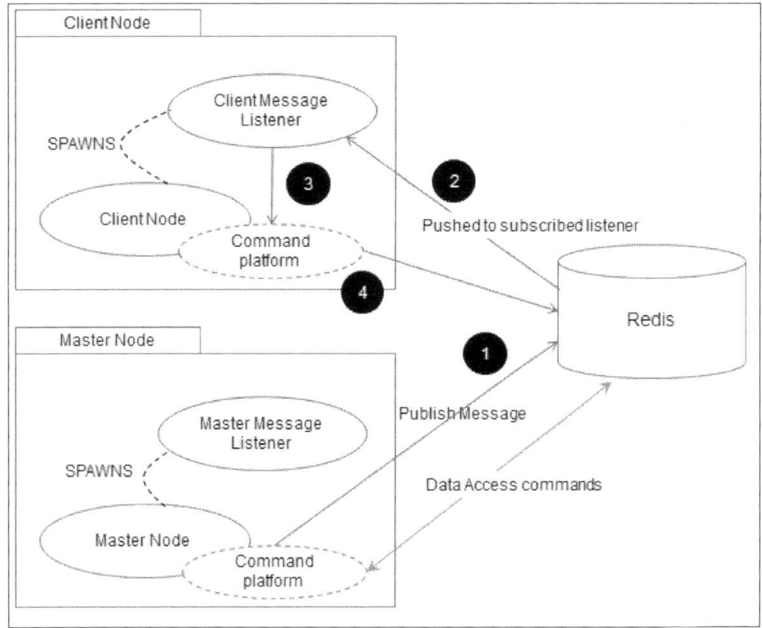

Messaging between master and client nodes

The syntax for this command is: mgs <node name> where command = set, field 1, field 2.

The following screenshot shows the response in the master shell console:

```
msg vinoo where command=set, p=300,z=600
command=set, p=300, z=600
:->true
:->Sent to desired channel
```

The response in the client node (vinoo) is as follows:

```
true
setting done in vinoo
```

Implementation of MessageCommand

The MessageCommand is implemented as shown here:

```
package org.redisch7.gossipserver.commands;
/* OMITTING THE IMPORT STATEMENTS TO SAVE SPACE */
public class MessageCommand extends AbstractCommand {
  Validator validator = new Validator();
  public MessageCommand() {
    validator.configureTemplate().add((new StringToken("msg"))).
add(new StringToken()).add(new StringToken("where"))
        .add(new MapListToken());
  }
  @Override
  public CheckResult execute(CommandTokens commandTokens) {
    CheckResult checkResult = new CheckResult();
    validator.setInput(commandTokens);
    checkResult = validator.validate();
    if (checkResult.getResult()) {
      List<Token> tokenList = validator.getAllTokens();
      checkResult = new MessageCommandHandler(this.getName()).
process(tokenList);
    }
    return checkResult;
  }
}
```

Implementation of MessageCommandHandler

The `messageCommandHandler` is implemented as shown in the following code snippet:

```
package org.redisch7.gossipserver.commandhandlers;
/* OMITTING THE IMPORT STATEMENTS TO SAVE SPACE */
public class MessageCommandHandler extends AbstractCommandHandler {
  public MessageCommandHandler(String nodename) {
    super(nodename);
  }
  public CheckResult process(List<Token> tokenList) {
    CheckResult checkResult = new CheckResult();
    JedisUtil jedisUtil = new JedisUtil();
    List<Boolean> result = jedisUtil.doesExist(this.getNodename(),
Arrays
        .asList(ConstUtil.registerationHolder,
            ConstUtil.activationHolder,
            ConstUtil.passivationHolder, ConstUtil.shutdownHolder));
    if (this.getNodename().equals("master")
        || ((result.get(0) == true) && (result.get(1) == true) &&
(result
            .get(2) == false)&& (result.get(3) == false))) {
      StringToken channel = (StringToken) tokenList.get(1);
      MapListToken data = (MapListToken) tokenList.get(3);
      checkResult = jedisUtil.publish(channel.getValue(),
          data.getValueAsMap());
    } else {
      checkResult
          .setFalse("Activation Validation :")
          .appendReason(
              ConstUtil.registerationHolder + " = "
                  + ((Boolean) result.get(0)))
          .appendReason(
              ConstUtil.activationHolder + " = "
                  + ((Boolean) result.get(1)))
          .appendReason(
              ConstUtil.passivationHolder + " = "
                  + ((Boolean) result.get(2)));
    }
    return checkResult;
  }
}
```

The kill command

The `kill` command is used to kill a node in the gossip server ecosystem. The precondition for executing this command is that the master node should be in the start mode. Here we'll do it via the `msg` command.

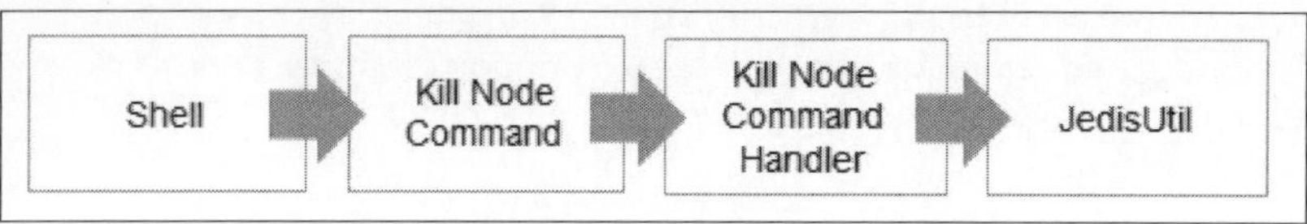

Sequence of flow of data in Kill command

The syntax for this command is: `mgs <node name> where command = kill`

The following screenshot shows the response in the master shell console:

```
msg vinoo where command=kill
command=kill
:->true
:->Sent to desired channel
```

The response in the client node (`vinoo`) is as follows:

```
Archiving the node..
Archived the node..
```

Implementation of KillNodeCommand

The `kill` command is implemented as shown here:

```
package org.redisch7.gossipserver.commands;
/* OMITTING THE IMPORT STATEMENTS TO SAVE SPACE */
public class KillNodeCommand extends AbstractCommand {
  private Validator validator = new Validator();
  public KillNodeCommand() {
    validator.configureTemplate().add((new StringToken("kill")))
        .add(new StringToken());
  }
  @Override
  public CheckResult execute(CommandTokens commandTokens) {
    CheckResult checkResult = new CheckResult();
    validator.setInput(commandTokens);
    checkResult = validator.validate();
```

```
    if (checkResult.getResult()) {
      List<Token> tokenList = validator.getAllTokens();
      checkResult = new KillNodeCommandHandler(this.getName())
          .process(tokenList);
      if (checkResult.getResult()) {
        String path = System.getProperty("user.home") + "\\archive\\"
            + this.getName() + ".json";
        File file = new File(path);
        if (file.exists()) {
          if (file.delete()) {
            System.exit(0);
          } else {
            checkResult.appendReason("Archive file for "
                + this.getName()
                + ".json could not get deleted!");
          }
        }
      }
    }
    return checkResult;
  }
}
```

Implementation of KillNodeCommandHandler

The `Kill` command handler is implemented as shown in the following code snippet:

```
package org.redisch7.gossipserver.commandhandlers;
/* OMITTING THE IMPORT STATEMENTS TO SAVE SPACE */
public class KillNodeCommandHandler extends AbstractCommandHandler {
  public KillNodeCommandHandler(String nodename) {
    super(nodename);
  }
  public CheckResult process(List<Token> tokenList) {
    CheckResult checkResult = new CheckResult();
    JedisUtil jedisUtil = new JedisUtil();
    List<Boolean> result = jedisUtil.doesExist(this.getNodename(),
        Arrays.asList(ConstUtil.registerationHolder,ConstUtil.
shutdownHolder));
    if ((result.get(0)) && (result.get(1) == false)) {
      checkResult = jedisUtil.killNode(this.getNodename());
    } else {
      checkResult.setFalse("Kill node failed ");
    }
    return checkResult;
  }
}
```

The clone command

The clone command is used to make a clone of a node in the gossip server ecosystem. The precondition for executing this command is that the master node should be in the start mode and a minimum of two client nodes should be in the activated mode.

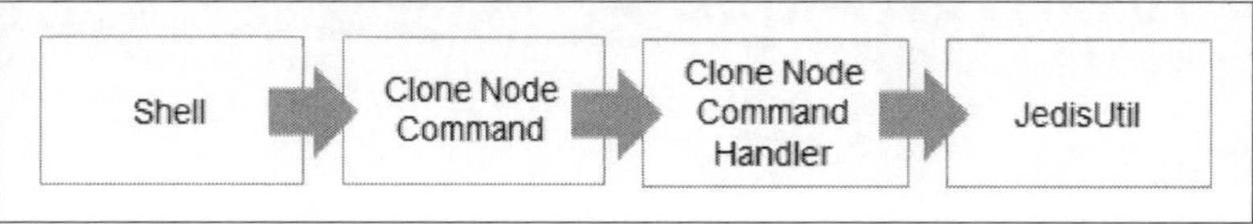

Sequence of flow of data in Clone command

The syntax for this code is: mgs <node name> where command = clone, target =<node name>, source=<node name>.

The following screenshot shows the response in the master shell console:

```
msg loki where command=clone,target=loki,source=vinoo
command=clone, target=loki, source=vinoo
:->true
:->Sent to desired channel
```

This is the response in the client node (loki):

```
clone lokitarget=loki, source=vinoo
true
OK
```

At this point, all the attributes in the source node will be copied to the target node.

Implementation of CloneNodeCommand

The clone command is implemented as shown here:

```
package org.redisch7.gossipserver.commands;
/* OMITTING THE IMPORT STATEMENTS TO SAVE SPACE */
public class CloneNodeCommand extends AbstractCommand {
        private Validator validator = new Validator();
        public CloneNodeCommand() {
    validator.configureTemplate().add((new StringToken("clone"))).
add(new StringToken())
         .add(new StringToken("from")).add(new StringToken());
}
```

```
@Override
  public CheckResult execute(CommandTokens commandTokens) {
    CheckResult checkResult = new CheckResult();
    validator.setInput(commandTokens);
    checkResult = validator.validate();
    if (checkResult.getResult()) {
      List<Token> tokenList = validator.getAllTokens();
      checkResult = new CloneNodeCommandHandler(this.getName()).
process(tokenList);
    }
    return checkResult;
  }
}
```

Implementation of CloneNodeCommandHandler

The `cloneCommandHandler` is implemented as shown in the following code snippet:

```
package org.redisch7.gossipserver.commandhandlers;
/* OMITTING THE IMPORT STATEMENTS TO SAVE SPACE */
public class CloneNodeCommandHandler extends AbstractCommandHandler {
  public CloneNodeCommandHandler(String nodename) {
    super(nodename);
  }
  public CheckResult process(List<Token> tokenList) {
    CheckResult checkResult = new CheckResult();
    MapListToken maptokens = (MapListToken) tokenList.get(1);
    String target = maptokens.getNValue("target");
    String source = maptokens.getNValue("source");
    JedisUtil jedisUtil = new JedisUtil();
    List<Boolean> target_validity_result = jedisUtil
        .doesExist(target, Arrays
            .asList(ConstUtil.registerationHolder,
                ConstUtil.activationHolder,
                ConstUtil.passivationHolder, ConstUtil.
shutdownHolder));
    List<Boolean> source_validity_result = jedisUtil
        .doesExist(source, Arrays
            .asList(ConstUtil.registerationHolder,
                ConstUtil.activationHolder,
                ConstUtil.passivationHolder, ConstUtil.
shutdownHolder));
    if ((target_validity_result.get(0) == true)
        && (target_validity_result.get(1) == true)
```

```
          && (target_validity_result.get(2) == false)&& (target_
validity_result.get(3) == false)) {
        if (((Boolean) source_validity_result.get(0) == true)
            && (source_validity_result.get(1) == true)
            && (source_validity_result.get(2) == false)&& (source_
validity_result.get(3) == false)) {
          checkResult = jedisUtil.clone(target, source);
        } else {
          checkResult.setFalse("The source =" + source
              + " is not in a proper state to clone");
        }
      } else {
        checkResult.setFalse("The target =" + target
            + " is not in a proper state to clone");
      }
      return checkResult;
    }}
```

Redis configuration – data management

To manage data in Redis, it's important to understand the application we are trying to build. Since the gossip server is meant to be a Config server, the reads are will be more than the writes. Redis provides a couple of data persistence mechanisms that we have already dealt with in the previous chapters, and the current section can act as a refresher. The mechanisms that Redis provides are the following:

- The RDB option
- The AOF option
- VM over commit memory (LINUX environments only)

The RDB option

The RDB option provides a mechanism to take a snapshot of the data at regular intervals. Since this is a periodic activity, which dumps the data into the `dump.rdb` file, it makes it a good option to take data backups. For our current application, the configuration in the `redis.conf` file for RDB can be one of the following:

- `save 60 10`: This will save data every 1 minute if 10 keys have changed
- `save 900 10`: This will save data every 15 minutes if 1 key has changed

The AOF option

This works for all the write operations. The AOF option dumps the write data commands to an `appendonly.aof` file by default. There are combinations that can be used to write commands to this file, but every strategy comes with a performance to data persistence rider. What this means is that Redis can be configured to write to this file every time it encounters a write command, but this can make the entire process slow. Leaving the persistence to the underlying operating system in order to flush the buffer to this file can take the control away from the system, but this makes the application very fast. For the gossip server, the configuration is as follows:

- `appendonly yes`: This will create an `appendonly.aof` file
- `appendfsync everysec`: This will call the `fsync()` function every second

VM overcommit memory

This is achieved by tuning the `/etc/stsctl.conf` of your Linux box. This command will take care of how virtual memory management will take place inside the Linux box. The problem occurs when the `BGSAVE` function is called and the parent process forks a child process. By rule, the child process will have as much memory in the shared memory pages as the parent process. So, if the data changes in the parent, the child process also needs to have the same dataset to flush to disk. If the combined memory requirement for the parent and child does not add up to the shared memory, then `BGSAVE` fails.

Discussion on VM memory management is outside the scope of the book. However, lack of this setting can cause Redis to fail in writing data to the disk. The change that should be made to the `/etc/stsctl.conf` is: `vm.overcommit_memory=1`.

Summary

In this application, you learned how to make a Config server, also called as a gossip server that can store properties and pass information around to its peer nodes. In this chapter, we have made provisions for the client node to store and access information and have a life cycle. Also, we provided a master node, which can have control over any of the client nodes.

In the subsequent chapters, we will take this further and add capabilities for the server to scale and have fault tolerance.

8
Clustering

If you are reading this, it would mean that you have fair amount of understanding of what Redis is and how it can be used in applications for web and business. Apart from that, it would be fair to assume that you also have fair amount of understanding of the data structures it can hold and how to use them in your application.

In this chapter, we will continue ahead and discuss the steps that need to be taken for a Redis application to get deployed in a production environment. Well, deployment in a production environment is always tricky and calls for a greater in-depth understanding of the architecture and the business requirement. Since we cannot envisage the business requirements that the applications have to fulfil but we can always abstract out the nonfunctional requirements, most of applications have and create patterns which can be used by the readers as they see fit.

Some of the most common nonfunctional requirements that come to mind when we think or talk about production environments are listed as follows:

- Performance
- Availability
- Scalability
- Manageability
- Security

All the mentioned nonfunctional requirements are always addressed in the way we create the blueprint for our deployment architecture. Going forward, we will take these nonfunctional requirements and map them to the cluster patterns that we will discuss.

Clusters

A computer cluster consists of a set of loosely or tightly connected computers that work together so that, in many respects, they can be viewed as a single system. The source of this information is `http://en.wikipedia.org/wiki/Computer_cluster`.

There are multiple reasons why we do clustering of systems. Enterprises have requirements to grow which have to be matched with cost effectiveness and future roadmap of solutions; therefore, it always makes sense to go for clustered solution. One big machine to handle all the traffic is always desirable but the problem with vertical scalability is the ceiling in compute capability of the chip. Moreover, bigger machines always cost more as compared to a group of smaller machines with aggregate same compute power. Along with cost effectiveness, the other nonfunctional requirements that a cluster can take care of are performance, availability, and scalability. However, having a cluster also increases efforts of manageability, maintainability, and security.

With the traffic that the modern websites are generating, clustering is not just a low cost option but the only option left. With that perspective in mind, let's look into various patterns of clustering and see how they fit with Redis. The two patterns that can be developed for Redis-based clusters are:

- Master-master
- Master-slave

Cluster pattern – master-master

This pattern of cluster is created for applications where read and writes are very frequent and the state across the nodes needs to be the same at any given point in time.

From a nonfunctional requirement perspective, following behaviors can be seen in a master-master setup:

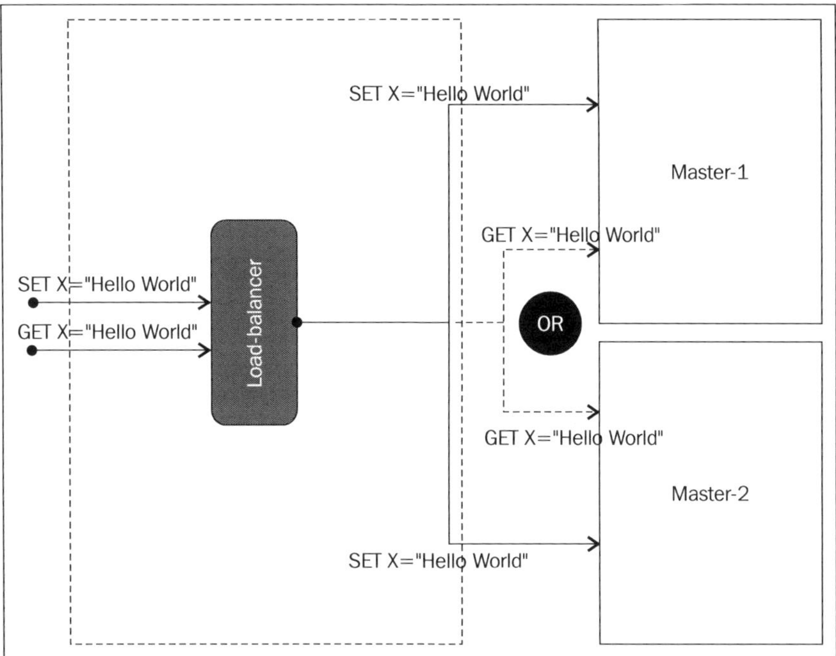

Getters and setters in master-master cluster pattern

Performance

The performance for reads and writes are very high in this kind of setup. Since the requests are load balanced across the master nodes, the individual load on a master reduces, thus resulting in better performance. As Redis inherently does not have this capability, this has to be provided outside the box. A write replicator and read load balancer kept in front of the master-master cluster will do the trick. What we are doing here is that, if there is a write request, the data will be written to all the masters, and all the read requests can be split among any of the master nodes, since the data in all the master nodes is in a consistent state.

Another dimension that we have to keep in mind is that when data quantity is very high. In case the data quantity is very high, then we have to create **shards (nodes)** inside the master node setup. These shards in individual master nodes can distribute the data based on the key. Later in the chapter, we will discuss the sharding capability in Redis.

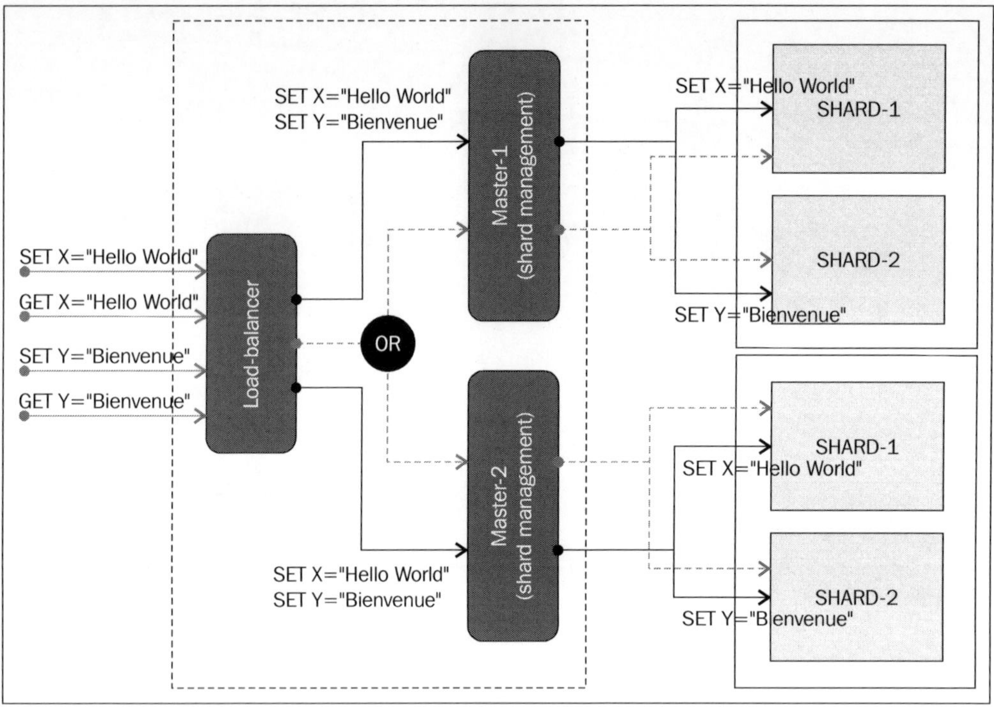

Read and write operations in a sharded environment

Availability

The availability of data is high or rather depends upon the number of master nodes maintained for replication. The state of the data is same across all the master nodes, so even if one of the master nodes goes down, the rest of the master nodes can cater to the request. During this condition, the performance of the application will dip since the requests have to be shared among the remaining master nodes. In case of data being distributed across shards inside the master node, if one of the shards were to go down, the request for that shard can be catered to by the replica shard in the other master nodes. This will still keep the affected master node working (but not to the full extent).

Scalability

The issue of scalability is a bit tricky in this case. While provisioning a new master node, following care has to be taken:

- The new master node has to be in the same state as the other master nodes.
- The information for the new master node has to be added in the client API, as the client can then take this new master node while governing the data writes and data reads.
- For these tasks, a period of downtime is required which will impact availability. Moreover, data volumes have to be factored in before sizing the master nodes or shard nodes in a master node to avoid these scenarios.

Manageability

Manageability of this type of cluster pattern requires efforts at both the node level and client level. This is because Redis does not provide an in-built mechanism for this pattern. Since the responsibility of doing data replication and data load is of the client adaptor, so following observations need to be addressed:

- The client adaptor has to factor serviceability in case the node (master or shard) goes down.
- The client adaptor has to factor in serviceability in case a new master node is added.
- Adding a new shard in to an already configured shard ecosystem should be avoided, as the sharding technique is based on the unique key generated by the client adaptor. This is decided on the basis of shard nodes configured at the beginning of the application, and adding a new shard will disturb the already set shards and the data inside it. This will render the entire application in an inconsistent state. This new shard will have some data replicated from the other shards in the master node's ecosystem. So the opted way for doing this would be to introduce consistent hashing to generate unique keys for assigning the master nodes.

Security

Redis, being a very light weight data store, has very little to offer from a security perspective. The expectation here is that the Redis nodes will be provisioned in a secured environment where the responsibility is outside the box. Nevertheless, Redis does provide some form of security in terms of username/password authentication to connect to node. This mechanism has its limitations since the password is stored in the `Config` file in clear text. Another form of security can be obfuscating the commands so that it cannot be called accidently. In the cluster pattern we are discussing it has limited use and is more from a program perspective.

Drawbacks of this pattern

This pattern has a few grey areas which we need to look out for before deciding to adopt it. A planned downtime is required for this pattern to work in a production environment. This downtime is essential if a node goes down and a new node is added to the cluster. This new node has to have the same state as the other replica master node. Another thing to look out for is data capacity planning, if underestimated, scaling horizontally would be a problem if done in a sharded environment. In the next section, we will run an example where we add another node and see a different distribution of data which can give us a hint of the problems. Data purging is another feature which is not addressed by Redis server as it's meant to hold all the data in the memory.

Sharding

Sharding is a mechanism of horizontally splitting data and placing it in different nodes (machines). Here, each partition of data residing in a different node or machine forms a shard. Sharding technique is useful in scaling a data store to multiple nodes or machines. Sharding, if done correctly, can improve the performance of the system at large.

It can also overcome the need to go for a bigger machine and can get the job done with smaller machines. Sharding can provide partial fault tolerance since if a node goes down then the request coming to that particular node cannot be served unless all the other nodes can cater to the incoming request.

Redis does not provide a direct mechanism to support sharding of data internally, so to achieve partitioning of data, techniques have to be applied from the client API when splitting the data. Since Redis is a key value data store, a unique ID can be generated based on an algorithm which can be mapped to nodes. So if a request to read, write, update, or delete comes, the algorithm can generate the same unique key or can direct it to the mapped node where the action can take place.

Jedis, the client API we are using in this book, does provide a mechanism to shard data based on keys. Let's try out a sample and see the distribution of data across the nodes.

Start with at least two nodes. The procedure has been discussed in the previous chapters. In the current sample, we will be starting one node on port 6379 and other on 6380. The first shard node should look similar to the following screenshot:

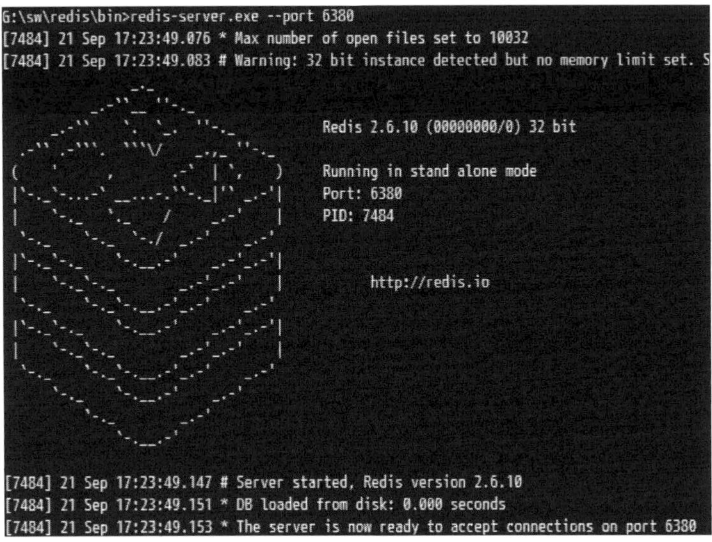
G:\sw\redis\bin>redis-server.exe --port 6380
[7484] 21 Sep 17:23:49.076 * Max number of open files set to 10032
[7484] 21 Sep 17:23:49.083 # Warning: 32 bit instance detected but no memory limit set. S
Redis 2.6.10 (00000000/0) 32 bit
Running in stand alone mode
Port: 6380
PID: 7484
http://redis.io
[7484] 21 Sep 17:23:49.147 # Server started, Redis version 2.6.10
[7484] 21 Sep 17:23:49.151 * DB loaded from disk: 0.000 seconds
[7484] 21 Sep 17:23:49.153 * The server is now ready to accept connections on port 6380

Screenshot for first shard node

The second shard node should look similar to the following screenshot:

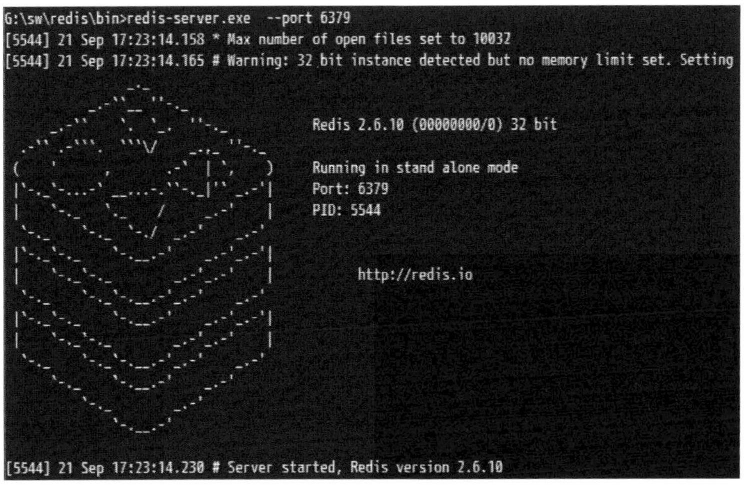
G:\sw\redis\bin>redis-server.exe --port 6379
[5544] 21 Sep 17:23:14.158 * Max number of open files set to 10032
[5544] 21 Sep 17:23:14.165 # Warning: 32 bit instance detected but no memory limit set. Setting
Redis 2.6.10 (00000000/0) 32 bit
Running in stand alone mode
Port: 6379
PID: 5544
http://redis.io
[5544] 21 Sep 17:23:14.230 # Server started, Redis version 2.6.10

Screenshot for second shard node

Let's open our editor and type in the following program:

```
package org.learningredis.chap8;
import java.util.Arrays;
import redis.clients.jedis.Jedis;
import redis.clients.jedis.JedisShardInfo;
import redis.clients.jedis.ShardedJedis;
public class Test {
  public static void main(String[] args) {
    Test test = new Test();
    test.evaluateShard();
  }
  private void evaluateShard() {
    // Configure Jedis sharded connection pool.
    JedisShardInfo shard_1 = new JedisShardInfo("localhost", 6379);
    JedisShardInfo shard_2 = new JedisShardInfo("localhost", 6380);
    ShardedJedis shardedJedis = new ShardedJedis(Arrays.
asList(shard_1, shard_2));
    // Looping to set values in the shard we have created..
    for (int i = 0; i < 10; i++) {
      shardedJedis.set("KEY-" + i, "myvalue-" + i);
    }
    // Lets try to read all the values from SHARD -1
    for (int i = 0; i < 10; i++) {
      Jedis jedis = new Jedis("localhost", 6379);
      if (jedis.get("KEY-" + i) != null) {
        System.out.println(jedis.get("KEY-" + i) + " : this is stored
in SHARD-1");
      }
    }
    // Lets try to read all the values from SHARD -2
    for (int i = 0; i < 10; i++) {
      Jedis jedis = new Jedis("localhost", 6380);
      if (jedis.get("KEY-" + i) != null) {
        System.out.println(jedis.get("KEY-" + i) + " : this is stored
in SHARD-2");
      }
    }
    // Lets try to read data from the sharded jedis.
    for (int i = 0; i < 10; i++) {
      if (shardedJedis.get("KEY-" + i) != null) {
        System.out.println(shardedJedis.get("KEY-" + i));
      }
    }
  }
}
```

The response in the console output should be as follows:

```
myvalue-1 : this is stored in SHARD-1
myvalue-2 : this is stored in SHARD-1
myvalue-4 : this is stored in SHARD-1
myvalue-6 : this is stored in SHARD-1
myvalue-9 : this is stored in SHARD-1
myvalue-0 : this is stored in SHARD-2
myvalue-3 : this is stored in SHARD-2
myvalue-5 : this is stored in SHARD-2
myvalue-7 : this is stored in SHARD-2
myvalue-8 : this is stored in SHARD-2
myvalue-0
myvalue-1
myvalue-2
myvalue-3
myvalue-4
myvalue-5
myvalue-6
myvalue-7
myvalue-8
myvalue-9
```

Observations

The following observations can be made about the sample:

- The data distribution is random which basically is dependent upon the hashing algorithm used to distribute the program or shards
- Multiple execution of the same program with result in same result. This signifies that hashing algorithm is consistent with the hash it creates for a key.
- If the key changes then the distribution of the data will be different, since a new hash code will be generated for the same given key; hence, a new target shard.

Add a new shard without cleaning the other shards:

1. Start a new master at 6381:
G:\sw\redis\bin>redis-server.exe --port 6381
   [6160] 21 Sep 18:50:08.326 * Max number of open files set to 10032

http://redis.io

   [6160] 21 Sep 18:50:08.401 # Server started, Redis version 2.6.10
   [6160] 21 Sep 18:50:08.404 * DB loaded from disk: 0.001 seconds
   [6160] 21 Sep 18:50:08.406 * The server is now ready to accept connections on port 6381

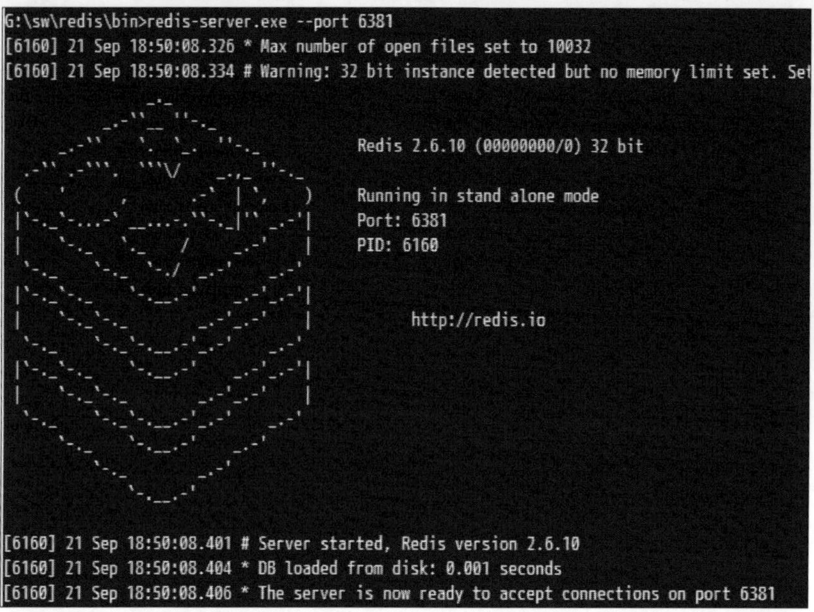

2. Let's type a new program wherein the client's new shard information is added:

```
package org.learningredis.chap8;
import java.util.Arrays;
import redis.clients.jedis.Jedis;
import redis.clients.jedis.JedisShardInfo;
import redis.clients.jedis.ShardedJedis;
public class Test {
  public static void main(String[] args) {
    Test test = new Test();
    test.evaluateShard();
  }
  private void evaluateShard() {
    // Configure Jedis sharded connection pool.
    JedisShardInfo shard_1 = new JedisShardInfo("localhost",
6379);
    JedisShardInfo shard_2 = new JedisShardInfo("localhost",
6380);
    JedisShardInfo shard_3 = new JedisShardInfo("localhost",
6381);
```

```
    ShardedJedis shardedJedis = new ShardedJedis(Arrays.
asList(shard_1, shard_2, shard_3));
    // Looping to set values in the shard we have created..
    for (int i = 0; i < 10; i++) {
      shardedJedis.set("KEY-" + i, "myvalue-" + i);
    }
    // Lets try to read all the values from SHARD -1
    for (int i = 0; i < 10; i++) {
      Jedis jedis = new Jedis("localhost", 6379);
      if (jedis.get("KEY-" + i) != null) {
        System.out.println(jedis.get("KEY-" + i) + " : this is
stored in SHARD-1");
      }
    }
    // Lets try to read all the values from SHARD -2
    for (int i = 0; i < 10; i++) {
      Jedis jedis = new Jedis("localhost", 6380);
      if (jedis.get("KEY-" + i) != null) {
        System.out.println(jedis.get("KEY-" + i) + " : this is
stored in SHARD-2");
      }
    }
    // Lets try to read all the values from SHARD -3
    for (int i = 0; i < 10; i++) {
      Jedis jedis = new Jedis("localhost", 6381);
      if (jedis.get("KEY-" + i) != null) {
        System.out.println(jedis.get("KEY-" + i) + " : this is
stored in SHARD-3");
      }
    }
    // Lets try to read data from the sharded jedis.
    for (int i = 0; i < 10; i++) {
      if (shardedJedis.get("KEY-" + i) != null) {
        System.out.println(shardedJedis.get("KEY-" + i));
      }
    }
  }
}
```

3. The result will be as follows as we can see data from `SHARD_1` and `SHARD_2` getting replicated in `SHARD_3`. This *replicated data* is nothing but older data in the `SHARD_1` and `SHARD_2` because of the previous executions. This, in production environment, can be dangerous as it increases the dead data which cannot be accounted for:

```
myvalue-1 : this is stored in SHARD-1
myvalue-2 : this is stored in SHARD-1
myvalue-4 : this is stored in SHARD-1
myvalue-6 : this is stored in SHARD-1
myvalue-9 : this is stored in SHARD-1
myvalue-0 : this is stored in SHARD-2
myvalue-3 : this is stored in SHARD-2
myvalue-5 : this is stored in SHARD-2
myvalue-7 : this is stored in SHARD-2
myvalue-8 : this is stored in SHARD-2
myvalue-4 : this is stored in SHARD-3
myvalue-6 : this is stored in SHARD-3
myvalue-7 : this is stored in SHARD-3
myvalue-8 : this is stored in SHARD-3
myvalue-9 : this is stored in SHARD-3
myvalue-0
myvalue-1
myvalue-2
myvalue-3
myvalue-4
myvalue-5
myvalue-6
myvalue-7
myvalue-8
myvalue-9
```

4. Add a new master node for the same set of data and clean all the previous data in the `SHARD_1` and `SHARD_2` nodes, and the result will be as follows:

```
The response in the output console should be as follows
myvalue-1 : this is stored in SHARD-1
myvalue-2 : this is stored in SHARD-1
myvalue-0 : this is stored in SHARD-2
myvalue-3 : this is stored in SHARD-2
myvalue-5 : this is stored in SHARD-2
myvalue-4 : this is stored in SHARD-3
myvalue-6 : this is stored in SHARD-3
```

```
myvalue-7 : this is stored in SHARD-3
myvalue-8 : this is stored in SHARD-3
myvalue-9 : this is stored in SHARD-3
myvalue-0
myvalue-1
myvalue-2
myvalue-3
myvalue-4
myvalue-5
myvalue-6
myvalue-7
myvalue-8
myvalue-9
```

We can see data getting distributed cleanly amongst all the shards with no repetitions such as older data is cleaned.

Cluster pattern – master-slave

This pattern of cluster is created for applications where reads are very frequent and writes are less frequent. Another condition necessary for this pattern to work is to have a limited size of data, or in other words, data capacity that can fit into the hardware provisioned for the master (the same hardware configuration is needed for the slaves too). Since the requirement is to cater to frequent reads, this pattern also has the capability to scale horizontally. Another point we have to keep in mind is that replication in slaves can have a time delay which can result in stale data getting served. The business requirement should be okay with that scenario.

The solution for this pattern would be to have all the writes done to the master, and have the slave cater to all the reads. The reads to slaves need to be load balanced so that performance can be met.

Redis provides an in-built capability to have master-slave configuration wherein the writes can be done to the master and the reads can be done to the slaves.

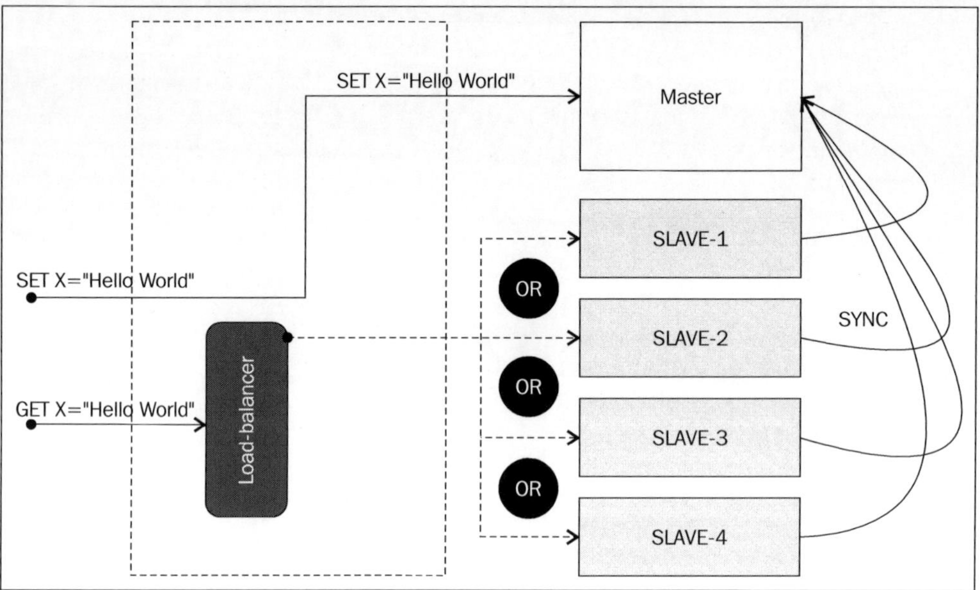

Getters and setters in master-slave pattern

From a nonfunctional requirement perspective, the behaviors that can be seen in a master-slave setup are discussed in the following sections.

Performance

The performance writes are very high in this kind of setup. This is because all the writes are happening to a single master node and the frequency of the writes is less as mentioned in the assumption. Since the read requests are load balanced across the slave nodes, the individual load on a slave reduces, thus resulting in better performance. As Redis inherently provides reads from slaves, nothing except for load balancing has to be provided outside the box. A read load balancer kept in front of the slave nodes will do the trick. What we are doing here is that if there is a write request the data will be written to the master and all the read requests will be split among all of the slave nodes since the data in all the slave nodes is in an eventual consistent state.

The thing to be noted in this case is that due to the time difference between master pushing the new updated data and the slave updating it, a scenario can be reached where the slave continues to serve stale data.

Availability

Availability in master-slave cluster pattern requires different approaches, one for the master nodes and the other for the slave nodes. The easiest part is slave availability. When it comes to availability of the slaves, it's pretty easy to handle since there are more slaves as compared to a master, and even if one of the slaves goes down, there are other slaves to cater to requests. In case of the master, since there is only one master, if that node goes down then we have a problem. While the reads will continue to happen unaffected, the writes will stop. In order to do away with data losses, there are two things that can be done:

- Have a message queue in front of the master node so that even in case the master goes down, the write message persists, which can be later written down.
- Redis provides a mechanism or an observer called Sentinel which can be used. Discussion on Sentinel has been done in some of the upcoming sections.

Scalability

The issue of scalability is a bit tricky in this case since we have two types of nodes here and both of them solve different kind of purpose. The scalability here will not be in terms of distributing the data across but more in terms of scaling out for performance. Following are some features:

- Master node has to be sized according to the data capacity that needs to be kept in RAM for performance
- The slave nodes can be attached to the cluster at run time but they eventually would come to the same state as master node, and the hardware capability of the slave should be on a par with the master
- The new slave node should be registered into the load balancer for the load balancer to distribute the data

Manageability

Manageability of this type of cluster pattern requires little effort at the master and slave node level and at the client level. This is because Redis does provide an in-built mechanism to support this pattern. Since the responsibility of doing data replication and data load is of the slave nodes, so what is left is managing the master and the client adaptors.

The following observations need to be addressed:

- The client adaptor has to factor serviceability in case the slave node goes down. The adaptor has to be intelligent enough to avoid the slave node that is down.
- The client adaptor has to factor in serviceability in case a new slave node is added.
- The client adaptor has to have a temporary persistence mechanism in case the master goes down.

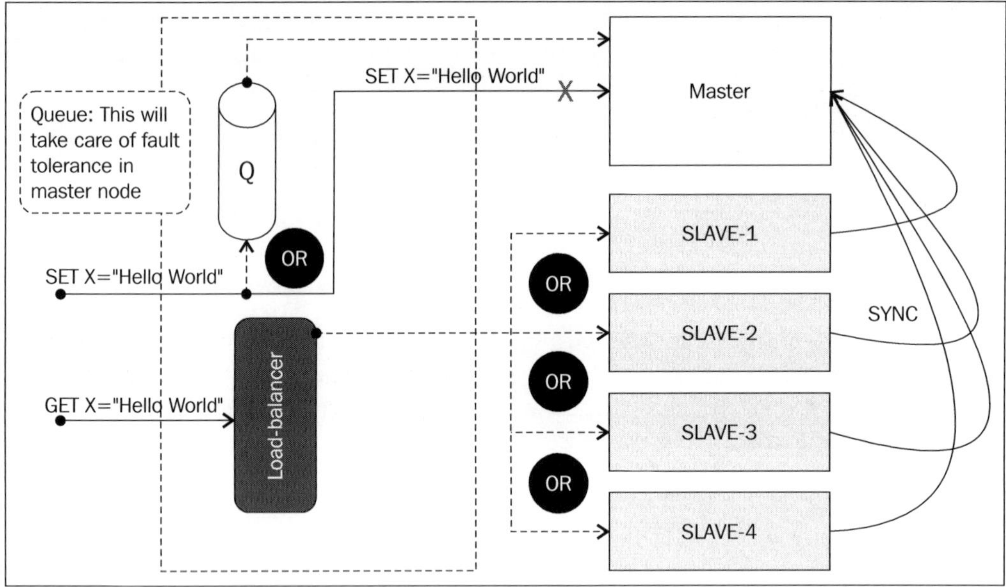

Fault tolerance in master node

Security

Redis, being a very light weight data store, has very little to offer from a security perspective. The expectation here is that the Redis nodes will be provisioned in a secured environment where the responsibility is outside the box. Nevertheless, Redis does provide some form of security in terms of username/password authentication to connect to node. This mechanism has its limitations since the password is stored in the `Config` file in clear text. Another form of security can be obfuscating the commands so that it cannot be called accidently.

In the cluster pattern we are discussing it has limited use and is more from a program perspective. Another good practice is to have separate APIs so that the program doesn't accidentally write to the slave nodes (though this will result in an error). Following are some APIs discussed:

- **WRITE API**: This component should be with the program interacting with the master node since the master can do writes in master-slave
- **READ API**: This component should be with the program interacting with the slaves which have to fetch the records

Drawbacks of this pattern

This pattern has few grey areas which we need to look out for before deciding to adopt it. One of the biggest problems is data size. The capacity sizing should be done in accordance to the vertical scaling capability of the master. The same hardware capability has to be done for the slaves. Another problem is the latency which can happen when the master copies the data to the slaves. This can sometimes result in stale data getting served in some conditions. Another area to look for is the time taken by the Sentinel to elect a new master if there is a failover in the master.

This pattern is best suited for scenarios where Redis is used as caching engine. In case it's used as a caching engine, then it's a good practice to evict the data after it's reached a certain size. In the section that follows, there are the eviction policies which we can use in Redis to manage the data size.

Configuring Redis Sentinel

Datastores provide capability in handling faulty scenarios. These capabilities are in-built and do not expose themselves in the manner in which they handle fault tolerance. Redis, which started with simple key value datastore, has evolved into a system which provides an independent node to take care of the fault management. This system is called **Sentinel**.

The idea behind Sentinel is that it's an independent node which keeps a track on the master node and the other slave nodes. When a master node goes down, it promotes the slave node to become the master. As discussed, in a master-slave scenario, master is meant to write and slaves are meant to read, so when a slave is promoted to master, it has the capability to read and write. All the other slaves will become slave to this new slave turned master. The following figure shows how Sentinel works:

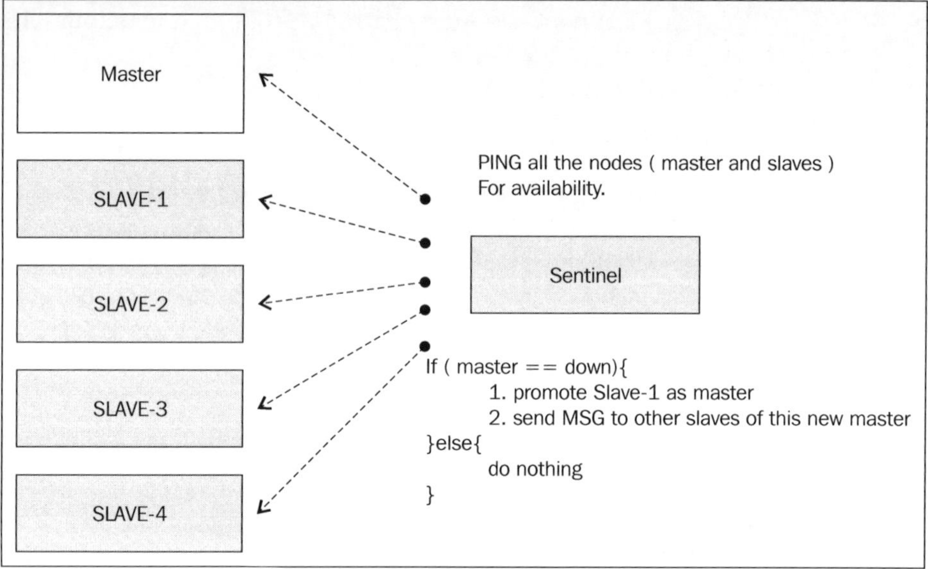
Master
SLAVE-1
SLAVE-2
SLAVE-3
SLAVE-4
PING all the nodes (master and slaves)
For availability.
Sentinel
If (master == down){
1. promote Slave-1 as master
2. send MSG to other slaves of this new master
}else{
do nothing
}

The working of Sentinel

Let's have an example now to demonstrate how Sentinel works as of Redis 2.6 Version. Sentinel has problems running in Windows machines, so this example is best executed out of *NIX machine. The steps are as follows:

1. Start a master node as shown:

```
[2831] 09 Sep 17:28:25.159 * DB loaded from disk: 0.000 seconds
[2831] 09 Sep 17:28:25.159 * The server is now ready to accept connections on port 6381
```

2. Start a slave as shown. Let's call it slave:

```
[2875] 09 Sep 17:40:33.931 * The server is now ready to accept connections on port 6382
[2875] 09 Sep 17:40:33.932 * Connecting to MASTER...
[2875] 09 Sep 17:40:33.932 * MASTER <-> SLAVE sync started
[2875] 09 Sep 17:40:33.932 * Non blocking connect for SYNC fired the event.
[2875] 09 Sep 17:40:33.932 * Master replied to PING, replication can continue...
[2875] 09 Sep 17:40:33.949 * MASTER <-> SLAVE sync: receiving 35 bytes from master
[2875] 09 Sep 17:40:33.949 * MASTER <-> SLAVE sync: Loading DB in memory
[2875] 09 Sep 17:40:33.949 * MASTER <-> SLAVE sync: Finished with success
```

3. Let's start Sentinel as shown next:

```
[2884] 09 Sep 17:42:07.528 # +redirect-to-master resque 10.207.78.5 6382 10.207.
78.5 6381
[2884] 09 Sep 17:42:07.528 * +slave slave 10.207.78.5:6382 10.207.78.5 6382 @ my
master 10.207.78.5 6381
[2884] 09 Sep 17:42:17.532 * +slave slave 10.207.78.5:6382 10.207.78.5 6382 @ resque 10.207.78.5 6381
```

4. Let's write a program in which we will do the following:
   1. Write to the master
   2. Read from the master
   3. Write to a slave
   4. Stop the master
   5. Read from the master after shutting the master
   6. Read from the slave after shutting the master
   7. Write to the slave
   8. Sentinel configuration
5. Let's type the program:

```
package simple.sharded;
import redis.clients.jedis.Jedis;
public class TestSentinel {
      public static void main(String[] args) {
        TestSentinel testSentinel = new TestSentinel();
            testSentinel.evaluate();
      }

      private void evaluate() {
            System.out.println("-- start the test ---------");
            this.writeToMaster("a","apple");
            this.readFromMaster("a");
            this.readFromSlave("a");
            this.writeToSlave("b", "ball");
            this.stopMaster();

            this.sentinelKicks();
            try{
            this.readFromMaster("a");
            }catch(Exception e){
              System.out.println(e.getMessage());
            }
            this.readFromSlave("a");
```

```
                this.sentinelKicks();
                this.sentinelKicks();
                this.writeToSlave("b", "ball");
                this.readFromSlave("b");
                System.out.println("-- end of test ------ -----");
        }
        private void sentinelKicks() {
                try {
                        Thread.currentThread().sleep(10000);
                } catch (InterruptedException e) {
                        e.printStackTrace();
                }
        }
        private void stopMaster() {
          Jedis jedis =  ConnectionUtill.
getJedisConnection("10.207.78.5", 6381);
              jedis.shutdown();
        }
        private void writeToSlave(String key , String value) {
              Jedis jedis =  ConnectionUtill.
getJedisConnection("10.207.78.5", 6382);
              try{
                System.out.println(jedis.set(key, value));
              }catch(Exception e){
                System.out.println(e.getMessage());

              }
        }
        private void readFromSlave(String key) {
              Jedis jedis =  ConnectionUtill.
getJedisConnection("10.207.78.5", 6382);
              String value = jedis.get(key);
              System.out.println("reading value of '" + key + "' from
slave is :" + value);
        }
        private void readFromMaster(String key) {
              Jedis jedis =  ConnectionUtill.
getJedisConnection("10.207.78.5", 6381);
              String value = jedis.get(key);
              System.out.println("reading value of '" + key + "' from
master is :" + value);
        }
```

```
        private void writeToMaster(String key , String value) {
            Jedis jedis =  ConnectionUtill.
getJedisConnection("10.207.78.5", 6381);
            System.out.println(jedis.set(key, value));
        }
}
```

6. You should be able to see the following result for the program you have written:

    1. Write to the master:

    ```
    OK
    ```

    2. Read from the master:

    ```
    reading value of 'a' from master is :apple
    ```

    3. Write to a slave:

    ```
    READONLY You can't write against a read only slave.
    ```

    4. Stop the master:

```
[10907] 11 Sep 09:44:49.262 # User requested shutdown...
[10907] 11 Sep 09:44:49.262 * Saving the final RDB snapshot before exiting.
[10907] 11 Sep 09:44:49.264 * DB saved on disk
[10907] 11 Sep 09:44:49.264 # Redis is now ready to exit, bye bye...
```

    5. Read from the master after shutting the master:

    ```
    java.net.ConnectException: Connection refused: connect
    ```

    6. Read from the slave after shutting the master:

    ```
    reading value of 'a' from slave is :apple
    ```

7. Write to the slave:

```
OK
```

8. Add the following text to the default Sentinel configuration:

```
sentinel monitor slave2master 127.0.0.1 6382 1
sentinel down-after-milliseconds slave2master 10000
sentinel failover-timeout slave2master 900000
sentinel can-failover slave2master yes
sentinel parallel-syncs slave2master 1
```

Let's understand the meaning of the five lines that we have added in the preceding code. The default Sentinel will have the information of the master running in the default port. If you have started the master in some other host or port, accordingly those changes have to be made in the Sentinel file.

- **Sentinel monitor slave2master 127.0.0.1 63682 1**: This gives us the information of the host and port of the slave node. Apart from that, `1` indicates the quorum agreement between the Sentinels for them to agree upon if the master fails. In our case, since we are running only one Sentinel, hence `1` is the value mentioned.
- **Sentinel down-after-milliseconds slave2master 10000**: This is the time for which the master should not be reachable. The idea is for the Sentinel to keep on pinging the master and if the master does not respond or responds with an error, than the Sentinel kicks in and starts its activity. If the Sentinel detects the master as down then it will mark the node as `SDOWN`. But this alone cannot decide if the master is down, there has to be an agreement between all the Sentinels to initiate the failover activity. When the agreement has been reached by the Sentinels that the master is down, then it's called `ODOWN` state. Think of this as democracy among the Sentinel before a master which is down is ousted and a new master is chosen.
- **Sentinel failover-timeout slave2master 900000**: This is time specified in milliseconds which takes care of the entire time span of the entire failover process. When a failover is detected, the Sentinel requests the configuration of the new master is written in all the slaves configured.
- **Sentinel parallel-syncs slave2master 1**: This configuration indicates the number of slaves that are reconfigured simultaneously after a failover event. If we serve read queries from the read-only slaves, we will want to keep this value low. This is because all the slaves will be unreachable at the time when the synchronization is happening.

Summary

In this chapter, we learnt how to use clustering techniques to maximize performance and handle growing datasets. Apart from that, we also had a glimpse of handing of data for availability and how well we can do fault handling. Though there are techniques which Redis provides but we also saw how we can use other techniques if we do not require Sentinel. In the next chapter we will focus on how to maintain Redis.

9

Maintaining Redis

To maintain data, it's important to understand the data that we are going to store in our Redis datastore. Data comes with various properties, which we covered in *Chapter 1, Introduction to NoSQL*, and we are again going to focus on one of these facets in deciding the strategies that we will undertake for data maintenance in this chapter. The facet that we will be focusing on is the ephemeral nature of data.

Maintaining ephemeral data

Data that has its importance for a certain duration of time, which is transient in nature, can be termed as **ephemeral data**. Such data needs to be flushed out of the system after the intended duration and computer resources have to be freed in order to be made available for newer datasets. In some datastores where there is no in-built capability to do this, scripts and programs have to be written to clean them, or in other words, the onus is on the user to cleanse the system. Before we get into details of the mechanisms Redis has to offer, let's look at the types of data that can be termed as ephemeral. Data types that fall in this category are the following:

- **Event data**: Stock tickers have importance over a small period of time and then lose their value in the context form in which they are viewed. Suppose the value of the tech stock of a dummy corporation is $100 at 1300 hours, and for all the algorithms interested in calculating the *whatever* index of the tech stock at 1300 hours this data is important. After, let's say, 1310 hours, this value of data is not important as it's old data or log data and can thus be viewed as ephemeral data.
- **Transient business data**: Transient business data, for example, promotion coupon discounts is an important feature of e-commerce businesses. They carry importance for a certain period of time and after the time period is over these promotional offers cease to exist. Again, this type of data can be categorized as ephemeral data.

- **Session data**: Every e-business has a component for session handling; it's basically the data that is maintained to record the data generated when the registered user is interacting with the portal.

The strategy to handle ephemeral data is easy in Redis. Redis has a built-in capability called **Time to Live (TTL)**, or the other option is P-TTL, which is more precise as it returns data with millisecond resolution. This capability keeps the data in the memory for a specified time, and after the time is over, the data is flushed out. Redis has an in-built process that keeps on monitoring the data that has a specified TTL and moves in a loop, cleaning data once the duration is over.

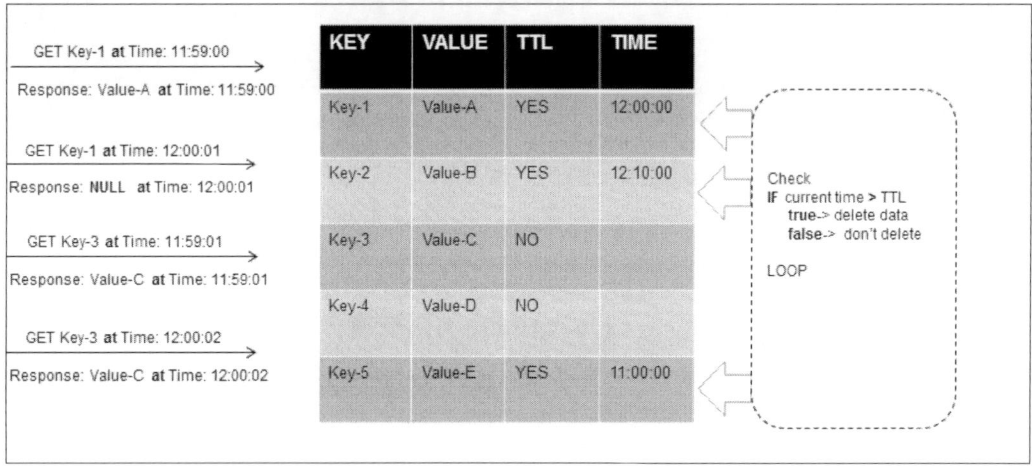

A diagrammatic representation of the TTL process in Redis

Another mechanism to cleanse data if TTL/PTTL is not specified is to use the `EXPIRE` or `PEXPIRE` commands. These commands set a time-out on the key as the data is volatile. An interesting thing that occurs in `PEXPIRE` is that if a key has been assigned with a value and an `EXPIRE` time, and if the value is set again before this time lapses, then the `EXPIRE` time attribute is removed.

For the `PEXPIRE` command in a clustered environment, the DEL command for the key is sent to all the slaves and to the **append-only file** (**AOF**) of the node. Redis makes sure that it is deleted from all the locations, either in memory (such as, in slaves) or in the filesystem (such as, in the AOF).

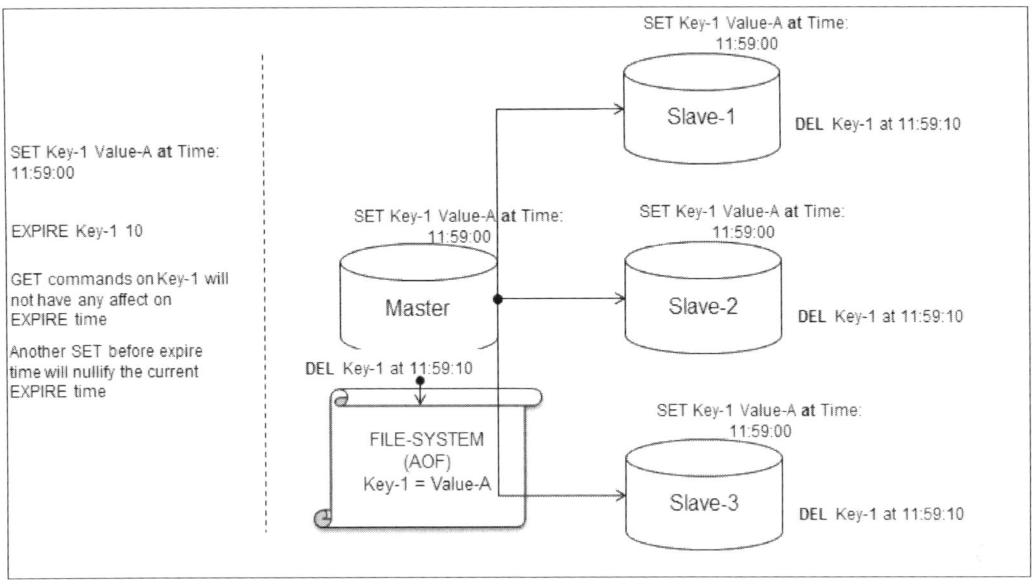

A diagrammatic representation of the EXPIRE command in a clustered environment

The behavior of TTL is similar to that of the `EXPIRE` command in a clustered environment.

Maintaining nonephemeral data

Nonephemeral type of data is not dependent on time and has usefulness throughout its existence in the system. Since this kind of data is time-independent, it is possible that the data can increase in due course of time. This can be problematic in Redis since data is stored in memory in Redis. Handling and maintaining this nonephemeral data is crucial for the maintenance of Redis since at the back of our minds, we have to keep the available memory and availability of data in mind.

Redis comes with some capabilities to handle the previously discussed scenarios, which is if the datastore grows at an alarming rate, as it can outgrow the memory available. In such scenarios, adding more RAM can solve the issue, or we can distribute the datasets using a programmatic technique called Sharding. However, in this chapter, we will discuss a mechanism to maintain data that is not required in an active application but needs to be stored.

Let's see a few in-built techniques or mechanisms to manage data in Redis and its evolution roadmap over the versions that have been released.

Redis 2.4

Redis has an in-built capability (deprecated since 2.4) of swapping datasets between the RAM and filesystem (disk or SSD). This capability of Redis is called **virtual memory** (**VM**). This capability can be configured by enabling it, `vm-enabled yes`, in the configuration file.

To understand this feature, let's imagine the entire dataset in Redis as a bucket sorted on the basis of the last accessed data. Here, last accessed refers to the instance it was last modified or accessed. The dataset that is least accessed is pushed to disk. This way the space is maintained for frequently accessed datasets. In case the dataset that has been pushed is accessed again, then this dataset is brought back to the main memory and the second to last least-accessed data is pushed to disk. The following figure is a representation of the behind-the-scenes activity when VM is enabled:

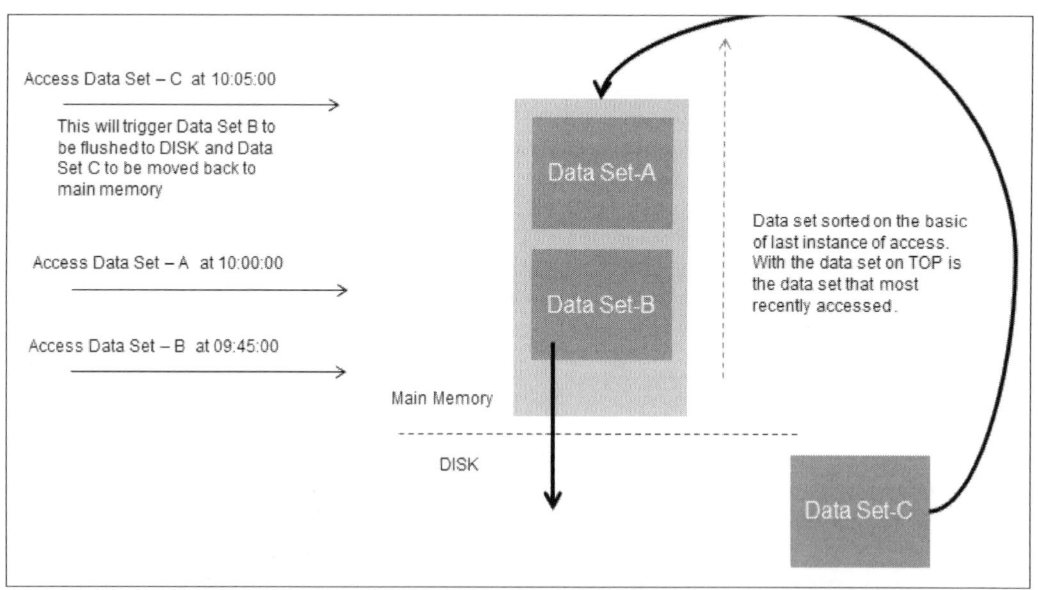

A simplistic representation of the handling of datasets of a VM-enabled system

Note that it's the values that are pushed to disk and not the keys. The keys are always in memory.

This VM option is suitable for business data that contains large datasets against a key. This option is also useful when there is a usage pattern wherein with time, some data is less frequently accessed.

This VM option is also suitable in scenarios where we have a large number of key-value pairs that can outgrow the memory. In this case, we can club these key-values in Hashes. For example, let's assume that we are maintaining customer records as shown here:

- *Customer 1 as (KEY) and some customer data "ABC" as (VALUE)*
- *Customer 2 as (KEY) and some customer data "XYZ" as (VALUE)*
- *Customer 3 as (KEY) and some customer data "123" as (VALUE)*
- *Customer 4 as (KEY) and some customer data "AQ@" as (VALUE)*

If we continue to store data in this fashion, then we have the danger of running out of space (memory) if the customer data grows (although it's good for business, it's not so good for the technical team supporting it). A better way of storing this customer data would be in a Hash.

A customer store will be `(KEY)` and the corresponding customer values will be of the type `(HASHES)` and contain the following data:

- *Customer 3 as (KEY) and some customer data "123" as (VALUE)*
- *Customer 4 as (KEY) and some customer data "AQ@" as (VALUE)*
- *Customer 1 as (KEY) and some customer data "ABC" as (VALUE)*
- *Customer 2 as (KEY) and Some Customer data "XYZ" as (VALUE)*

If we store values in this way, in a worst-case scenario, the entire value dataset will be pushed to disk and can be brought back to memory again, if need be.

To configure a VM capability apart from `vm-enabled yes`, the following configurations need to be looked into:

- `vm-max-threads`: This provides the maximum number of threads to perform I/O activity between memory and disk. Setting the value to `0` will burden the single thread, which is managing the client request, stall the entire process and load the dataset back into the main memory.
- `vm-max-memory`: This option tells the Redis server the amount of memory it should reserve to store datasets. The moment this threshold is reached it starts to swap datasets from memory to disk.
- `vm-swap-file`: This setting provides the location in the filesystem where the datasets can be dumped.
- `vm-pages`: This setting will hint the Redis server about the number of pages that need to be created to swap the file.

- `vm-page-size`: This setting will hint the Redis server about the amount of disk storage to be allocated to store a value dataset. The combination of `vm-pages` and `vm-page-size` is important for the storage and faster retrieval of the datasets from the disk.

In business case scenarios where performance is paramount and there's a constraint of using the VM option, performance can be improved by using **solid-state devices** (**SSD**). These devices have faster reads and writes as compared to disk, which is limited by the read/write speed of the disk.

Note that the VM option will be getting deprecated as of Redis 2.4.

Redis 2.6 to 2.8

Unlike Version 2.4—where the VM option was the way out to handle data bigger than memory—in newer versions, it's better to clear the data and store it in a separate location (here, location can be a different instance or a filesystem). The problems faced in the VM option were taken care of in the newer version.

Dump and restore

For Redis Version 2.6, one of the mechanisms is to issue the `Dump` key command, which will return the serialized version of the data for the key. This data can be used along with the `Restore` command in the target instance of Redis from where it can be converted to readable data. As discussed earlier, the best pattern to handle large data is to collect the key-values in a collection, such as Hashes, and then to operate on it to manage the data.

The following diagram is a simple representation of the actions that can be taken to handle data (which is no longer accessed but need to be kept in the system):

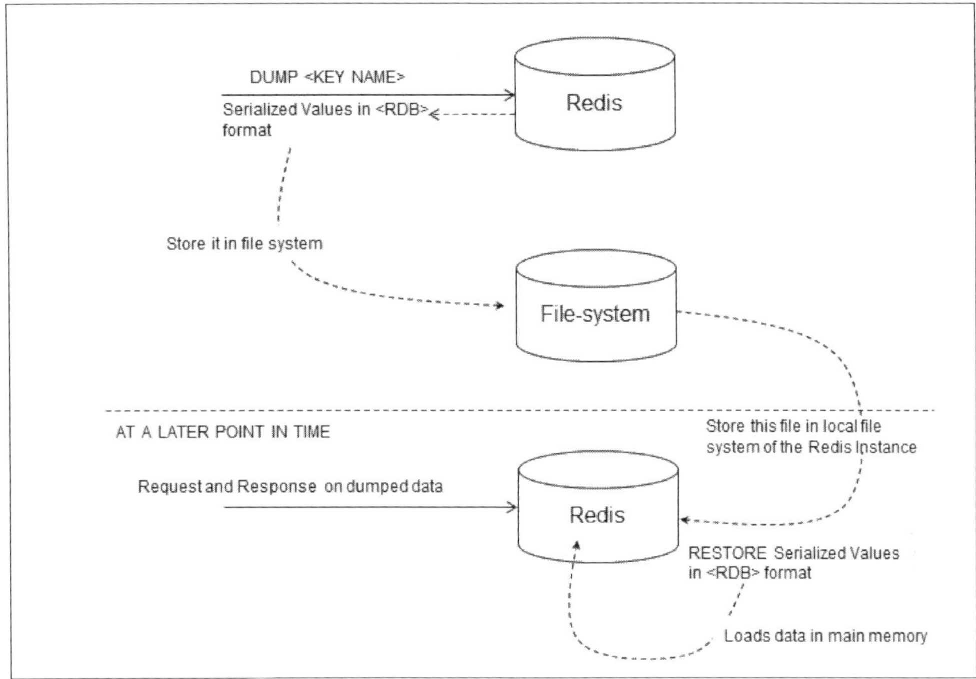

A diagrammatic representation of the DUMP and RESTORE commands

The benefit of storing keys and values in a collection, such as Hashes, is that you can fire one command that will act on the entire collection and then use one command to restore it back. This technique is useful when you already have a pocket of data that needs to be purged. However, when you want to store the entire dataset, you have to look into *snapshotting*, which is discussed later.

This mechanism has a caveat; that is, it records data in a serialized RDB version, so this serialized data cannot be used for any other Redis version.

Snapshotting

An in-built technique to handle large datasets is called *snapshotting*. This technique, as discussed in the previous chapters, is used to persist data in AOF. This process will dump data into an AOF, as specified in the configuration file. The means and mechanism to do this is to execute commands in order to dump data into the file either in the background (`BGSAVE`) or foreground (`SAVE`). In a highly concurrent environment, if these activities cause a strain on the system performance, one clever way to solve this issue is to have a bigger machine.

The idea to bring in a bigger machine and make it a slave to the node (master) under stress and at a suitable time promotes this bigger machine to master node. So, now the entire datasets are in the bigger machine with more resources. The following diagram is a simple representation of the entire activity. In many production environments, since the data layer is usually behind a router, it's general practice to use a router to make a switch of traffic rather than depend on Sentinel to make the switch. In an environment where the router is not present, Sentinel can be used to make the switch, and the process to do so has been dealt with in previous chapters.

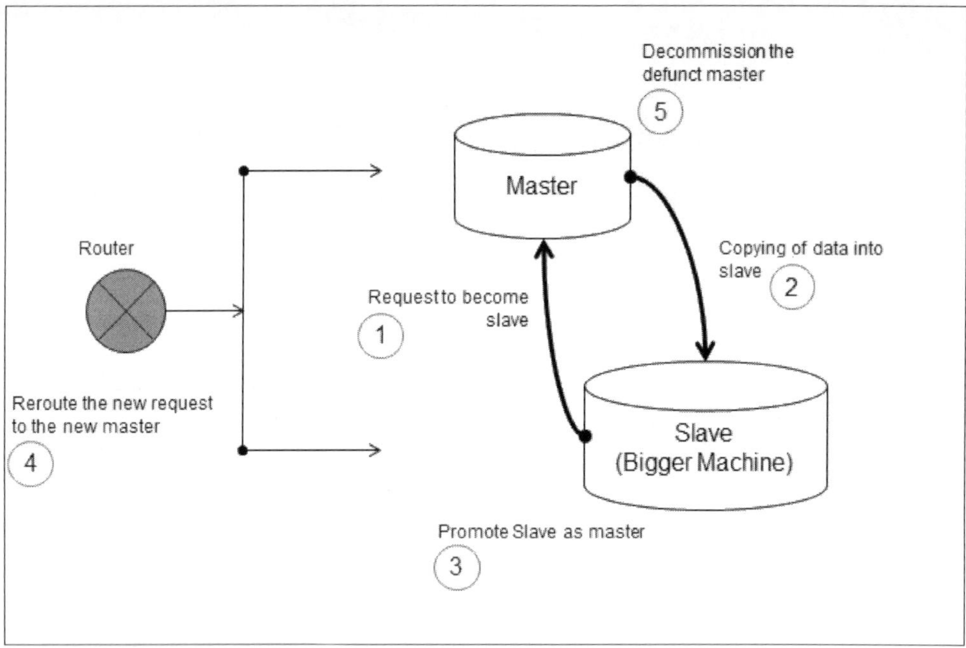

A simplistic representation of migrating data from a small to a large machine

Redis 3.0

Another mechanism to keep the Redis dataset limited to the available memory is to purge old data. Redis doesn't have an in-built mechanism to purge data; instead, it has a combination of `MIGRATE` and `RESTORE` data. Let's look at this process in detail.

Let's assume that we have a collection of Hashes, which maintain the purchase history of all the customers for the year 2012; so, typically the key will look like **PURCHASE_HISTORY_2012**, and the value will be a Hash of datasets, containing the customer's ID as the key and the customer purchase details as values.

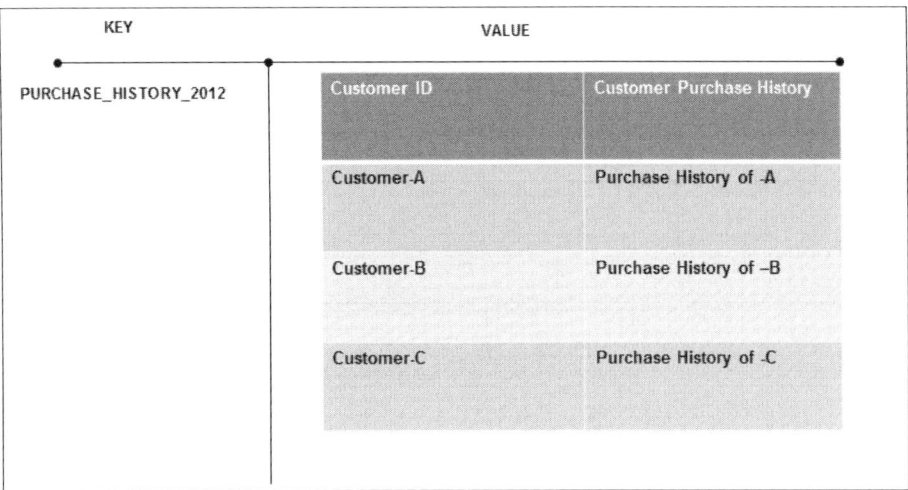

KEY
VALUE
PURCHASE_HISTORY_2012
Customer ID
Customer Purchase History
Customer-A
Purchase History of -A
Customer-B
Purchase History of –B
Customer-C
Purchase History of -C

A representation of the key-value datasets to be migrated

Likewise, **PURCHASE_HISTORY_2013**, **PURCHASE_HISTORY_2014**, and **PURCHASE_HISTORY_2015** will be maintained for subsequent years. Any business requirement to show the purchase data for the last 4 years for a user, let's say **Customer-A**, will pick data from the key for 2012, 2013, 2014, and 2015. The business requirement will append the data from these years, thereby forming a composite response. Now, in 2016, another key will be created, but the same function to get the purchase history for **Customer-A** will pick data from the key for 2013, 2014, 2015, and 2016. In this case, **PURCHASE_HISTORY_2012** will be left out, but for legal reasons, we cannot delete it. Yet, it occupies memory space in the online system. In this scenario, we can issue the `MIGRATE` command, which is a combination of `DUMP` and `DEL`. When we issue the `MIGRATE` command internally, Redis will issue a `DUMP` key to serialize the data and I/O into the target instance. Once the target instance is restored, the serialized key then sends an `OK` command back to the source machine, which can then delete the **PURCHASE_HISTORY_2012** key. We can now issue a `SAVE` command in the target instance and make an AOF file, which can be stored in the filesystem for later reference, if need be.

The following figure is a representation of the migration of data for a given key:

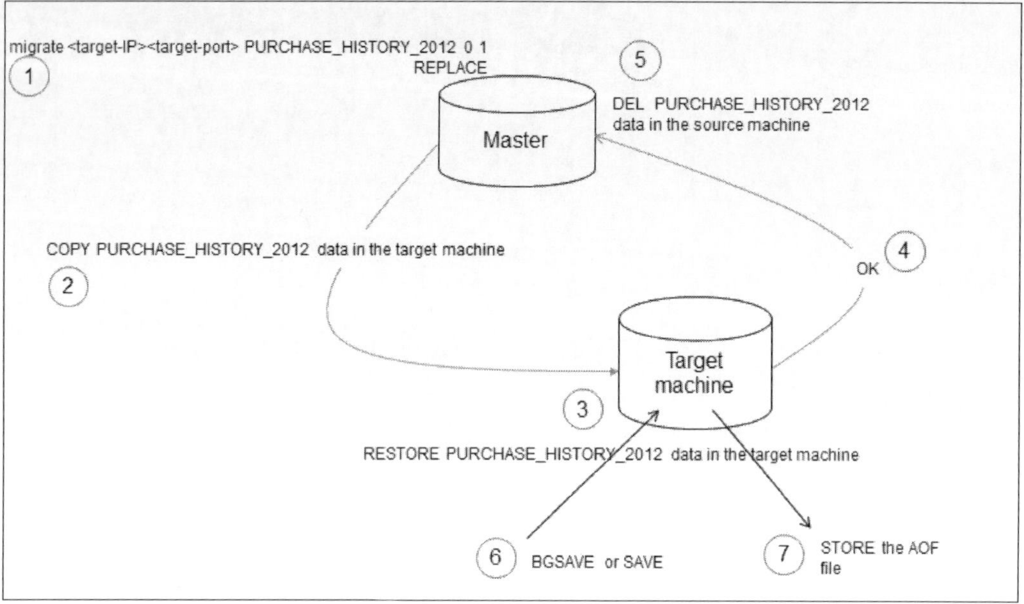

A representation of the migration process in Redis

Note that the `MIGRATE` command will work in Redis 3.0 Version.

Summary

In this chapter, you saw various mechanisms to maintain data in Redis, either using the in-built capability in Redis or by employing clever mechanisms to achieve it.

Index

D

E

F

G

H

I

J

K

L

P

R

S

T

U

V

W

Thank you for buying
Learning Redis

About Packt Publishing

Packt, pronounced 'packed', published its first book, *Mastering phpMyAdmin for Effective MySQL Management*, in April 2004, and subsequently continued to specialize in publishing highly focused books on specific technologies and solutions.

Our books and publications share the experiences of your fellow IT professionals in adapting and customizing today's systems, applications, and frameworks. Our solution-based books give you the knowledge and power to customize the software and technologies you're using to get the job done. Packt books are more specific and less general than the IT books you have seen in the past. Our unique business model allows us to bring you more focused information, giving you more of what you need to know, and less of what you don't.

Packt is a modern yet unique publishing company that focuses on producing quality, cutting-edge books for communities of developers, administrators, and newbies alike. For more information, please visit our website at `www.packtpub.com`.

About Packt Open Source

In 2010, Packt launched two new brands, Packt Open Source and Packt Enterprise, in order to continue its focus on specialization. This book is part of the Packt Open Source brand, home to books published on software built around open source licenses, and offering information to anybody from advanced developers to budding web designers. The Open Source brand also runs Packt's Open Source Royalty Scheme, by which Packt gives a royalty to each open source project about whose software a book is sold.

Writing for Packt

We welcome all inquiries from people who are interested in authoring. Book proposals should be sent to `author@packtpub.com`. If your book idea is still at an early stage and you would like to discuss it first before writing a formal book proposal, then please contact us; one of our commissioning editors will get in touch with you.

We're not just looking for published authors; if you have strong technical skills but no writing experience, our experienced editors can help you develop a writing career, or simply get some additional reward for your expertise.

Building Databases with Redis [Video]

ISBN: 978-1-78328-411-5 Duration: 03:13 hours

Acquire practical experience and skills in designing databases using Redis

1. Harness the power of the Redis to build storages as per your needs.
2. Execute Redis commands and discover ways to perform them on the database.
3. Filled with practical examples close to real-life tasks and situations.

Rapid Redis [Video]

ISBN: 978-1-78439-545-2 Duration: 00:49 hours

Get to grips with Redis; an open source, networked, in-memory, key-value data store that will solve all your storage needs

1. Understand the difference between SQL and NoSQL databases.
2. Use Redis interactively through its command-line interface (CLI).
3. Understand the basic data structures of Redis and their usage.

Please check **www.PacktPub.com** for information on our titles

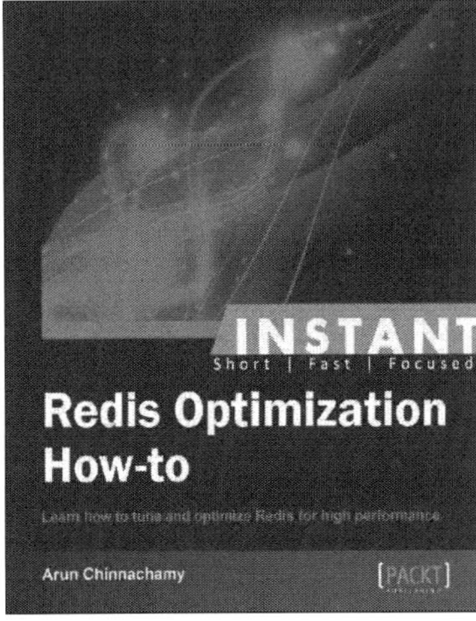

Instant Redis Optimization How-to

ISBN: 978-1-78216-480-7 Paperback: 56 pages

Learn how to tune and optimize Redis for high performance

1. Learn something new in an Instant! A short, fast, focused guide delivering immediate results.
2. Install, fine-tune, and add Redis to your application stack.
3. Perform bulk writes into Redis efficiently.
4. Debug and troubleshoot Redis.

Building Scalable Apps with Redis and Node.js

ISBN: 978-1-78398-448-0 Paperback: 316 pages

Develop customized, scalable web apps through the integration of powerful Node.js frameworks

1. Design a simple application and turn it into the next Instagram.
2. Integrate utilities such as Redis, Socket.io, and Backbone to create Node.js web applications.
3. Learn to develop a complete web application right from the frontend to the backend in a streamlined manner.

Please check **www.PacktPub.com** for information on our titles

Printed in Poland
by Amazon Fulfillment
Poland Sp. z o.o., Wrocław